COMPUTE!'s
Beginner's Guide to

Machine
Language
on the
IBM PC and PCjr

Christopher D. Metcalf
and
Marc B. Sugiyama

Foreword by Richard Mansfield

COMPUTE! Publications,Inc.abc
One of the ABC Publishing Companies
Greensboro, North Carolina

Printed in the United States of America

ISBN 0-942386-83-3

10 9 8 7 6 5

COMPUTE! Publications, Inc., Post Office Box 5406, Greensboro, NC 27403, (919)
275-9809, is one of the ABC Publishing Companies, and is not associated with any
manufacturer of personal computers. IBM PC and IBM PCjr are trademarks of International Business Machines, Inc.

Contents

Foreword

Machine language (ML) is the native language of any computer. When you program in a high-level language like BASIC, each program statement must be translated into machine language while the program is running. That seriously slows up execution speed.

For many applications, BASIC is the language of choice because its slow speed doesn't matter. But if speed is significant, ML is the answer. What's more, you'll gain significantly more control over your computer when you can give it instructions in its own language. You bypass the limitations and blind spots of BASIC.

Unfortunately, many BASIC programmers have come to believe that machine language is too complex to be easily understood, that it's beyond their reach. This is a popular misconception, but it's a misconception nonetheless. In fact, people who learned to program in ML have claimed that learning BASIC was about as difficult. What's more, if you already know BASIC, you already know most of the concepts and structures that you'll need to program in ML.

COMPUTE!'s Beginner's Guide to Machine Language on the IBM PC and PCjr makes learning 8088 ML easy. The authors introduce you to the tools you'll need and start you off by showing you, step by step, how to write simple programs. Slowly, with numerous examples, they describe each ML command. You'll soon be telling your assembler (either MASM or the *Small Assembler*) exactly what you want it to do. And, after you've got the basics down, you'll learn everything you need to know to write complex programs entirely in ML.

This book includes more than 15 complete ML programs for you to type in and assemble. Each program is more complex than the one before and guides you through new techniques. Many programs contain routines which can be simply lifted as is and inserted into your own programs.

Do you want to use ML and BASIC together? Do you want to merge one of your ML routines with a Pascal program? *COMPUTE!'s Beginner's Guide to Machine Language on the IBM PC and PCjr* shows you how. You'll even learn about Macros: how and why they're used in ML programs, and how to create a library of them.

Once you've learned the techniques of 8088 ML programming on the IBM, you'll find yourself returning to this book again and again. It not only teaches, but is also an excellent reference for the experienced programmer.

For almost every level of 8088 ML programming, from rank beginner to veteran programmer, *COMPUTE!'s Beginner's Guide to Machine Language on the IBM PC and PCjr* can be your guide to greater understanding of your machine and effective, powerful programming methods. But if you're just starting out with ML, you'll soon be writing your first ML program and can begin to explore the amazing world in the interior of your machine.

Richard Mansfield
Author of *Machine Language For Beginners*

Acknowledgments

This book has been the result of the efforts of many people. We would like to thank the following who have been of great assistance: Orson Scott Card, former book editor of COMPUTE! Publications, without whom we would have never even considered writing a book; Rosemary Morrissey, of Entry Systems Division information at IBM, Boca Raton, for answering our questions and for providing us with several useful products; and Jeff Sensabaugh and Will Clemens for taking the time to review our book. Their comments were most helpful in the final editing process.

Christopher Metcalf
Marc Sugiyama
September 1984

1

Introduction

The PC is a powerful tool, whether for business uses, mathematic calculations, or game playing. It is sometimes astonishing to observe the speed at which some programs work, whether spreadsheets, word processors, or flashy videogames.

Sometimes, however, BASIC is simply too slow. For fast-moving games, complex calculations, and rapid communication with external devices, BASIC often fails to perform as you might wish. The answer to that problem is the subject of this book. *Machine language*, the computer's native language, executes many times faster than BASIC or even Pascal.

BASIC is useful in many situations, and is often all you need to write a program. BASIC (or Pascal) programs are usually much simpler to write, modify, and debug than machine language. Furthermore, programs written in BASIC can be transported from computer to computer almost without modification.

There are times, though, that the benefits of machine language outweigh the advantages of BASIC and Pascal. Machine language is fast, faster than BASIC or any of the other high-level languages. Machine language also provides for a greater degree of precision and control when dealing with the computer and all its associated hardware. Finally, machine language programs are often more compact than BASIC, and invariably far shorter than the equivalent programs would be in Pascal. When you need speed, precision, or compactness, machine language is the best answer.

What You'll Need

This book assumes that you are using one of the IBM family of personal computers (PC, PC/XT, Portable, or PCjr), or one of the many PC compatibles. PCjrs must be the expanded version, with a disk drive and at least 128K of RAM. Other computers require at least 64K (with DOS 1.10) or 96K (with DOS 2.00 and above) and a disk drive. Any programmer using

1

a noncompatible version of MS-DOS can use this book, but don't be too surprised if some of the sample programs fail to give the proper results.

That's the hardware needed. Below is a list of the software you will need.

DOS. We assume that you are using either DOS 2.00 or 2.10 (or their Microsoft equivalent); however, most of the explanation applies to DOS 1.10 as well.

Text editor. Those who have never written a program in an assembled or compiled language (like Pascal) may not be familiar with *text editors* or *source files*. A text editor allows you to enter your program (the source file) into the computer and store it on disk. Assembly language source files are generally given the extension .ASM.

Any editor or word processor which generates standard DOS files can be used to enter your programs. A standard DOS file, sometimes called a *pure ASCII* file, doesn't contain any special word processor control codes. IBM's assembler will assemble only standard DOS files.

Some word processors *(WordStar* and *WordPerfect,* for example) don't store their text files in this standard format; however, most provide a way to handle DOS files. Word processors vary considerably, so check with your manual for the specifics. If your word processor doesn't handle DOS files, use EDLIN. EDLIN is quite adequate as a program editor; besides, it came on your DOS disk, and you might as well use it. If you would prefer a more powerful text editor, IBM sells two: the *Personal Editor* and the *Professional Editor.*

The assembler. The most important software requirement is an *assembler.* In this book, we'll assume you have the IBM assembler. The assembler is the program which converts your assembly language source file into an *object file,* usually given the extension .OBJ. This file contains the actual machine language instructions which the computer will execute. We can also have the assembler produce a *list file.* This file, with the extension .LST, contains both the original source file and the actual machine language program, generated by the assembler, in the margin.

In writing the sample programs and the assembly examples, we have assumed that you are using the *IBM Macro Assembler.* The *Macro Assembler* is available from your IBM dealer or product center, and is nearly identical to the version of MASM provided free with some MS-DOS computers. Although there are other assemblers available, the *IBM Macro Assembler* is the most popular, as well as standard for IBM equipment.

When you buy the *IBM Macro Assembler* package, you are supplied with two assemblers, MASM.EXE and ASM.EXE. MASM requires at least 96K of RAM, while ASM needs only 64K. If you have the memory, use MASM. There is little difference in the performance of the two assemblers; however, MASM offers additional commands and options, which will be detailed in Chapter 15.

The linker. Before you can execute your object file, you must link it using the LINK program provided on your DOS disk. The LINK program converts the object file into an executable file (with the extension .EXE). The LINK program can also be used to join many object files (IBM calls these *object modules*) together into a large program. These object modules can be created with the assembler or other language compilers such as the BASIC and the Pascal compilers.

How to Use This Book

In order to use this book to its fullest potential, we recommend that you have at least some knowledge of BASIC or Pascal, enough so that you can write your own programs. Although a knowledge of BASIC is not essential, there will be some sample programs written in BASIC when added clarity is necessary. We assume that you know some of the computer technical jargon, such as the words *loop* and *subroutine.* If you are completely in the dark, take some time to read through the glossary at the end of this book.

In addition, we assume that you are familiar with your operating system, whether PC-DOS or MS-DOS. By this we mean you know how to name files, to copy files from one disk to another, and know how to format your own disks.

Machine language should not be the beginner's first computer language. It's not that it's harder to learn than other computer languages—it's just less forgiving of mistakes. High-level languages perform many error checks while executing your program; assembly language performs almost none.

Before You Get Started

Before you go on, make a working copy of the assembler and your editor (whether EDLIN.COM, *WordStar*, or some other word processor). You should also copy the assembler to your working disk (either ASM.EXE or MASM.EXE; you don't need both). You will also need LINK.EXE and DEBUG.COM from your DOS program disks. Your work disk does not have to be a boot disk, but copy COMMAND.COM onto the disk anyway, since DOS reloads it after every assembly. If you're using a word processor, it's a good idea to copy it and all its associated program files onto your work disk, so you don't have to trade disks every time you assemble.

In the next chapter we'll be discussing some of those esoteric terms you may have heard from your hacker friends: binary, hexadecimal, memory addressing, segments, registers, and flags. If you're a hacker yourself, you should at least glance through Chapter 2 and be sure you understand it before starting on Chapter 3.

2
Fundamentals

In this chapter we will discuss some of the basic concepts necessary for learning machine language. Most of these concepts will be general to all computers, but we will also talk about some features specific to the 8088, the microprocessor—the brain—of your computer. First we'll discuss the computer's numbering system, binary, and some related topics. Then we'll examine the basic structure of the computer's microprocessor, as well as some of the ideas that must be understood to program in machine language.

Our system of numbering is called decimal. In this system, each digit, as we move to the left, has ten times more weight than the preceding one. So in the number 4782 we have a one's digit, a ten's digit, a hundred's digit, and a thousand's digit, each with a value ten times the preceding one. In other words, we have what is called a *base 10* numbering system.

The base 10 numbering system is not the system used by computers. Microprocessors everywhere use base 2.

Binary

A computer is essentially a series of switches. Each switch is either on or off. Thus the use of the *base 2* numbering system, in which each digit, instead of being 0 to 9, is either on or off, either a 0 or a 1. This is the system called *binary*. This binary system of numbering is responsible for much of a computer's architecture: the size of the largest number it can store in a memory location, the amount of memory it can have, even the size of the screen.

As in the decimal system, each digit, as we move to the left, has an increased value. But instead of ten times, each digit as we move left has a value two times the preceding digit: a one's digit, a two's digit, a four's digit, an eight's digit, a sixteen's digit, and so on.

Look at the binary number

10011

Reading from right to left, it has one *1*, one *2*, no *4*'s or *8*'s, and one *16*. Adding them all up (1 + 2 + 0 + 0 + 16), we can see that 10011 in binary represents the number 19 in decimal.

Table 2-1 shows the binary values of the decimal numbers 0 to 9.

Table 2-1. Binary-Decimal Illustration

Decimal number	eight's	four's	two's	one's	Binary number
zero	0	0	0	0	0
one	0	0	0	1	1
two	0	0	1	0	10
three	0	0	1	1	11
four	0	1	0	0	100
five	0	1	0	1	101
six	0	1	1	0	110
seven	0	1	1	1	111
eight	1	0	0	0	1000
nine	1	0	0	1	1001

Table 2-1 may seem reminiscent of elementary school lessons in addition, but in fact an understanding of binary is critical to many aspects of 8088 programming and to comprehending the structure and workings of the microprocessor.

Hexadecimal

As you can see from Table 2-1, even small numbers require three and four digits in binary. Long strings of 1's and 0's may be fine for the computer, but for the human programmer they can get a little overpowering. Base 16, or the hexadecimal (hex for short) number system, is used to get around this problem. In this system, as you may have guessed, each succeeding digit to the left is greater than the last by a factor of 16. Thus, we have the 1's digit, a 16's digit, a 256's digit, and so forth. For example, the number 47 corresponds to seven 1's and four 16's; (4 × 16) + (7 × 1) = 71.

But wait. In base 10 (our decimal system), we have ten different characters (0–9); in base 2 we have two (0 and 1). For base 16 we need 16 characters. We can understand this need more easily by thinking of what 9 and 10 represent in hex: the decimal numbers 9 and 16. Therefore, to represent in hex the numbers between 9 and 16, the one's place must be able to hold more than 9. In fact, we must be able to represent up to 15 ones in each place. For the first ten we use the base 10 digits 0 to 9. For the remaining six we use the letters A, B, C, D, E, and F, to stand for 10, 11, 12, 13, 14, and 15 respectively. This is shown in Table 2-2.

Table 2-2. Decimal-Binary-Hexadecimal Numbers

Decimal	Binary	Hexadecimal
0	00000000	0
1	00000001	1
2	00000010	2
3	00000011	3
4	00000100	4
5	00000101	5
6	00000110	6
7	00000111	7
8	00001000	8
9	00001001	9
10	00001010	A
11	00001011	B
12	00001100	C
13	00001101	D
14	00001110	E
15	00001111	F
16	00010000	10
17	00010001	11
18	00010010	12

3A uses both letters and numbers; A represents 10 (10 ones). This, added to the three 16's, gives us 58 (3 × 16 + 10) decimal.

Notice in Table 2-2 there's a correspondence between four binary digits and one hexadecimal digit: Four binary digits make up one hexadecimal digit. If you think about it, this makes sense: The most that four binary digits can represent is 1111 or 1 + 2 + 4 + 8, which equals decimal 15. And 15 is the largest number that one hexadecimal digit can represent (F in hex). In fact, any combination of four binary digits can be represented by a single hex digit.

binary 0010 = hex 2
binary 0000 = hex 0
binary 1111 = hex F
binary 1011 = hex B

For this reason hexadecimal is often used for computer programming in lieu of binary. It's compact (one digit instead of four) and it fits in well with binary. Thus, many aspects of machine language are best represented by hex.

Decimal, on the other hand, doesn't work well with binary. You would need about three and a third binary digits to make up one decimal number, and that's not possible. Decimal, therefore, is often not the numbering system of choice when dealing with computers. Some computers do have a provision to handle decimal directly, for the benefit of the programmer; we'll discuss these in "Advanced Arithmetic" (Chapter 8) later in the book.

Another system that works well with binary is base 8, octal. In this system three binary digits make up one octal digit, and we represent numbers in 1's, 8's, 64's, and so forth. Although it's not very common, IBM BASIC and the IBM assembler provide for it.

The concept of base 2 and base 16 requires an extension to our usual way of thinking about numbers. As you have seen, a two-digit number is not merely composed of 1's and 10's, but 1's and 2's, or 1's and 16's. Now that you have gained some understanding of the binary and hexadecimal numbering systems, we'll turn our attention to arithmetic. Once you've mastered the ideas inherent in using a new base, arithmetic in that base is surprisingly simple.

Arithmetic

Addition. Since binary arithmetic is somewhat complex and rarely used, we'll deal only with hexadecimal in our discussion of computer arithmetic. Let's begin with a few simple two-digit additions:

```
  47
+ 26
────
  6D
```

The idea is exactly the same as decimal addition. First you add the one's digits. In this case, 7 + 6 = D. (Remember D is the hex symbol for 13.) Then, we add the sixteen's digits, 4 + 2, and get 6.

Now for a somewhat more complex example:

```
  1A
+ 39
────
  53
```

Here, we have A plus 9 in the one's digit. This would add up to hex 13 (decimal 19), which is too big for a single hex digit. So we adopt the same strategy we use in decimal: Take only the 3 from hex 13, and add the 1 to the next column as a carry. Thus, we have 3 in the one's column, and in the sixteen's column we have 1 plus 3, plus 1 from the carry, to equal 5 in all. Here are a few more examples of hex addition for you to study:

```
  31      5A      A3      99
+ 48    + 5A    + 3A    + 2B
────    ────    ────    ────
  79      B4      DD      C4
```

Subtraction. Subtraction in hex is also similar to decimal.

```
  E3
- 79
────
  6A
```

Here we must subtract 9 from 3. So, just as in decimal, we borrow 10 (decimal 16) from the next column. That gives us 13 hex − 9, which works out to A. (Convert to decimal, if you like: 19 − 9 = 10, or hex A.) Now we move to the next column, the sixteen's. First we subtract 7 from E, to get a result of 7 (in decimal, 14 − 7 = 7). However, we must subtract one from this result, since we borrowed hex 10 in the one's column. So, we have six 16's in the final answer. Here are a few more practice hex subtractions:

```
  74      AA      23      F2
- 42    - 3B    - 1A    - BC
────    ────    ────    ────
  32      6F      09      36
```

Multiplication. Multiplication and division in hex are easier than you would think. When dealing with computers, most multiplying and dividing is in powers of 2 or 16. Thus, it's often the case that you have to take some number and multiply by 16. To do this, all you have to do is add a 0 to the end of the number.

45A9 × 10 = 45A90

or (using computer notation)

45A9 * 10 = 45A90

As you can see, multiplying by 10 hex (decimal 16) in hex math is much like multiplying by decimal 10 in decimal math.

Division. Division works the same way; if you need to divide a number by 16, just shift it over one digit. Since computers rarely use fractions or decimal points, the digit on the end just drops off:

45A9 / 10 = 45A

Again, you may notice the similarity to decimal: Dividing a decimal number by decimal 10 also shifts the number one place to the right.

A calculator that allows hex math can be an important tool when programming in machine language. If you plan to do any serious programming in ML, you should consider purchasing one.

For the moment there are just a few important concepts about these alternate bases to remember:

• Why it is that computers use binary at the lowest level, and why programmers prefer to use hex.
• How to add (most important) as well as subtract and multiply in hex. This knowledge is necessary for understanding and working with segments, which we shall discuss shortly.

Notation and Terminology

In our discussion of arithmetic, you may have been occasionally confused about whether a 10, for example, referred to decimal, binary, or hexadecimal. To distinguish between the systems, we sometimes follow the number by the base as a subscript. Thus,

71_{16}

would refer to 71 base 16. Computers can't handle subscripts, so the assembler uses a letter suffix to indicate the base. Decimal numbers don't have a suffix. Binary numbers have a B suffix (110110B); hexadecimal numbers, an H suffix (45H or 8AH). Since the assembler does not allow a number to begin with a letter, any hex number that begins with a letter (A–F) must begin the number with a zero (for example, FFH is represented as 0FFH; A0H becomes 0A0H). A more complete discussion of the assembler's numeric notation can be found in Chapter 14.

Bits, bytes, and nybbles. A *bit* is one binary digit, a 0 or a 1. A byte is two hex digits, eight bits.

A *byte* is the basic unit of 8088 memory storage, and so is particularly important. A byte can hold values from 0 to 255 decimal (00 to FF hex, or 00000000 to 11111111 binary).

A *nybble* is a four-bit quantity, usually thought of as half a byte. A nybble can be represented by a single hex digit.

Finally, a *word* is two bytes, four hex digits, 16 bits. A word can have a value from 0000 to FFFF hex.

More and larger units exist, but these are uncommon and will be discussed later.

Most and least significant. Least and most significant are terms usually applied to the bits and bytes making up larger numbers. For example, in a byte (eight bits) the most significant bit (binary digit) is the leftmost one. This is the bit with the highest value (128 in decimal) and thus the *most* significant. The least significant bit is the rightmost one (with a value of one). The other common use of these terms is in reference to words.

As we mentioned above, a word is composed of two bytes (each holding up to FF hex). One often refers to the two component bytes of words as most significant and least significant. For example, in the hex word 03AB, the 03 byte is the most significant, and the AB byte is the least significant.

Computer Fundamentals

In order to successfully program in machine language, it is essential to understand how to store numbers, and how to use them when doing math. In this section, we'll discuss the topics relating to storing and using numbers, as well as examining the 8088's internal registers.

Addressing. All computers have a certain amount of memory, consisting of RAM (read/write memory) and ROM (read only memory). In this memory are stored both programs and numbers. The computer keeps track of all this data (both programs and numbers) by placing it at different *addresses*, or locations, within this memory. This concept may already be familiar to those of you who have had a need to use the BASIC keywords POKE and PEEK. With the POKE statement, we POKE a number (a byte) into an address. PEEK, the counterpart of POKE, tells us what number is already stored at a specified address.

For example, load up BASIC on your computer and enter

POKE 10000,123

The POKE puts the number 123 at location 10000 (decimal). We can use PEEK to tell us what is there:

PRINT PEEK(10000)

The computer should display

  123
Ok

Try PEEKing around in memory a little more. You'll find that addresses range from 0 to 65535 and that the numbers that can be placed in an address range from 0 to 255. Above, we mentioned that a word can hold 0000 to FFFF hex, which corresponds to 0 to 65,535 decimal.

Memory. From the point of view of PEEK, all that is stored in memory is numbers. How then does the computer store a program? The answer is simple: as numbers. Most of the numbers from 0 to 255 can serve both as numbers and as machine language instructions. For example, the five numbers 198 6 16 39 123 (in decimal) represent one machine language instruction, telling the computer to put the number 123 into location 10000 (as you did above with POKE). Luckily, using the assembler, you will never need to know which numbers make up which instructions.

An enormous variety of things are stored in a computer's memory (machine language programs, BASIC programs, numbers, and text), but in the end, everything is stored as a number from 0 to 255. Of course, not all of this memory is RAM: Some is empty space, some holds the Operating System, some is used to display information on the screen, and so on. At first, our programs will be using memory only as machine language programs and the data accompanying these programs. Later, we will discuss storage of large numbers (up to 32 bits in length) and of strings of characters.

Segments. Since the computer uses a word to hold addresses, and a word can hold only numbers from 0 to 65,535, many computers can therefore address only 65,536 bytes. This is not true for the IBM's 8088 microprocessor.

Instead of using one word to address memory, the 8088 uses two. To address any particular location, the 8088 adds the two words together to find the actual address. However, to increase the amount of memory that can be accessed by a factor of 16, the 8088 multiplies one of the words by hexadecimal 10 before adding it to the other. Multiplying by 16, as you may recall, is the same as simply adding a 0 to the end of a hex number. So, if one number is 1234 hex and the other (to be multiplied) is 5678 hex, the computer would calculate the actual address as:

```
  1234
+ 56780
  579B4
```

This *segmented* memory system, as you can imagine, allows a huge amount of memory to be addressed. The 8088 uses its segments to make available (in hex) 10000 * 10 = 100000 bytes or (in decimal) 65,536 * 16 = 1,048,576 bytes. This number is known as a *megabyte* (metricized readers may note the mega, or million, prefix). If you wish to put it in truly impressive terms, think one thousand K.

The number that is multiplied by 16 is referred to as the *segment.* The segment is almost always used to define the beginning of a block of memory. Then, the *offset,* a word value, is used to address one of 65,536 bytes within that segment. The segment usually remains the same throughout a program, so machine language programs usually only need to specify the appropriate offset. Different segments are used for the program, the data, and so forth. We'll discuss how segments are used in more detail in a few moments.

Figure 2-1 diagrams one possible arrangement of four segments. Note that the segments can overlap. The shaded areas indicate the possible range of the offset values within each segment.

Registers

Little machine language programming is done directly to memory (in fact, some of it cannot be done directly to memory). To improve performance and to simplify programming, the 8088 uses registers. A *register* is one word that the 8088 holds within itself, directly available to the microprocessor, not

Figure 2-1. Sample Segment Locations

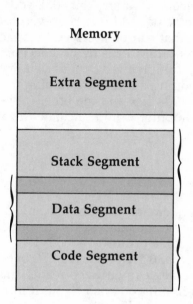

in memory. Using a register is always faster than using data in memory, because registers are, in a sense, part of the 8088. Furthermore, less space is used in program memory to specify one register out of, perhaps, eight, as opposed to one address out of 65,536.

General-purpose registers. The most used registers on the 8088 are the four general-purpose registers, AX, BX, CX, and DX (registers are named, not numbered, to distinguish them from memory). Each of these holds a word (0–FFFF hex), and each is often used for a different purpose.

For now, a few mnemonics will suffice to give a necessarily simplified picture. AX is the Accumulator; it often holds (or accumulates) the values used by the various functions. As a rule, the AX register serves as the pivotal register. BX is the Base register (to be explained in Chapter 7, "Addressing Modes"). CX is the Count register (as explained in "Program Flow," Chapter 5, and "String Instructions," Chapter 9) ; DX is the Data register. Most of the time, however, you can use these registers interchangeably.

Byte registers. Each of the general-purpose registers can also be used as two separate bytes. When we discussed most and least significant above, we mentioned that a word is often separated into its two component bytes. Likewise, for each general-purpose register, there is a *high byte* (most significant) and a *low byte* (least significant). If AX is holding 487A, the high byte holds 48 and the low byte holds 7A. The high and low byte parts of the registers are symbolized by H and L; thus we have AL and AH, BL and BH, CL and CH, and DL and DH. The general-purpose registers are the only registers that can be used both as bytes and words.

Index and pointer registers. The 8088's other registers are more specialized, and more time will be devoted to them in later chapters. For now, just remember that SI and DI are index registers, and SP and BP are pointer registers. Most of these registers can be used just like the general-purpose registers above, but they have other uses, which we'll discuss in due course.

Segment registers. The 8088 also has four specialized registers it uses to hold the segment addresses of the different parts of your program (code, data, and so forth). These *segment registers* are named CS, DS, SS, and ES. CS stands for *Code Segment*. CS holds the segment address for your program code. DS is the *Data Segment;* your program's data is usually in this segment. SS is the *Stack Segment;* this is where the stack for the computer is based. If you're a machine language novice, don't despair; the stack is discussed in detail in Chapter 6. Finally, ES, the *Extra Segment,* is used to address the screen, the Operating System, and so forth, as the programmer wishes.

The Instruction Pointer. The IP, or *Instruction Pointer,* holds an offset value that points into the code segment. This register can't be directly accessed by your programs. Instead, it serves as a pointer into your program. The 8088 uses this pointer to execute the instructions one by one.

Learning machine language is like a giant jigsaw puzzle. And parts of the puzzle are easier to find if you can look at the entire picture. The problem with ML is that it is difficult to see the whole picture before you understand the parts. At this point the parts may seem disjointed and abstract. Don't worry if this discussion of registers doesn't make sense now; as we continue to use these registers throughout the book, their use

15

will become more and more clear as you see the parts fitting in to make the whole picture.

The flags register. One final word-sized register in the 8088 is devoted to the so-called flags. A flag is one bit, either on or off; the on and off states of these flags tell the programmer about various states in the microprocessor. The flags are used with *conditional jumps*, much like IF-THEN statements, to make your program take different actions at critical points.

Some of the flags are *processor flags*, telling the computer what to do when certain situations occur (in this group are the trap flag, the interrupt enable flag, and the direction flag). The other flags are used for arithmetic on the computer. You'll find that two of these other flags, the zero flag and the carry flag, are very useful when doing math of all kinds. Two other flags that are useful when doing signed math are the sign and overflow flags. Table 2-3 is a complete list of the 8088's flags.

Table 2-3. The 8088's Flags

carry flag	trap flag
parity flag	interrupt enable flag
auxiliary carry flag	direction flag
zero flag	overflow flag
sign flag	

Each of these flags will be explained in their appropriate chapters. For now, just remember that a flag is a signal that indicates various states in the microprocessor.

Machine language is no harder to learn than BASIC. Many of the operations in machine language are similar to those in BASIC: moving information from variable to variable, adding, subtracting, multiplying, dividing, dealing with strings, and the like. In fact, many early programmers who had to learn machine language as their first language had difficulty making the transition to BASIC once it became available. Both languages seem to require about as much effort to master.

Now that you have been introduced to the fundamentals of the 8088—the numbering system, the uses of memory, segments, registers, and flags—you are ready to begin your first program, and be introduced to your first machine language command.

Figure 2-2. Registers on the 8088

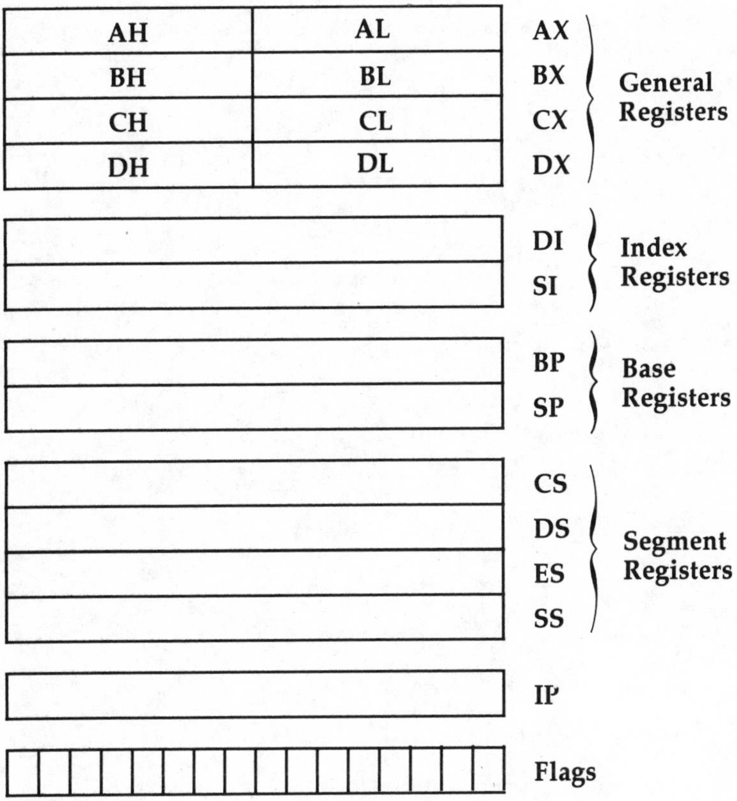

AH	AL	AX	General Registers
BH	BL	BX	
CH	CL	CX	
DH	DL	DX	

	DI — Index Registers
	SI

	BP — Base Registers
	SP

	CS — Segment Registers
	DS
	ES
	SS

	IP

	Flags

1
Basic ML
Programming

3
Getting Started

We'll begin our discussion of the 8088 assembly language with the simple MOV instruction and some of the assembler's pseudo-ops. You will also learn how to use the utility program DEBUG.

The MOV Instruction

The MOV instruction is the most used, and often most useful, of the 8088 instructions. (Note that, by tradition, most assembly language mnemonics are three letters long.) It allows you to move bytes or words between two registers or between registers and locations in memory. The MOV instruction takes the following format:

MOV *destination,source*

MOV takes the source value and moves it to the destination. We will examine three variations on the MOV instruction in this chapter: MOV immediate to register, MOV between registers, and MOV with register indirect addressing.

MOV immediate to register. This first kind of MOV is very straightforward—it moves an immediate value into a register. An *immediate value* is a number that's stored with the machine language instruction itself, not in a separate data segment. For example, the instruction

MOV BX,1234H

moves the hex number 1234 into the BX register. The immediate value is stored as part of the instruction and is moved directly into the register. This is similar to the BASIC LET statement BX=&H1234.

The only limitation on the MOV instruction is that you cannot move an immediate value into a segment register (CS, DS, ES, or SS). Here are a few examples of valid MOV instructions:

```
MOV DX,0A2H        ;a hexadecimal number
MOV BL,4FH         ;hexadecimal
MOV DL,241         ;decimal
MOV AH,10110101B   ;binary
```

(See Chapter 2 for a discussion of the notation used to distinguish binary, decimal, and hexadecimal.)

The immediate value must be the same size as the destination register. In other words, you cannot move a word into a byte register. For example, this is illegal:

MOV DL,4567H

DL is a byte register and 4567H is a word-sized number.

Moving data between registers. Moving a value from one register to another is also quite simple. Below are just a few of the numerous possible register-to-register moves. Notice that the source and the destination registers must be the same size (both either words or bytes).

```
MOV AX,BX
MOV DL,AH
MOV SI,DI
MOV ES,AX
MOV AH,CH
```

Register indirect addressing. This final kind of MOV instruction uses *register indirect* addressing. This too is easy to understand—once you get past the name. With this MOV the computer uses the contents of a register as a memory address's offset, while the DS register provides the segment. In the first example below, the number stored in BX is used as an offset into the data segment. (The computer multiplies the value in the DS register by 10 hex, 16 decimal, and adds the contents of BX. See Chapter 2 for more details on offsets.)

```
MOV AX,[BX]
MOV DL,[SI]
MOV [BX],AL
MOV [DI],DX
```

The contents of the memory location pointed to by BX are moved to AX. The square brackets around BX mean "use the quantity stored in BX as an indirect address." As we shall see in later chapters, these square brackets are common to all indirect addressing modes.

In the next example above, MOV DL,[SI], SI is used as the offset, and the contents of the memory location pointed to by

SI are moved to DL. Notice, in the first example above, that a word is moved, while in the second only a byte is moved. The size of the number to be transferred is determined by the size of the register involved. In the final two examples the destination of the data is another register indirect address. The last example moves the number in DX to the memory location pointed to by DI.

Only four registers can be used in *register indirect* addressing: BX, BP, SI, and DI. Note that you cannot move a number directly from one memory location to another, so something like

MOV [DI],[SI]

is illegal. If you need to move from memory to memory, you must use two MOV instructions and a register. As we shall see, the sample program "Switch" uses this technique.

The 8088 offers almost 20 different ways of addressing data. In Chapter 8 all of the addressing modes will be brought together and examined in detail. However, now that you are familiar with at least some aspects of the MOV command, let's take a look at the sample program Switch.

Writing a Program
The sample program, Switch (Program 3-1), will work with any 8088 computer. Switch is accompanied by a brief tutorial on the use of DEBUG, the machine language debugging tool supplied with your DOS disk. Program 3-2 is a BASIC version of Switch which may help improve your understanding of the machine language version.

Switch is a fairly simple program. It copies the contents of one eight-byte area (labeled SOURCE) to another eight-byte area (labeled DEST, for destination). In the process, it reverses the order of the bytes, so that the DEST area becomes a mirror image of the SOURCE area.

Commenting the program. Before you enter Switch, take a look at its structure. At the beginning of the program, there are a number of lines preceded by semicolons. These are comments, like the single quote (') or REM statements in BASIC programs. They are ignored by the assembler, but are crucial in documenting your program. The first few lines of any program should give the name of the author and explain what the program does. You might also want to include a date or version number for your own reference. Remember, each comment line must be preceded by a semicolon.

Instruction lines. Lines which are not comments (instruction lines) have a definite format and can be broken down into specific fields:

Symbol	Instruction	Comment
NO_RESET:	MOV [BX],AH	;store attribute
A_VERY_LONG_LABEL:		;this is a legitimate symbol
	ADD AH,16	
	MOV AL,34	;initialize AL

The first field contains a name, called a *symbol*. A symbol can be of any length, but only the first 31 characters are recognized as significant. In other words, the first 31 characters of each symbol must be unique. The alphabet characters (the letters A to Z), the digits (the numbers from 0 to 9), and the characters ?, @, _, $, and . are all legal characters. Uppercase and lowercase letters are considered identical; so the symbols "sample", "Sample", and "SAMPLE" are all the same. The first character in a symbol cannot be a digit; if it is, the assembler thinks that the symbol should be a number. If a period is used in a symbol, it must be the first character. When a symbol is used to identify a position within a program (like NO_RESET above), it is called a *label*. A label must be defined with a colon after its name. When a symbol is used to reference data, it is called a *variable*. A variable is never defined with a colon.

The second field is the *instruction field* and contains the operation and the operand. There are basically two kinds of operations: those that produce actual machine code (opcodes, a cryptic abbreviation for operation codes), and those that are interpreted by the assembler and produce no machine code. These operations which produce no code are called *pseudo-ops* for false operations. Only a small number of the pseudo-ops are detailed here. See Appendix C for a list of other pseudo-ops available with the *Macro Assembler*.

The second part of the instruction field is the operand, the information that the operation acts on. The number of operands depends on the particular operation. Some operations take only one operand, others take two, and a few take none.

Comment field is the last field of the line and is optional. Comment must be preceded by a semicolon.

On an instruction line, only the operation and any associated operands are required. The label and the comment are optional. Remember that the assembler considers lines which start with semicolons comments and it ignores them entirely.

Pseudo-Operations

PAGE pseudo-op. The first operation in Switch is the PAGE command. This pseudo-op tells the assembler the width and length of a printed page in the list file. In Switch, PAGE is used as follows:

PAGE ,96

The first parameter is the page length. Since none is specified, 58 is assumed. The next parameter is the width of the page. The second operand, 96, sets the width to 96 characters, which corresponds to a standard printed page at 12 characters per inch.

The SEGMENT pseudo-op. The SEGMENT pseudo-op is used three times in Switch. Its purpose is to define the various segments for the DS, SS, and CS registers. SEGMENT first appears in the program as:

```
DATA    SEGMENT
SOURCE  DB 1,3,5,7,11,13,17,19
DEST    DB 0,0,0,0,0,0,0,0
DATA    ENDS
```

Here, SEGMENT is used to create a separate segment for the program's data. The label preceding the pseudo-op names the segment DATA. The name is arbitrary; we could have called it PAUL, ALEX, or AXZDFG, but naming the segment DATA identifies its purpose. The ENDS pseudo-op at the end of the segment declaration tells the assembler that the segment named by the ENDS command is ending.

Program data. The source and destination areas, named SOURCE and DEST respectively, are within the segment DATA. The initial values of these data areas are defined with the DB (Define Byte) pseudo-op. The eight bytes at SOURCE are filled with the numbers 1, 3, 5, 7, and so forth, and the eight bytes at DEST are filled with zeros.

Stack segment. The next use of the SEGMENT command is to assign the stack segment. This is a special kind of segment and for now must be included in all your programs.

```
STACK   SEGMENT STACK
        DW 128 DUP (?)
STACK   ENDS
```

We will be using this exact format in future programs for the stack segment. Note that we have somewhat arbitrarily assigned the stack segment the name STACK. In Chapter 6, we will explain how and why to use this segment.

Code segment. The last segment we define is the code segment. This is where the machine language instructions are located. This segment has been given the name CODE. Within the segment CODE, however, we must define a "FAR procedure." This is accomplished with the SWITCH PROC FAR instruction. We have named the procedure SWITCH. This procedural declaration is necessary if the program is to return to DOS properly (right now, don't worry about why).

The ASSUME pseudo-op. The last pseudo-op before the actual machine language instructions is ASSUME. The ASSUME command tells the assembler what the segment registers are supposed to be holding. This is necessary for the program to assemble properly. It will be explained in more detail in Chapter 14.

The Machine Language

Now, finally, comes the assembly language. The PUSH DS instruction stores DS on the stack. DS is stored this way so that we can return to DOS. The next operation puts a zero in the AX register (MOV AX,0). Then, we PUSH AX onto the stack, the same way we pushed DS. This, too, is necessary in order to return to DOS properly (this will all be explained in Chapter 6).

Next we must set up the data segment, DS, so that we can address our own data. We do this by assigning the DS register to the location of our data segment. Unfortunately, the 8088 cannot move an immediate value directly into a segment register. To overcome this limitation we first move the value of DATA (which identifies our data segment's position) to AX and then from AX to DS. At this point DS points to the first address of our data segment. Note that setting up the DS register is much like using the DEF SEG command in BASIC (before using PEEKs and POKEs).

The registers SI (Source Index) and DI (Destination Index) are now given their initial values. These registers will act as offsets into the segment DATA. SI is set to zero so that it points to the first byte of the SOURCE area. DI is assigned the value 15 so that it points to the end of the DEST area. The next instruction, MOV AL,[SI], moves into AL the byte pointed to by SI. This is the so-called register indirect addressing that we discussed earlier. Notice, too, that this is the first line with a label as well as a machine language instruction.

SUB DI,1 subtracts 1 from the value of DI. DI now points to the next lower memory location. At the same time, we add 1 to the SI register with the ADD SI,1 instruction. SI now points to the next piece of data in SOURCE.

Finally, we check to see if all the bytes have been moved. If they have not, we jump to MOVE_BYTES (JNE, Jump if Not Equal). If they have, we execute the RET (RETurn) instruction, which returns us to DOS.

After the RET, we must tell the assembler that the procedure has ended (SWITCH ENDP), that the segment has ended (CODE ENDS), and finally, that the program has ended (END). The block-ending statements must be in the opposite order as the beginnings (that is, you must maintain the correct nesting order as with BASIC's nested FOR-NEXT structures). If you get the ENDP and the ENDS out of order, the assembler will give you a block-nesting error.

Entering Source Code

Now that you have at least some idea of how SWITCH works, enter the source code into your computer. Below is a short tutorial on the use of EDLIN. If you have a line editor or word processor which produces DOS-compatible files (see Chapter 1), use it and skip the EDLIN tutorial. If you're using your own word processor, for best results set its formatting options as follows: Set the margins at 0 and 79 and the tab stops every eight spaces. Remember to press Enter after each line, and to save the files as standard DOS (pure ASCII) text files. Do not use line numbers.

Using EDLIN

Make sure that EDLIN.COM is in the default disk, and enter the command:

A> EDLIN SAMPLE.TST

from the DOS prompt. This will load EDLIN and open a file named SAMPLE.TST on the default disk. If you want SAMPLE.TST somewhere else, enter the appropriate device (and path name for DOS 2.00 users); for example, EDLIN B:SAMPLE.TST will put SAMPLE.TST on drive B even though you are logged onto drive A.

If SAMPLE.TST is a new file, you will get the message New File. On the next line, you will see an asterisk. This is EDLIN's prompt. If you get the End of Input File message, you already have a file named SAMPLE.TST and EDLIN is ready to edit it. Since we want to edit a new file, however, leave EDLIN with the Q (Quit) command and answer Y to the Abort edit (Y/N)? prompt. Try a new name for the file, one that does not already exist on the disk.

Now that you have opened a new file, you can enter text with the I (Insert) command. Type I and press Enter. You will see the following:

*I
  1:*_

You may now enter text. You can enter only one line at a time, and pressing Enter moves you to the next line. Note that the star after the line number tells you that this is the current line.

If you make a mistake while entering a line, the Backspace key will delete the last character. Pressing the Esc key erases the entire line (as in BASIC). Pressing F5 (or Fn-5 on the PCjr) allows you to edit the line just as you can edit a DOS command string. Try this as an example.

Type the text shown below and press F5.

1:* This is a sample line

An at sign (@) will appear at the end of the line. The message "This is a sample line" is now stored as a string template. Pressing the cursor-right key copies a character from this template to the displayed string. Pressing the Del deletes the next character in the template; pressing the Ins key allows you to add text without moving the template pointer. If you press cursor right after you insert text, the insert mode will be turned off and the next character will be taken from the template and displayed. Pressing F3 copies the remainder of the template to the input string. Pressing F2, followed by a character, copies all of the characters in the template up to the specified character into the input string. F4 is similar, except that it skips all of the characters in the template up to the specified character. This may all seem confusing, but after some experimentation and practice, it will become clear.

For practice, use the same sample line as above and press F5. Now press the Del key five times and press F3. The line should now read "is a sample line". Now, press F5 again, press Ins and type "That was ", and press F3. Now the line reads "That was is a sample line". To correct our grammar, press F5 again, press F2 and space, then F2 and space again, press F4 and space, and F3. Finally, press Enter to go on to line 2. Now the line should read "That was a sample line". When you are done, you should have the following on your screen:

1:*This is a sample line@
** is a sample line@**
** That was is a sample line@**
** That was a sample line**
2:*_

You can return to the command level of EDLIN by pressing Ctrl-Break (or Fn-Break on the PCjr). The last line is not inserted into your text.

Editing the entire file. Once you have entered a file with EDLIN, you can review your work by entering the command L (List). This will list the lines immediately before and after the line you last entered. If you want to list other lines, precede the L command with the starting and ending line numbers separated by commas. For example, 3,5L will list lines 3 through 5.

If you need to insert additional lines, use the I (Insert) command preceded by the number of the line you want to insert. Remember that EDLIN will insert lines *before* the line you specify. For example, if you want to insert text between lines 4 and 5, use 4I as below:

```
* 1,5L
    1: this
    2: is
    3: a
    4: short
    5: file
*4I
    4:*very
    5:*^C
*1,6L
    1: this
    2: is
    3: a
    4: very
    5: short
    6: file
```

After we inserted the new line 4, all of the lines after the old line 3 have been moved down one to make room for the new line 4. You can append lines to the end of the file with the #I command.

To delete lines you merely specify the lines (as you did with the List command) to remove and the D (Delete) command. Specifying only one line number deletes just that line; not specifying a line number deletes the current line. For example, if we decided that line 4 in the above sample file is not needed after all, we can use the command 4D from the * prompt. Line 4 will be deleted and lines 5 and 6 will automatically be renumbered to lines 4 and 5. Deleting lines one at a time can be confusing because the line numbers are constantly updated. So check the line numbers carefully to avoid deleting the wrong lines.

Editing the text. You can edit a line from the * prompt by entering the number of the line you wish to change. The line which you specify will be printed on the screen. On the following line, EDLIN will print an input prompt. The text of the specified line will be placed in the template buffer (as described above). You can edit the line just as if you had pressed F5. For example ,entering 3 from the * lets you edit line 3 (see below).

```
*3
    3: This is a sample line
    : _
```

There are two ways to leave EDLIN. Use the Q (Quit) command if you do not want to save the file you are working on. Answer the prompt Abort Edit (Y/N)?, with Y if you do not want to save your file, or with N if you have second thoughts. The E (End) command exits EDLIN and saves your file.

You can reenter EDLIN just as you entered it the first time; however, you will receive an End of Input File rather than a New File message. You can now list and edit your file. Remember to leave EDLIN through the E command if you want to save your changes. Your old file is automatically re-named as a backup file (with a .BAK extension).

For a more detailed explanation of EDLIN, see your DOS manual's section on EDLIN.

Entering Your Source Code with EDLIN

Now that you are acquainted with EDLIN, let's enter the sample program Switch. From the DOS prompt, enter the command EDLIN SWITCH.ASM (or whatever name you wish to use). Make sure you are starting a new file (you should get a New File message). Enter the I command and type the first few lines of SWITCH.ASM. Your screen should look something like the text below:

A> EDLIN SWITCH.ASM
 New file
*I
   1:* ; SWITCH.ASM
   2:* ;
   3:* ; Reverses an eight-byte buffer. DEBUG
   4:* ; must be used to analyze the results.
   5:* ; This program should work in any
   6:*_

Enter Program 3-1, Switch. Be certain that you have entered it correctly, editing the text as necessary. When you are done, exit EDLIN. If all goes well, you should now be ready to assemble your program.

The Assembler

After you save your source code file on disk, enter the command MASM (or ASM, depending on which assembler you are using). The computer should respond as follows:

A> MASM
The IBM Personal Computer MACRO Assembler
Version 1.00 (C)Copyright IBM Corp 1981

Or, if you are using ASM:

The IBM Personal Computer Assembler
Version 1.00 (C)Copyright IBM Corp 1981

Answer the questions as follows (assuming that SWITCH.ASM is the name of your source file). The name of the source file is SWITCH.ASM, so type SWITCH and press Enter. The assembler will automatically use the extension .ASM. It will also assume that the name of the object file is SWITCH.OBJ, so just press Enter. We want a list file, so type SWITCH and press Enter. The assembler will append the .LST extension. We do not want a cross-reference file so just press Enter. You should have the following on your screen:

Source filename [.ASM]: SWITCH
Object filename [SWITCH.OBJ]:
Source listing [NUL.LST]: SWITCH
Cross reference [NUL.CRF]:

If you prefer, you can specify different extensions. Also note that the name of the .LST file defaults to "NUL.LST"; if you do not want a list file, then just press Enter at this prompt.

After you have answered all of the questions, the assembly process will begin. The assembly is done in two passes. The assembler reads the source code once, doing a mock assembly. This first pass determines the position of all the labels within the program. The second pass produces the actual object file.

After a short while, the assembler should print:

Warning Severe
Errors   Errors
0   0

on the screen. If you received any errors, either Warning or Severe, reenter your editor and correct the problems. Reassemble the program. Only when you receive no errors are you ready to go on.

The assembler .LST file. Enter the command "TYPE SWITCH.LST" to print the list file to the screen. You should get a listing much like Program 3-3. If you want to send this to the printer, turn on the printer echo (Ctrl-PrtSc, or Fn-Echo on the PCjr) and use the TYPE command. When the entire file has been printed, you should turn off the printer echo by pressing Ctrl-PrtSc (or Fn-Echo) again. If you prefer, you can tell the assembler to output the list file directly to the printer by naming the list file PRN (for printer). However, this latter method often does not work on non-IBM printers. Now let's look at the list file's key components.

At the top of each page the assembler prints

The IBM Personal Computer MACRO Assembler 8-18-84 PAGE 1-1

After the assembler's name comes the date and the page number. The number before the dash is the chapter number, while the number after the dash is the page number. The chapter number is not important.

The numbers which are printed on the left edge of the page are the offsets into the current segment. Notice that the first offset number does not appear until we define the first segment. The numbers to the right of the offset are the data which is stored at that offset. The data and the offset values are always printed in hexadecimal. Starting about halfway across the page is a listing of the source file. Bear in mind that long lines will wrap around the edge of the page. This makes reading the printout difficult, so use as many columns as possible (96 is generally sufficient).

Also notice that on the line which moves DATA (the address of our data segment) into AX, there is no hexadecimal value for DATA, only four dashes. This means that the assembler does not know where the segment DATA is going to be located; the address of the data segment will be calculated only when the program is loaded into memory.

The last page of the assembly listing is the *symbol table*. It has information about the labels and variables used in the program. They are in two groups and are arranged alphabetically within the groups. The first group, titled Segments and Groups, is a table of the segments which we defined in the program. Their size (again in hexadecimal), alignment, and combine class are also given. These last two entries are not important until you know more about the assembler. The second list, titled Symbols, is a table of the labels and variables which are used in the program. For now, don't worry about their type and attributes.

The LINK Program

Once SWITCH assembles without errors, you are ready to link the program. From the DOS prompt, execute the LINK program by typing LINK and pressing Enter:

A> LINK
IBM Personal Computer Linker
Version 2.00 (C)Copyright IBM Corp 1981, 1982, 1983

If you are using DOS 1.10, you will see

IBM Personal Computer Linker
Version 1.10 (C)Copyright IBM Corp 1982

The LINK program will convert the .OBJ file generated by the assembler into an executable .EXE file. The .EXE file can be loaded and run like any other DOS program. Answer the questions as follows. The name of the object file is SWITCH.OBJ, so type SWITCH and press Enter. LINK will automatically append the .OBJ extension. We want the .EXE file to be called SWITCH.EXE, so just press Enter. Since we do not want a .MAP file, nor have we defined any Libraries, just press Enter to the last two prompts. You should have the following on your screen:

Object Modules [.OBJ]: SWITCH
Run File [SWITCH.EXE]:
List File [NUL.MAP]:
Libraries [.LIB]:

You can specify a different extension for the object file if you desire. However, you can't change the extension of the run file, which is always .EXE. It is unlikely that you will receive an error from the LINK program other than a Cannot Find File error. If you receive such an error, be certain that you have entered the name of the object file correctly.

Running Switch

Now that we have assembled and linked SWITCH, you are ready to execute it. From the DOS prompt type

A> SWITCH

and press Enter. The DOS prompt should return after a moment or two. If it does not, the computer has probably crashed. Try pressing Ctrl-Break (Fn-Break on a PCjr). If this does not return you to DOS, you will have to reset the computer with Ctrl-Alt-Del. If the crash is very severe, even this may not revive the computer, in which case you will have to turn the computer off and back on again. If your computer crashes when you run Switch, you must double-check the source program for any typing errors, correct them, and re-assemble the program. Unfortunately, we still do not know if Switch actually works since it does everything internally. How can we tell if it is doing anything at all? We must use DEBUG, which allows us to examine our program and to watch it execute instruction by instruction (using the Trace command). It can also dump and unassemble memory, as well as change the contents of registers and memory locations. DEBUG is supplied on your DOS disk.

Using DEBUG: the Unassemble Command

Type the command DEBUG SWITCH.EXE from the DOS prompt. The DEBUG prompt, a dash (–), will appear on the screen. Type U (for Unassemble) and press Enter. The unassembly of the Switch program should be printed as below:

```
-U
091B:0000    1E          PUSH    DS
091B:0001    B80000      MOV     AX,0000
091B:0004    50          PUSH    AX
091B:0005    B81F33      MOV     AX,091D    our data segment
091B:0008    8ED8        MOV     DS,AX
091B:000A    BE0000      MOV     SI,0000    start of source
091B:000D    BF0F00      MOV     DI,000F    end of destination
091B:0010    8A04        MOV     AL,[SI]
091B:0012    8805        MOV     [DI],AL
091B:0014    83EF01      SUB     DI,+01
091B:0017    83C601      ADD     SI,+01
091B:001A    83FE08      CMP     SI,+08
091B:001D    75F1        JNZ     0010
091B:001F    CB          RETF               program ends
```

If you are using DEBUG from DOS 1.10, the last line of the program will look like this:

```
091B:001F    CB          RET     L          DEBUG 1.10 differs
```

From now on, DOS 1.10 users should read RET L every time RETF is used. Note that the number before the colon (the 091B) may be different in your computer.

Let's take a close look at DEBUG's output. The example below breaks a typical line down into three fields.

Address   Bytes   Assembly Instruction
091B:0012   8805   MOV [DI],AL

The first field indicates the address of the instruction in hexadecimal. The number before the colon is the segment address and the number after the colon is the offset into the segment. This is known as the *segment:offset* form of representing an address.

The next field, Bytes, is the group of bytes that make up the assembly language instruction. In the example above, the two bytes which make up the instruction MOV [DI],AL are 88H and 05H.

If you compare the DEBUG output with the source code, you will notice that there are no longer any labels. Also notice that our JNE (Jump if Not Equal) has been turned into a JNZ (Jump if Not Zero) instruction. These are identical operations. The difference in name is for the sake of the human, not the computer (all of the conditional jumps will be explained in Chapter 5). Our RET has also been changed into a RETF. RETF stands for Far Return, and will be explained in Chapter 6.

Also note how DEBUG shows bytes when a word value is part of an operand. For example, the assembler .LST file may unassemble an instruction as:

Assembler: BF 000F MOV DI,15

while DEBUG reverses the order of the last two bytes:

DEBUG: BF0F00 MOV DI,000F

(Remember that it takes two bytes to make up a 16-bit word.) In fact, the assembler is actually reversing the bytes, not DEBUG. The two bytes which make up a word are stored in a low byte/high byte format. This means that the least significant byte precedes the most significant byte (the byte which represents the bigger value comes last). In the actual program, the bytes appear as 0F 00, not 00 followed by 0F, as the assembler .LST file seems to imply.

The purpose of unassembling the file was to find the data segment. If you look carefully, DATA has been turned into the hex value 091D (this value varies; it depends on how your particular computer is configured). In our case, the data, which is a short series of prime numbers, can be found at 91D:0.

Using the Dump command. To check to see if the data is there, we can instruct DEBUG to display a portion of memory.

Enter D followed by the desired segment and the offset. In this case we would type (remember to use the segment you determined, which might not be the same as the one given below):

- D 91D:0

DEBUG should print something similar to the following:

```
- D 91D:0
091D:0000  01 03 05 07 0B 0D 11 13-00 00 00 00 00 00 00 00   . . . . . . . . . . . . . . . .
091D:0010  00 00 00 00 00 00 00 00-00 00 00 00 00 00 00 00   . . . . . . . . . . . . . . . .
091D:0020  00 00 00 00 00 00 00 00-00 00 00 00 00 00 00 00   . . . . . . . . . . . . . . . .
091D:0030  00 00 00 00 00 00 00 00-00 00 00 00 00 00 00 00   . . . . . . . . . . . . . . . .
091D:0040  00 00 00 00 00 00 00 00-00 00 00 00 00 00 00 00   . . . . . . . . . . . . . . . .
091D:0050  00 00 00 00 00 00 00 00-00 00 00 00 00 00 00 00   . . . . . . . . . . . . . . . .
091D:0060  46 FE EB D5 C4 1E A0 13-B0 00 26 38 07 75 09 A2   F   kUD.   . 0 . & 8 . u . "
091D:0070  AC 13 26 88 47 01 EB 05-C6 06 AC 13 FF B0 00 A2   , . & . G. k. F . , . . 0 . "
```

The format of the memory dump can be broken down into three sections as shown below.

Address   091D:0060

Sixteen bytes of data in hex format
    46 FE EB D5 C4 1E A0 13-B0 00 26 38 07 75 09 A2

Character format F kUD. .0.&8.u."

The first field is the address, much like in the Unassemble command. In the next section are the 16 bytes starting from the address shown in the first field. In the last field are the characters which represent the 16 bytes shown in the previous field. Any unprintable characters are represented by a period.

The Go and Enter commands. The Go command is used to execute the program. Type G (for Go) and press Enter. DEBUG should print Program Terminated Normally and give you the dash prompt. Now reexamine the data segment:

- D 91D:0
```
091D:0000  01 03 05 07 0B 0D 11 13-13 11 0D 0B 07 05 03 01  .....
```

(Only the first line is shown here; the rest is unimportant.) Notice that the eight zero bytes (the DEST data) are now filled with the prime numbers in reverse order.

Now that we know that the program works, let's play with it a little. We can use DEBUG to modify the SOURCE memory area with the E (Enter) command. Type E 91D:0 "compute!" (remember to use your data segment address) and press Enter. Then display the SOURCE area again:

```
E 91D:0 "compute!"
- D 91D:0
091D:0000  63 6F 6D 70 75 74 65 21-13 11 0D 0B 07 05 03 01  compute! . . . . . . . .
```

Notice how the ASCII string *compute!* has filled the eight bytes of the SOURCE area. The format of the E command is very simple. The numbers after the E are the location, and the string in quotes is the data. The ending quote is required, or you will get an error from DEBUG. Now run Switch again, using the G command, and dump the data in the SOURCE buffer area.

```
- G
```

Program terminated normally

```
- D 91D:0
091D:0000  63 6F 6D 70 75 74 65 21-21 65 74 75 70 6D 6F 63  compute!!etupmoc
```

The *compute!* has been reversed to *!etupmoc*.

This has demonstrated one method of entering data into memory. See your DOS manual for the other available options with this command.

The Register command. Type R and press Enter. DEBUG should respond with something similar to the following:

```
- R
AX=0000  BX=0000  CX=0080  DX=0000     SP=01FC  BP=0000 SI=0000  DI=0000
DS=090B  ES=090B  SS=091E  CS=091B     IP=0005    NV UP DI PL NZ NA PO NC
091B:0005  B81D09        MOV        AX,091D
```

(The output on a 40-column screen will be different.) The first two lines indicate the current values of the registers. At the end of the second line is a list of the flags and their current statuses. Table 3-1 gives the abreviations that DEBUG uses to indicate the statuses of the 8088's flags (the different flags will be explained in the following chapters).

Table 3-1. DEBUG Flag Status Names

Name of Flag	Set (Flag=1)	Clear (Flag=0)
Overflow	OV = overflow	NV = no overflow
Direction	DN = decrement	UP = increment
Interrupt	EI = enabled	DI = disabled
Sign	NG = negative	PL = plus
Zero	ZR = zero	NZ = not zero
Auxiliary Carry	AC = yes	NA = no
Parity	PE = even	PO = odd
Carry	CY = carry	NC = no carry

The third line of DEBUG's response shows the address of the next instruction, the bytes which make up that instruction, and the unassembled instruction itself (this is the same format as the Unassemble command). This is the instruction which will be executed first when you enter the G command.

An option of the R command allows you to change the values of the registers. Type R AX and DEBUG will respond:

- R AX
AX 0000
:_

DEBUG is now waiting for you to enter the desired value for the register AX. You can enter any word-sized value to be placed in AX. Pressing Enter without any other input means that you do not want to change the value in AX. Any of the registers can be changed in this way.

The Trace command. Type T (for Trace) and press Enter. The format of the output is identical to that of the R command. If you enter T again, you will step through the next machine language instruction. You can step through more than one instruction at a time by specifying a number after the Trace command. For example:

- T 10

will trace through the next 16 instructions (remember, DEBUG does everything in hexadecimal).

This feature of DEBUG can be very useful in the debugging of a program. You can go through the program step by step and examine the effects of different instructions on the flags and the contents of the registers. Note that DEBUG occasionally skips instructions. There is nothing wrong with DEBUG; this is perfectly normal. This skipping will be discussed in Chapter 11.

For more examples of how to use DEBUG, see Section 5, "Sample Programs," or your DOS manual. Play with DEBUG and Switch. When you have had enough, you can exit the DEBUG utility program with the Q (Quit) command.

Writing Your Own Programs

Program 3-4 is a fill-in-the-blank program, a program template, which you can use until you are more familiar with the assembler and assembly language. Keep in mind that the structure of the sample programs is not fixed, nor is it standardized. You are free to format and structure your programs as you will. The examples are simply guides that represent a format which we like to use. Feel free to devise your own system.

Program 3-1. SWITCH.ASM

```
;   SWITCH.ASM
;
;   Reverses an eight byte buffer. DEBUG
;   must be used to analyze the results.
;   This program should work in any
;   MS-DOS computer.
;
;   Marc Sugiyama 8/15/84
;
            page  ,96

data        segment                         ;segment which holds buffers
source      db 1,3,5,7,11,13,17,19          ;source buffer
dest        db 0,0,0,0,0,0,0,0              ;empty destination buffer
data        ends
;
stack       segment stack                   ;stack segment
            dw 128 dup (?)                  ;give the stack 256 bytes
stack       ends
;
code        segment                         ;segment for code
switch      proc far                        ;for proper return to DOS
            assume cs:code,ds:data,ss:stack
;
            push ds                         ;set up for FAR RETurn to DOS
            mov ax,0
```

```
        push ax

        mov ax,data        ;set up DS for data segment
        mov ds,ax

        mov si,0           ;first byte of source area
        mov di,15          ;last byte of destination area
move_bytes:
        mov al,[si]        ;move from source to AL
        mov [di],al        ;move from AL to destination
        sub di,1           ;reduce dest pointer by one
        add si,1           ;increase source pointer by one
        cmp si,8           ;moved all of the bytes?
        jne move_bytes     ;if not, do more.

        ret                ;return to DOS

switch  endp               ;end of procedure declaration
code    ends               ;end of code segment
        end                ;end of program
```

Program 3-2. SWITCH.BAS

```
100 ' SWITCH.BAS
110 '
120 '
130 '
140 DEFINT A-Z
150 '
160 DIM DATASEG(15)
170 FOR I=0 TO 15:READ DATASEG(I):NEXT
180 DATA 1,3,5,7,11,13,17,19:          'sourc
    e
190 DATA 0,0,0,0,0,0,0,0      :         'dest
200 '
210 PRINT"Before":GOSUB 380 'dump "memory"
220 '
230 SI = 0                             '
        MOV SI,0
240 DI = 15                            '
        MOV DI,15
250                                    'MOVE_
    BYTES:
260 AL = DATASEG(SI)                   '
        MOV AL,[SI]
270 DATASEG(DI) = AL                   '
        MOV [DI],AL
```

```
280 DI = DI - 1
    SUB DI, 1                               '
290 SI = SI + 1
    ADD SI, 1                               '
300 ZF = (SI = 8)
    CMP SI, 8                               '
310 IF NOT ZF THEN 260
    JNE MOVE_BYTES
320 '
330 PRINT:PRINT"After":GOSUB 380 'dump "memory
    "                                       '
340 '
350 END
    RET
360 '
370 ' Dump "memory" in hex
380 PRINT"memory: ";:I=0:GOSUB 410:PRINT "- ";
    :I=8:GOSUB 410:PRINT
390 RETURN
400 '
410 FOR J=0 TO 7:PRINT RIGHT$("0"+HEX$(DATASEG
    (I+J)),2);" ";:NEXT
420 RETURN
```

Program 3-3. SWITCH.LST

The IBM Personal Computer MACRO Assembler 01-01-80   PAGE   1-1

```
                               ; SWITCH.ASM
                               ;
                               ; Reverses an eight byte buffer. DEBUG
                               ; must be used to analyze the results.
                               ; This program should work in any
                               ; MS-DOS computer.
                               ;
                                       page  ,96
0000                           data    segment              ;segment which holds buffers
0000  01 03 05 07 0B 0D        source  db 1,3,5,7,11,13,17,19   ;source buffer
      11 13
0008  00 00 00 00 00 00        dest    db 0,0,0,0,0,0,0,0      ;empty destination buffer
0010  00 00
0010                           data    ends
                               ;
0000                           stack   segment stack        ;stack segment
0000  80 [                     stack   dw 128 dup (?)        ;give the stack 256 bytes
          ????
      ]
0100                           stack   ends
                               ;
0000                           code    segment              ;segment for code
0000                           switch  proc far             ;for proper return to DOS
                                       assume cs:code,ds:data,ss:stack
                               ;
```

44

```
0000  1E            push ds           ;set up for FAR RETurn to DOS
0001  B8 0000       mov ax,0
0004  50            push ax
              ;
0005  B8 ---- R     mov ax,data       ;set up DS for data segment
0008  8E D8         mov ds,ax
              ;
000A  BE 0000       mov si,0          ;first byte of source area
000D  BF 000F       mov di,15         ;last byte of destination area
0010          move_bytes:
0010  8A 04         mov al,[si]       ;move from source to AL
0012  88 05         mov [di],al       ;move from AL to destination
0014  83 EF 01      sub di,1          ;reduce dest pointer by one
0017  83 C6 01      add si,1          ;increase source pointer by one
001A  83 FE 08      cmp si,8          ;moved all of the bytes?
001D  75 F1         jne move_bytes    ;if not, do more.
              ;
001F  CB            ret               ;return to DOS
              ;
0020          switch endp             ;end of procedure declaration
0020          code   ends             ;end of code segment
              end                     ;end of program
```

The IBM Personal Computer MACRO Assembler 01-01-80   PAGE   Symbols-1

Segments and groups:

Name	Size	align	combine class
CODE	0020	PARA	NONE
DATA	0010	PARA	NONE
STACK.	0100	PARA	STACK

Symbols:

Name	Type	Value	Attr	
DEST	L BYTE	0008	DATA	
MOVE_BYTES	L NEAR	0010	CODE	
SOURCE	L BYTE	0000	DATA	
SWITCH	F PROC	0000	CODE	Length =0020

Warning Severe
Errors Errors
   0   0

Program 3-4. Program Template

```
; program name
;
; description
;
; author and date/version
;
        page ,96

data    segment                    ;segment for data
        [put your data ...
         ... in here]
data    ends
;
```

```
stack   segment stack
        dw 128 dup (?)          ;stack segment
                                ;give the stack 128 words
stack   ends
;
code    segment                 ;segment for code
program proc far                ;for proper return to DOS
assume cs:code,ds:data,ss:stack
;
        push ds                 ;for far return to DOS
        mov ax,0
        push ax
;
        mov ax,data             ;set up your data segment in DS
        mov ds,ax
;
        [put your...
        ...program...
        ...code...
        ...in here]
;
        ret                     ;return to DOS
;
program endp                    ;end of procedure declaration
code    ends                    ;end of segment code declaration
        end                     ;end of program
```

4
Arithmetic

Computers are known for their number-crunching abilities.
The 8088 is no exception; it is a very powerful microprocessor.
In this chapter, you will be introduced to the basic mathematical operations of addition, subtraction, multiplication, and division.

Negative Numbers

In Chapter 2 you learned that binary digits can be chained together into eight-bit bytes. You were also told that a byte could represent the numbers from 0 to 255 (0 to FF hex). This is the unsigned number range of the byte. A byte can also represent the *signed* number from −128 to +127. There are still eight bits to a byte; only the interpretation of the bits is different. When a byte is meant to represent a signed number, the most significant bit (the bit representing 128) is the *sign bit*.

When the sign bit is zero, the byte is positive (0 to 127). When the sign bit is one, the byte is negative (−128 to −1).

Signed words are similar to signed bytes. Recall that a word is made up of 16 bits and can represent the numbers from 0 to 65,535 (0 to FFFF hex). This is a word's unsigned range. The signed range of a word is −32,768 to 32,767. The sign bit is still the most significant bit of the number (the bit representing 32,768). As with signed bytes, a sign bit with the value of zero means that the word is positive (0 to 32,767), while a sign bit with the value of one means that the word is negative (−32,768 to −1).

The actual storage of signed numbers is complex. The method which is used is called *twos complement*. This method of representing negative numbers is very similar to the one used by counters on tape players. Most tape recorders have a three-digit counter which can represent the numbers from 000 to 999. Let's pretend that the tape in the recorder is a number line. The tape counter tells us where we are on the line.

Try this exercise: Fast-forward the tape to the middle, and zero the tape counter. Now, fast-forward the tape some more. Note that the counter starts from 0 and counts up. When the counter reads 005, we understand that we are five counts away from 0 in the positive direction. Now rewind the tape. The counter will begin to count down. When it passes 000, it will start again from 999. We understand that when the counter reads 999, we are one count away from 0; but this time we are on the negative side. If we stop the tape when the counter reads 990, we know that we are ten counts away from 0—we are at the position −10 on the tape.

Negative binary numbers are similar. For the moment, consider only signed bytes. A byte can represent the numbers from 0 to 255. You can think of a byte as a tape counter which can count up only to 255. If we rewind from 0 with this byte counter, the first number we will get is 255 (like we get 999 on a real tape counter), so 255 is like −1. Notice that the most significant bit, the sign bit, is 1; thus the number is negative.

For words, the only difference is that the maximum count is not 255 but 65,535. When our "word counter" counts backwards from 0, we get 65,535.

ADD, SUB, and NEG

ADD and SUB, add and subtract, are versatile instructions which allow you to add to or subtract from registers or memory addresses. The format of both instructions is the same:

ADD *destination,source*
destination = destination + source

SUB *destination,source*
destination = destination − source

Notice the mathematical representations of the operations. ADD takes the source value, adds it to the destination, and places the sum in the destination. SUB does the same, only it subtracts rather than adds.

The source for these instructions can be a general register (any register except the segment registers, the flags, and IP), a memory location, or an immediate value. The destination can be a general register or a memory location. As with the MOV instruction, the source and destination cannot both be memory locations.

Because the 8088 is a 16-bit microprocessor with an 8-bit heritage, the ADD and SUB instructions come in two forms, one for 16 bits and the other for 8 bits. The assembler automatically determines which instruction you need to use. Below are some examples of the ADD and SUB commands.

ADD AX,4   ;add 4 to the contents of AX
ADD BX,DX   ;add contents of DX to BX, result in BX
ADD DL,DH   ;8-bit addition
SUB DX,AX   ;subtract AX from DX, result in DX
SUB [BX],AL   ;subtract AL from indirectly addressed memory

The NEGate instruction changes the sign of a number. If the number was positive, it is made negative, and if it was negative, it is made positive. NEG takes the form shown below:

NEG *operand*

The operand can be any general byte, word register, or memory location. This instruction can be used when you need to subtract a register from an immediate value. For example, you cannot use SUB to subtract AL from 100:

SUB 100,AL

This is illegal because the destination cannot be an immediate value. Instead, you have to use something like:

NEG AL
ADD AL,100

First we negate AL (so AL $= -$AL), then we add it to 100. In other words, we have:

AL $= -$AL   'negate AL
AL $= 100 +$ AL   'add (the negated) AL to 100

There are three processor flags which are important to addition and subtraction. These flags are used for error checking and for program decision making. Decision making and program flow are the topics of the next chapter.

The *sign* flag (abbreviated SF) indicates the sign of the result of the last operation; however, only certain operations, such as addition and subtraction, set this flag. If you are unsure whether SF is set by an operation, check Appendix A. If SF is set (has a value of one), the last result was negative. If it is clear (has a value of zero), the result was positive.

The *overflow* flag (OF) is set whenever a mathematical operation overflows the range for signed numbers. OF is set if the result is greater than 127 or less than −128 for bytes, or greater than 32,767 or less than −32,768 for words. If the result is within the range of signed numbers, the overflow flag is clear.

The last flag which should be mentioned in connection with ADD and SUB, is the *carry* flag (CF). During addition, CF is used to hold any carry out of the highest bit. Thus, for byte addition, the carry represents the "ninth bit," and for word addition, the carry is the "seventeenth bit." With subtraction, CF is used to indicate a borrow into the highest bit. CF will be important only when we begin to investigate advanced arithmetic in Chapter 8.

INC and DEC

INC (INCrement) and DEC (DECrement) are used to increment and decrement a register or memory location by 1. The form of both these instructions is:

INC *memory location*
memory location = memory location + 1

DEC *memory location*
memory location = memory location − 1

INC and DEC set the sign and overflow flags, but do not set the carry flag. Both instructions can operate on bytes or words.

INC and DEC are useful in addressing memory. We can move a pointer up or down one byte within a table. For example, in the program "Switch" we could have used INC SI and DEC DI rather than the ADD and SUB instructions. They can also be used in loops; more about loops later.

MUL

The multiply and divide functions are somewhat less versatile than their addition and subtraction counterparts. However, the 8088 is the first microprocessor in wide use which offers multiply and divide operations. In the past—with 8080, Z80, and 6502 systems—programmers had to write special subroutines to multiply and divide.

MUL, the multiply instruction, allows you to find the product of two numbers. There are two MUL instructions: one for multiplying bytes, and another for multiplying words.

Byte multiplication multiplies the AL register by another general byte register or an addressed memory location. You cannot multiply by an immediate value. The format of this instruction is:

MUL *source*

Since the product of two bytes can be greater than 255 (in fact, it can be as great as 65,025), the 8088 uses all of AX to store the result of byte multiplication; so AX = AL * *source*.

If the product is greater than 255, OF and CF are set (they have the value of 1). For example, if we multiply 57 by 24, using byte multiplication, the product is 1368, far too large to fit in a single byte. Since all of AX is used to store the result, the carry and overflow flags will be set, indicating that the result uses the high-order byte to store part of the product. If, on the other hand, we multiply 45 by 4, the product is only 180, small enough to fit into one byte. The entire product will fit in AL, so the carry and overflow flags are cleared. Note that the other arithmetic flags are undefined.

Word multiplication multiplies the AX register by another general word register or an addressed memory location. Again, you cannot multiply by an immediate value. The format of word multiplication is identical to that of byte multiplication, only the source is a word, not a byte.

The product of two words can be considerably greater than 65,535 (the capacity of a word), so the 8088 uses the AX and DX registers to hold the result of word multiplication. AX holds the least significant word, DX the most significant word. In other words, AX and DX hold a 32-bit number. A 32-bit number is often referred to as a double word.

If the result of word multiplication is greater than 65,535, CF and OF are set to indicate that the high-order word (DX) is used to hold part of the product.

You select which multiplication you want, either byte or word, with the operand. If the operand is byte-sized, then byte multiplication is used. If, on the other hand, the operand is word-sized, word multiplication is used. For example, if you use:

MUL BL

BL will be multiplied by AL. However, if you use:

MUL BX

BX will be multiplied by AX.

If you wish to square the value in AL (AL^2), you can use

MUL AL

This also works with AX.

IMUL

The IMUL instruction is identical to MUL in every respect, except that IMUL takes the sign of the number into consideration before it multiplies. In other words, MUL is used only for unsigned numbers, while IMUL is used only for signed numbers. It is very important that you make this distinction. If MUL is used on signed numbers, or IMUL on unsigned numbers, the results are interesting, but entirely meaningless.

DIV

Using the DIV instruction, you can divide two numbers to find the quotient and the remainder.

Byte division is used to divide a word by a byte. The general format of byte division is

DIV *source*

The source can be any general byte register or a memory location. As with MUL, the source cannot be an immediate value. With byte division, the word stored in AX is divided by the source byte. The quotient is stored in AL, while the remainder is stored in AH. For example, the code:

```
MOV AX,97
MOV BL,13
DIV BL
```

divides 97 by 13. After the division, AL will hold 7 (the quotient) and AH will hold 6 (the remainder). Note that all of the arithmetic flags are undefined after division.

If you want to divide a single byte by another byte, you have to set AH to 0 before you divide. For example, if you would like to divide a number in AL by BL, you need to clear AH first:

```
MOV AH,0
DIV BL
```

The second DIV instruction is used to divide a double word by a word. The double word is stored in AX and DX, as was described in the word multiplication discussion. The format of word division is identical to that of byte division, only the source must be a word, not a byte. Thus, the source must be a general word register, or a word-sized variable.

With word division the quotient is stored in AX, and the remainder in DX. Note that if you are only dividing a word by another word, you must set DX to 0 before you divide. For example, if you want to divide 15,837 by 1,343, you can use something like:

```
MOV AX,15837
MOV DX,0
MOV CX,1343
DIV CX
```

After the division, AX will hold 11 (the quotient) and DX 1064 (the remainder). As with byte division, all of the arithmetic flags are undefined after word division.

When using the DIV instruction you select which division you want, byte or word, by the size of the operand. If the operand is byte-sized, byte division is used. For example, if you use

```
DIV BL
```

AX will be divided by BL. If, on the other hand, you use a word-sized operand, then word division is used:

```
DIV CX
```

Here, the double word stored in AX and DX will be divided by CX.

The 8088 has a rather dramatic way of indicating an error in division. If there is a divide overflow, the 8088 generates a type zero interrupt (interrupts are discussed in Chapter 11). This causes the computer to print the message Divide Overflow and exit the program. For example, the code below will generate an overflow error:

```
MOV AX,900
MOV BL,3
DIV BL
```

In this example, the quotient is 300 (900 divided by 3). This is a byte division (the divisor is a byte quantity), so the quotient must fit in the AL register. As you can see, it does not. The computer will print the message Divide Overflow and program execution will cease.

One solution to this problem is to use word division even though you are dividing by a byte.

```
MOV AX,900
MOV DX,0
MOV CX,3
DIV CX
```

DOS 2.00 users note that, because of a bug in DOS 2.00, the computer will crash when it tries to print the Divide Overflow error message. You will probably be unable to reset the computer with the Ctrl-Alt-Del combination. So, you'll have to turn the computer off and reboot. This problem has been corrected in DOS 2.10. DOS 1.10 works fine as well.

IDIV

As there are signed and unsigned versions of the multiplication instructions, there are signed and unsigned divisions. DIV only works on unsigned numbers. If you are using signed numbers, you must use IDIV. In all other respects, IDIV and DIV are identical.

A Sample Program

The sample program for this chapter, "Primes," finds prime numbers. Since it uses a word to store all of its results, it can find primes up to only 65535 (there are over 6500 of them). Primes was written to demonstrate some of the instructions introduced in this chapter; there are more efficient ways to write this program.

A prime number is a number that is divisible only by one and itself. The numbers 2, 3, 5, 7, and 11 are all prime. Prime numbers occur at uneven intervals and have been the object of much scrutiny in recent years. As you might imagine, determining whether or not a number is prime is not very difficult; just divide the number in question by all the numbers between one and itself. For example, if we were testing the number 15, we would divide 15 by the numbers 2 through 14. If any of the numbers divided without remainders, we would know that 15 is not prime. For smaller numbers this is a good system; after all, the computer is very fast. Consider, however, what would happen with very large numbers—for instance, 2003. The computer would have to do 2001 divisions to find out whether it is prime. Even for a computer, that would take a noticeable amount of time.

We must find a way to reduce the length of the search for even divisors. To begin with, the search can be shortened by remembering that we need only check for possible factors. If a number is not prime, its lowest possible factors will be prime numbers. For example, 21 has two factors, 7 and 3 (both prime numbers). (We could limit our search for factors still further by searching up only to the square root of the number, but then we would have to write a square root routine.)

Outlined below is the general flow of a program which uses this method to find prime numbers. This is not what programmers call a flow chart, but an English version of how the program is supposed to work.

1. Divide the number in question by all of the previously found primes.
2. If any of the numbers divide evenly, select a new number and start checking to see if it is prime.
3. If the number is prime, add it to our list of prime numbers, print the number, and look for the next prime.

The only hard part in our algorithm is printing the prime numbers on the screen. DOS, however, helps out by providing a Print Character routine. This DOS function is called by the routine BYTE_OUT towards the end of Primes. DOS function calls will be explained in Chapter 13.

The only difficulty in printing the number is converting it from its binary form to a decimal form. The routine which conducts this conversion is named DECIMAL_OUT. DECIMAL_OUT divides the number it is trying to output repeatedly by 10. This routine will be explained in more detail in Chapter 6.

PRIMES.ASM

The first few lines are the comment header, common to all of the sample programs. It identifies the program and its purpose, and gives the name of the author and the last date the program was modified. Following these comments is the PAGE pseudo-op, which defines the size of the printed page as discussed in the last chapter.

After the PAGE pseudo-op is a constant declaration. Declaring a constant is much like assigning a value to a variable in BASIC. The constant NUMBER_TO_FIND is assigned the value 6542 through the EQU pseudo-op. NUMBER_TO_FIND represents the index of the last prime number we can find using unsigned words to store the prime numbers. Constants will be discussed in more detail in Chapter 14.

The SEGMENT pseudo-op which follows sets up the segment for data. The DUP instruction in the primes declaration tells the assembler to repeat what is inside the parentheses the number of times specified to the left of the DUP instruction. For details about the DUP instruction, see Chapter 14. The question mark in the operand section of the DW and DB pseudo-ops tells the assembler that it does not matter what is stored in these locations during assembly and load. The assembler simply makes note that these locations are there and must be reserved for the program. Next we define the required stack segment (as in "Switch"), and finally, the program segment.

Primes uses the 8088's addition, subtraction, multiplication, and division instructions. It does so largely with unsigned numbers. As the program shows, it is not very difficult to convert this particular mathematical procedure into a program which the computer can execute.

Program 4-1. PRIMES.ASM

```
; PRIMES.ASM
;
; Finds prime numbers
; This program should work in any
; MS-DOS computer
;
        page ,96
;
number_to_find equ 6542              ;number of primes to find
;
data    segment
prime_number    dw 2,number_to_find dup(?) ;has first prime
number_found    dw ?                 ;number of primes found
last_check      dw ?                 ;last number to divide by
base            dw 10                ;base to print the numbers in
data    ends
;
stack   segment stack                ;stack segment
        dw 128 dup (?)               ;give the stack 256 bytes
stack   ends
;
code    segment                      ;segment for code
primes  proc far                     ;for proper return to DOS
        assume cs:code,ds:data,ss:stack
;
```

```
        push ds                                   ;for far return to DOS
        mov ax,0
        push ax
        mov ax,data                               ;set up data segment in DS
        mov ds,ax
;
        mov di,0                                  ;zero index in table of primes
        mov number_found,0                        ;zero number of primes found
;
next_prime:
        inc number_found                          ;found another prime
        cmp number_found,number_to_find           ;found all primes?
        je done                                   ;yes, we're done
        mov ax,prime_number[di]                   ;take current prime from table
        add di,2                                   ;point to next entry
        mov prime_number[di],ax                   ;start checking with last prime
;
next_test:
        add prime_number[di],1                    ;check next number as prime
        mov si,0                                  ;zero index into primes table
next_divisor:
        mov ax,prime_number[di]                   ;set current value
        mov dx,0                                  ;prepare to divide
        div prime_number[si]                      ;divide by a prime
        cmp dx,0                                  ;remainder zero?
        je next_test                              ;yes, do next number
        add si,2                                  ;set for next prime
        cmp si,di                                 ;run out of primes?
```

```
        jne  next_divisor         ;no, then divide by next prime
;
        call output               ;output the info
        jmp  next_prime           ;and find another prime
;
done:   ret                       ;return to DOS
primes  endp                      ;end of procedure declaration
;
; Output number_found and the prime number (with cr-lf)
; DI preserved
;
output  proc near
        push di                   ;preserve DI
        mov  ax,number_found      ;print number of primes found
        call decimal_out
        mov  al,':'               ;output a colon
        call character_out
        mov  ax,prime_number[di]  ;print the last prime
        call decimal_out
        mov  al,13                ;do cr-lf
        call character_out
        mov  al,10
        call character_out
        pop  di                   ;restore DI
        ret
output  endp
;
; Output a hex word in decimal
```

```
; CX, AX, DX destroyed
;
decimal_out proc near
        mov cx,0              ;counts digits to print
another_digit:
        inc cx                ;increment counter
        mov dx,0              ;prepare to divide
        div base              ;divide by base
        push dx               ;remainder is less sig digit
        cmp ax,0              ;is the quotient zero?
        jne another_digit     ;if not, more number to convert
print_digits:
        pop ax                ;retrieve digit from stack
        add al,'0'            ;convert to ASCII
        call character_out    ;print the character
        loop print_digits     ;do all of the digits
        ret                   ;return to caller
decimal_out endp
;
; output a single character
; character to print in AL
; AX and DL destroyed
;
character_out proc near
        mov dl,al             ;character to output
        mov ah,2              ;output character function
        int 21h               ;print character
```

```
        ret
character_out endp
;                       ;end of segment declaration
code    ends
        end             ;end of program
```

Program 4-2. PRIMES.BAS

```
100 ' BASIC VERSION OF PRIMES
110 '
120 '
130 '
140 DEFINT A-Z
150 '
160 NUMBERTOFIND = 300
170 DIM PRIMES(NUMBERTOFIND)
180 '
190 PRIMES(0)=2
200 '
210 NUMBERFOUND=NUMBERFOUND+1:IF NUMBERFOUND=N
    UMBERTOFIND THEN END
220 PRIMES(DI+1)=PRIMES(DI):DI=DI+1
230 PRIMES(DI)=PRIMES(DI)+1:SI=0
240 IF (PRIMES(DI) MOD PRIMES(SI))=0 THEN 230
250 SI=SI+1:IF SI<DI THEN 240
260 PRINT NUMBERFOUND;":";PRIMES(DI)
270 GOTO 210
```

very slow

186 sec for prime first 167 numbers

5
Program Flow

Program flow refers to the order in which a program's instructions are executed. Programs written in BASIC, or any other high-level language, tend to loop back on themselves, and to skip over portions which do not need to be executed. This is also true of machine language programs.

In this chapter, you will be introduced to ways of changing program flow, jumps. There are two basic types of jump instructions, conditional and unconditional. Both will be examined in this chapter. This chapter also explains how to create machine language versions of BASIC's IF-THEN-ELSE and FOR-NEXT structures using assembly's CMP and LOOP instructions.

The CMP Instruction

In high-level languages, decision making is usually based on the IF-THEN-ELSE construction; in machine language it is not quite so easy. In machine language, the CMP (compare) instruction is used with conditional jumps to change program flow. The conditional jumps jump only if a certain condition is satisfied. For example, JZ (Jump if Zero) jumps only if the last operation resulted in zero; if the result was nonzero, the computer "falls through" the conditional jump and executes the next instruction following JZ. The CMP instruction corresponds to the IF part of BASIC's conditional construction, while the conditional jumps provide for the THEN and ELSE.

The general form of the CMP instruction is:

CMP *first,second*

CMP compares the values of two numbers. They both must be either words or bytes—you can't mix and match. Any operand legal with instructions such as MOV, ADD, or SUB is legal with CMP. Remember that the 8088 does not allow both the operands to be memory locations.

It is important to remember that there is only one CMP instruction. The type of comparison (whether signed or unsigned) depends solely on the operands. Signed and unsigned comparisons are identical to one another. However, the flags after signed and unsigned comparisons must be interpreted differently. For this reason, there are two sets of conditional jumps, one for unsigned and another for signed comparisons.

Conditional Jumps After CMP

A comparison is often followed by one of the numerous conditional jumps. The 18 conditional jumps generally used after a CMP instruction are summarized in Table 5-1.

Table 5-1. Conditional Jumps Used after CMP

Instruction		Jump if...(unsigned comparisons)
JE	label	first equals second
JNE	label	first not equal to second
JA	label	first above second
JAE	label	first above or equal to second
JB	label	first below second
JBE	label	first below or equal to second
JNA	label	first not above second
JNAE	label	first not above or equal to second
JNB	label	first not below second
JNBE	label	first not below or equal to second

Instruction		Jump if...(signed comparisons)
JG	label	first greater than second
JGE	label	first greater than or equal to second
JL	label	first less than second
JLE	label	first less than or equal to second
JNG	label	first not greater than second
JNGE	label	first not greater than or equal to second
JNL	label	first not less than second
JNLE	label	first not less than or equal to second

These conditional jumps can be summarized more concisely, as in Table 5-2. Many of the conditional jumps come in pairs: one with a positive condition, and another with a negative. For example, JA (Jump if Above) is identical to JNBE (Jump if Not Below or Equal to). Intel provides these alternate terms entirely for the programmer's convenience.

The naming scheme of the jump instructions is very consistent. Note that all instructions with *below* or *above* in their names are used after the comparison of unsigned values, while *greater* or *less* conditional jumps are used after comparing signed values. The JE and JNE instructions apply to the comparison of both signed and unsigned values.

Table 5-2. Summary of Jumps

Jump if...		Use with unsigned operands	Use with signed operands
First >	Second	JA/JNBE	JG/JNLE
First ≥	Second	JAE/JNB	JGE/JNL
First =	Second	JE	JE
First <>	Second	JNE	JNE
First ≤	Second	JBE/JNA	JLE/JNG
First <	Second	JB/JNAE	JL/JNGE

It is important to remember that the names of the conditional jumps refer to the first operand versus the second. For example, JG means jump if the first operand is greater than the second. Below are some examples of comparisons and conditional jumping.

```
CMP AX,BX
JA AX_ABOVE_BX

CMP CX,AX
JB CX_BELOW_AX

CMP DX,SS
JE DX_EQUALS_SS

CMP AL,DL
JG AL_GREATER_THAN_DL

CMP BX,156H
JLE BX_LESS_THAN_OR_EQUAL_TO_156H
```

Machine Language IF-THEN-ELSE

The combination of the CMP instruction with conditional jumps gives the machine language programmer the equivalent of the high-level IF-THEN-ELSE construction. There are a number of ways to implement such a structure in machine language. Here are two examples:

```
              CMP AX,10        ;IF AX>10 ...
              JA THEN
              ADD AX,1         ;ELSE AX=AX+1
              JMP CONTINUE
THEN:         MOV AX,0         ;THEN AX=0
CONTINUE:     (more code)
```

Notice that, in the above example, the ELSE and THEN parts of the construction are not placed as they would be in BASIC. Unless the condition is satisfied (first is above second), the computer falls through JA to the next instruction (ADD AX,1) and then performs a JMP to skip over the THEN portion.

```
            CMP AX,10       ;IF AX>10
            JNA ELSE        ;(a negative condition)
            MOV AX,0        ;THEN AX=0
            JMP CONTINUE
ELSE:       ADD AX,1        ;ELSE AX=AX+1
CONTINUE:   (more code)
```

In this example the THEN and ELSE are placed in the familiar order of BASIC, because JNA tests for the condition opposite that of JA. Unless this condition is satisfied (first is *not* above second), we fall through JNA to MOV AX,0, and then JMP past the ELSE portion.

Both examples produce the same result, but with reversed logic. Some people find the first example easier to follow, because it tests for a positive rather than a negative condition. Others find the second construction more natural. It is important that you understand both.

The unconditional jump. JMP is an *unconditional* jump, like the GOTO statement in BASIC; the jump is always performed. It is used to skip over the unneeded parts of the conditional structure. With more complex conditional structures, you may begin to feel that your program plays leapfrog with itself as it executes the ELSEs and skips the THENs, and vice versa.

Conditional Jumps After Other Instructions

So far, conditional jumps have always followed a CMP instruction; however, they may be placed anywhere within a program. There is no rule that says conditional jumps must follow the CMP instruction. In fact, they can follow ADD, SUB, or any of the other instructions that affect the flags. As you may recall, there are six arithmetic flags in the 8088:

The *zero flag* is set by certain operations (such as ADD, SUB, INC and DEC) when the result of the operation is 0. Otherwise, this flag is clear.

The *carry flag* is used as the overflow flag for unsigned arithmetic. It becomes set when the result is less than 0 or greater than 255, for bytes, or 65535, for words. This flag is set by operations such as ADD and SUB. Note that INC and DEC do not set the carry flag. In addition, the carry flag is often used with subroutines in machine language.

The *sign flag* indicates the sign of the last result. When the flag is set, the last result was negative. If the flag is clear, the last result was positive. Again, only certain operations set this flag; they include ADD, SUB, INC, and DEC. Essentially, this flag mimics the most significant bit (the sign bit) of the result.

The *overflow flag* is used to indicate an overflow error. When this flag is set, there has been an overflow; otherwise, this flag is clear. An overflow error occurs when the result is beyond the representable range of signed numbers (-128 to 127 for bytes or -32768 to 32767 for words). Only certain operations such as ADD, SUB, INC, and DEC set this flag.

The other two arithmetic flags, the *auxiliary carry flag* (AF) and the *parity flag* (PF), will not be detailed here (please refer to the glossary); they are very rarely important to machine language programming.

Table 5-3 lists the conditional jumps which depend solely on the value of one flag:

Table 5-3. Conditional Jumps Relying on Only One Flag

Instruction	Jump if...	Flag status
JC	carry	CF = 1
JNC	no carry	CF = 0
JO	overflow	OF = 1
JNO	no overflow	OF = 0
JS	sign (negative)	SF = 1
JNS	no sign (positive)	SF = 0
JZ	zero	ZF = 1
JNZ	no zero	ZF = 0
JP/JPE	parity	PF = 1
JNP/JPO	no parity	PF = 0

These ten conditional jumps can be used after any operation (you can even use them after the compare instruction if you like). Below are some examples.

ADD AX,BX
JO OVERFLOW_ERROR   ;if sum >32767 or <-32768

SUB CX,DX
JZ RESULT_WAS_ZERO   ;if CX and DX are equal

```
MUL BL
JC WORD_RESULT            ;if product uses all of AX
DEC COUNTER
JNZ COUNTER_NOT_ZERO      ;if counter is not zero
```

Instructions which do not affect the flags (such as MOV) can be placed between an instruction which does and the conditional jump itself, as shown below. See Appendix A for a table detailing which instructions affect which flags.

```
              CMP AX,BX        ;finds which is greater...
              MOV CX,AX        ;...AX or BX, and stores...
              JG AX_GREATER    ;...larger value in CX
              MOV CX,BX
AX_GREATER:   (more code)

              MUL BX           ;perform 16 bit multiply
              MOV CX,0         ;use CX to indicate
                               overflow...
              JNO DX_CLEAR     ;...into DX register
              MOV CX,1
DX_CLEAR:     (more code)
```

Conditional Jumps for Looping

Another common use of conditional jumps is controlling loops. The most familiar looping statements in BASIC are FOR and NEXT. In a FOR-NEXT structure, the following operations are performed: The index (counter variable) is given an initial value; it is incremented (or decremented) for each iteration of the loop; and, it is checked against an end value. The BASIC structure, FOR I=1 TO 100:(do something):NEXT, could be coded into machine language, assuming I is a variable in the data segment, as:

```
              MOV I,1           ;set up the index variable
LOOP:         (do something)    ;do the instructions within the loop
              INC I             ;increment the loop variable
              CMP I,100         ;is the index variable 100?
              JNE LOOP          ;if so, end the loop
```

A more efficient version of the same loop looks like:

```
              MOV I,100         ;set up the index variable
LOOP:         (do something)    ;do the instructions within the loop
              DEC I             ;decrement the loop variable
              JNZ LOOP          ;if it's not zero, continue looping
```

The second example is more efficient because there are fewer instructions to accomplish the same task. A decremented loop variable is more efficient because the zero flag will be set automatically when the index becomes zero. With an incremented variable you must use the CMP instruction to end the loop. However, often a loop must increment so both techniques are used.

There are many ways to structure a loop. You can increment or decrement the index variable. The incrementing or decrementing can be at the beginning of the loop or at the end. In addition, you can increment or decrement by some number other than one. When you use ADD or SUB it might be necessary to use a JNC rather than a JNZ. Remember, the carry flag acts like an overflow for unsigned operations.

LOOP, LOOPE-LOOPZ, and LOOPNE-LOOPNZ

With the loops described above you must do everything, from adjusting the index variable to deciding which kind of jump to use. There are other, more specialized 8088 machine language instructions, which facilitate the looping operation. The three loop instructions described below give the programmer a completely automatic looping system.

LOOP is the simplest looping instruction. Study the example below. Notice that the LOOP instruction uses the CX register as its counter. This example does "something" 300 times. The LOOP instruction automatically decrements the CX register and loops back to START_OF_LOOP if CX is not zero.

```
                      MOV CX,300
START_OF_LOOP:        (do something)
                      LOOP START_OF_LOOP
```

Variations of the LOOP instruction, LOOPE-LOOPZ and LOOPNE-LOOPNZ, offer added versatility to the LOOP instruction. LOOPE (loop if equal), also called LOOPZ (loop if zero), loops back if CX is not zero and the zero flag indicates a zero status. LOOPNE (loop if not equal), or LOOPNZ (loop if not zero), loops back if CX is not zero and the zero flag indicates nonzero status. Thus, LOOPE can be considered *loop while equal*, and LOOPNE, *loop while not equal*. CX merely serves to put a limit to the number of possible loops. Both of these instructions will be examined in more detail in the chapter on string instructions.

69

JCXZ and the LOOP Instructions

Unfortunately, the LOOP instructions decrement CX before checking to see if it is zero. So, if you enter a LOOP structure when CX is zero, the loop will be executed 65,536 times. If this is what you intended, this is fine. If, on the other hand, you want the loop to be skipped when CX is zero, you can use the JCXZ (Jump if CX is Zero). Place the JCXZ instruction before the loop as shown below. Now the loop will be skipped when CX is zero.

```
          JCXZ NO_LOOP
DO_LOOP:  (whatever)
          LOOP DO_LOOP
NO_LOOP:  (continue)
```

The Unconditional Jump

JMP simply transfers control of the program from one place to another, just like the BASIC GOTO statement. There is no decision making involved with this instruction; in other words, the computer jumps *unconditionally.*

There are five kinds of unconditional JMPs. The assembler automatically selects the correct JMP on the basis of the operand (the label you are jumping to).

Near jumps. Near jumping (referred to as an *Intra Segment Direct* jump by IBM literature) has the general format as shown below.

```
     JMP label      ;displacement to label
          .         ;is calculated by the
          .         ;assembler.
     (some code)

          .
label:  (more code)
```

Near JMPs can jump anywhere within the code segment. Near JMPs are called *direct* jumps because the position of the next instruction is stored with the JMP instruction.

Short jumps. A short jump, or an *Intra Segment Direct Short* jump, is identical to a near JMP. A short jump can be only 127 bytes forward or 128 bytes backward. Trying to jump too far with a short jump will result in a *Relative jump out of range* error from the assembler. Note that, whenever possible, the assembler will automatically use short jumps.

Short jumps are important because all conditional jumps are short jumps, and all LOOP instructions use short jumps. The range limitation on short jumps can become a problem when you need a conditional jump to skip a very large part of your program. You can overcome this limitation by reversing the logic of your jump condition and skipping over an unconditional (near) jump. For example, if this jump resulted in a Relative Jump Out of Range error:

JGE SOME_PLACE
(more program)

You could replace it with:

JNGE SKIP   ; (a negative condition)
JMP SOME_PLACE
SKIP: **(more program)**

Remember that the unconditional JMP can jump anywhere within the current code segment. Unfortunately, there is no way to overcome the limitation on LOOP instructions. Just use short loops.

Far jumps. The far jump allows you to transfer control to another segment. This kind of jump is also known as an *Inter Segment Direct* Jump. Note IBM's careful use of the prefixes Inter (between) and Intra (within).

The format of the far JMP is identical to that of near JMP; however, the operand label must have a far attribute; that is, the label must be the name of a far procedure. You will need to use this instruction only if you write programs with more than one code segment, but the assembler will use far jumps automatically if the label has a far attribute.

Indirect jumps. Indirect jumps are jumps in which the address of the next instruction is not coded as the operand of the JMP operation, but is held in a data table or in a general register. There are two kinds of indirect jumps, one for *Intra Segment* jumps, and another for *Inter Segment* jumps. Advanced programmers can use indirect jumps just as BASIC programmers use the ON-GOTO construction.

A Sample Program

"Flash," as its name implies, flashes the screen several times. With a color/graphics screen adapter, the background color of the screen is changed as it is flashed. Flash_M (Program 5-1) is for IBM PC users who have the monochrome screen adapter. Flash_C (Program 5-2) is designed for a PC computer with the color/graphics screen adapter and for the PCjr. They should work with any of the compatibles, as long as the screen adapters are fully compatible with the IBM boards. If you are using a PC with both monochrome and color/graphics adapters, try entering both programs. However, DOS 2.00 users should execute the MODE command to change to the appropriate adapter before running the program; otherwise, the results are unpredictable. DOS 1.10 users will have to load BASIC and change monitors according to the BASIC manual. Users of noncompatible systems should still look at these programs, as they are good examples of short machine language programs.

Flash uses the register DX as a counter; it determines how many times the screen should be flashed. The BX register acts as a pointer into the screen memory. We will use it to read and write the screen attributes. The CX register, the counter for the LOOP instruction, is used to determine how many attributes to change. It is initialized to the value of the constant SCREENSIZE, the size of the screen page. AH is used to hold and check the attribute.

These programs introduce our first use of the SEGMENT command. The SEGMENT command is being used to locate the screen memory. The AT operand tells the assembler that we want the segment to be located at a specific segment address; B000H for the monochrome screen, and B800H for the color graphics screen. Note that these are not absolute addresses (0 to FFFFF hex), but segment addresses (0 to FFFF hex).

Notice the use of the assembler pseudo-op EQU. This pseudo-op is used to assign a constant value to a symbol (not a memory location, but an assembler value). The format is

symbol **EQU** *value*

Symbol is equal to the value.

At this point it is important to understand how IBM computers handle screen memory. There are 2000 characters on an 80-column screen. IBM computers use 4000 bytes (note that this is 4000 bytes, not 4K bytes) to represent the characters. The even-numbered bytes (0, 2, 4, etc.) hold the actual character. The odd-numbered bytes (1, 3, 5, etc.) hold the character's attribute. So the character in byte 0 has the

attribute defined by byte 1. The attribute byte of the monochrome screen adapter can be broken down as shown in Figure 5-1. The F and I symbols show where flashing and
intensity attributes can be set.

The attribute byte for the color adapter is used as shown
in Figure 5-2.

Figure 5-1. Monchrome's Attribute

0	0	0	0	0	0	0	0	- no display

F	0	0	0	I	0	0	1	- underline

F	0	0	0	I	1	1	1	- white on black

F	1	1	1	0	0	0	0	- black on white

Figure 5-2. Color Attribute Byte

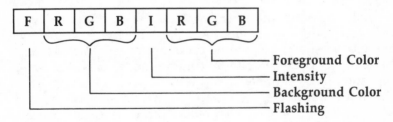

F	R	G	B	I	R	G	B

Foreground Color
Intensity
Background Color
Flashing

You can combine the different color bits to mix your own colors. For example, if blue and red are on at the same time, the
screen displays purple.

Let's look at the basic flow of the program Flash_M. At
the start of the loop, AH is assigned the value of the normal,
white on black, screen attribute. AH is compared with the
attribute pointed to by the BX register. If AH and the attribute
are different, we use AH as the new attribute, changing the
screen attribute to normal.

If AH and the attribute are the same, we move the
reverse, black on white, attribute, into AH and use this as the
new attribute. Next, BX, the pointer into screen memory, is incremented and the LOOP instruction executed. As mentioned

above, screen memory is set up as a character byte followed by an attribute byte, so we must add two to BX. We change every other byte to get all of the attributes. Once this inner loop is complete, we must manually decrement DX and jump to LOOP0 if it is not zero. When it is zero, we perform the RET operation which returns us to DOS.

Flash_C is a little more complex. The bulk of the program is the same; the only differences lie in the section which changes the screen attribute. The first instruction retrieves the current screen attribute. Next, 16 is added to the attribute byte. This increments the background color by one. However, we do not want to change the most significant bit, which controls the flashing attribute of the screen. Here we can use a little trick; remember that the most significant bit can be considered the sign bit. If this sign bit is changed by the ADD operation, the Overflow Flag (OF) is set, so if the OF is set, the attribute is reloaded and the background color set to black. The rest is the same as Flash_M.

Running FLASH

Assemble the program as FLASH.ASM. When complete, type FLASH from the DOS prompt and press Enter. There may be some picture snow or lightning on the color/graphics screen when FLASH is executed in 80-column mode. This is normal. The static can be eliminated if you use 40 columns. Remember to be in a color mode, not a black-and-white mode. Execute MODE CO40 or MODE CO80 before running FLASH just to be sure (DOS 1.10 users must enter BASIC and use a SCREEN 0,1 and a WIDTH 40 or WIDTH 80 command).

If all goes well, the screen should flash for a few moments and the DOS prompt should return. If nothing happens, and the DOS prompt does not return, the computer has probably locked up. Try resetting with the Ctrl-Alt-Del combination. If this does not work, you will have to turn the computer off and back on. Check the program carefully before reassembling. If the DOS prompt returns after a few seconds, but the screen does not flash, check to be certain you are using the correct version of FLASH. Monochrome screen adapter users should have assembled Flash_M and color/graphics users the Flash_C program. If you have both adapters, use the MODE command from DOS to switch between the two displays before you execute the appropriate program. PCjr users should have entered the Flash_C program.

If your compatible computer does not seem to be working, take a close look at the program before you assume the hardware is at fault. Any of the full compatibles should be able to execute these programs. If your machine is only slightly compatible, the program may not work correctly.

Once you get the appropriate version of Flash running, there are a number of modifications you can make to produce your own version of Flash. You can change the number of times the screen flashes by changing the constant FLASHES to another value. In Flash_M, FLASHES should be an even number if you want the screen to return to white on black; in Flash_C, FLASHES should be a multiple of eight if you want the screen to return to its original color. Try using Flash_M on the color screen by changing the SCREEN segment to point to the color screen. Try making the program flash only the top half of the screen (easy) or only the bottom half (a little harder).

Conditional Jumps

All 31 different conditional jumps are summarized in Table 5-4. Note that there are really only 17 different conditional jump instructions, but that some of the instructions have been given more than one name. Some instructions have obvious aliases; for example, JA (Jump if Above) is the same as JNBE (Jump if Not Below or Equal to). Other instructions are less obvious: JC is the same as JB. When you use DEBUG to unassemble programs, all of the conditional jumps will appear as the names shown in Table 5-5 (since the instructions are identical, DE-BUG has no way of knowing if your source code has JA or JNBE).

Table 5-4. The Conditional Jump Instructions

(* indicates conditional jumps for signed comparisons)

Operation Name	Full Explanation	Jump if...
JA	jump if above	CF = 0 and ZF = 0
JAE	jump if above or equal	CF = 0
JB	jump if below	CF = 1
JBE	jump if below or equal	CF = 1 or ZF = 1
JC	jump on carry	CF = 1
JCXZ	jump if CX zero	CX = 0
JE	jump if equal	ZF = 1
*JG	jump if greater	ZF = 0 and SF = OF
*JGE	jump if greater or equal	SF = OF
*JL	jump if less	SF <> OF
*JLE	jump if less or equal	ZF = 1 or SF <> OF
JNA	jump if not above	CF = 1 or ZF = 1
JNAE	jump if not above or equal	CF = 1
JNB	jump if not below	CF = 0
JNBE	jump if not below or equal	CF = 0 and ZF = 0
JNC	jump if no carry	CF = 0
JNE	jump if not equal	ZF = 0
*JNG	jump if not greater	ZF = 1 or SF<>OF
*JNGE	jump if not greater or equal	SF <> OF
*JNL	jump if not less	SF = OF
*JNLE	jump if not less or equal	ZF = 0 and SF = OF
*JNO	jump if no overflow	OF = 0
JNP	jump if no parity	PF = 0
JNS	jump if no sign (positive)	SF = 0
JNZ	jump if not zero	ZF = 0
*JO	jump on overflow	OF = 1
JP	jump on parity	PF = 1
JPE	jump if parity even	PF = 1
JPO	jump if parity odd	PF = 0
*JS	jump on sign (negative)	SF = 1
JZ	jump on zero	ZF = 1

CF—Carry Flag
OF—Overflow Flag
PF—Parity Flag
SF—Sign Flag
ZF—Zero Flag

Table 5-5. Conditional Jumps and Their Aliases

(*—for comparisons of signed values)

DEBUG names	Aliases
JA	JNBE
JB	JC, JNAE
JBE	JNA
*JG	JNLE
*JGE	JNL
*JL	JNGE
*JLE	JNG
JNB	JAE, JNC
JNZ	JNE
JPE	JP
JPO	JNP
JZ	JE

Program 5-1. Flash_M.ASM

```
; FLASH_M.ASM
;
; This program flashes the IBM
; monochrome screen.  It will only work
; with computers with IBM's monochrome
; screen adapter or compatible product.
; If you are using both a monochrome
; and color graphics screen adapters,
; switch to the monochrome screen
; before executing this program.
;
;
        page  ,96
;
; Constants definition
flashes         equ 80                          ;number of times to flash
screensize      equ 2000                        ;size of the screen (80x25)
normal          equ 7                           ;normal attribute
reverse         equ 112                         ;reverse attribute
;
screen  segment at 0B000h                       ;screen starts at B000:0000
scrnmap dw screensize dup(?)                    ;length of screen
screen  ends
;
stack   segment stack                           ;stack segment
```

78

```
stack    dw 128 dup (?)        ;give the stack 256 bytes
         ends

;
code     segment               ;segment for code
program  proc far              ;for proper return to DOS
         assume cs:code,es:screen,ss:stack
         push ds               ;for far return to DOS
         mov ax,0
         push ax
         mov ax,screen         ;set up screen segment in ES
         mov es,ax
         mov dx,flashes        ;Number of times to flash
loop0:   mov bx,1              ;Where first attrib is stored
loop1:   mov cx,screensize
         mov ah,normal         ;normal attribute
         cmp ah,es:[bx]        ;is it reversed already?
         jne nochange          ;if it is, make it normal
         mov ah,reverse        ;make attribute reversed
nochange:
         mov es:[bx],ah        ;point to next attribute
         add bx,2
         loop loop1            ;loop until CX is zero
         dec dx                ;done all flashes?
         jne loop0             ;if we have not, flash again
         ret                   ;return to DOS
program  endp                  ;end of procedure declaration
code     ends                  ;end of segment declaration
         end                   ;end of program
```

Program 5-2. Flash_C.ASM

```
; FLASH_C.ASM
;
; This program flashes the IBM color
; screen.  It will only work with
; computers with IBM's color/graphics
; adapter or compatible product.  If
; you are using both monochrome and
; color graphics adapters in your
; computer, switch to the color/graphics
; screen before executing this program.
; PCjr users should use this version of
; the FLASH.  If you are using a 40-
; column screen, change screensize
; to 1000
;
;
            page  ,96
;
;constants definition
flashes       equ 80                      ;number of times to flash
screensize    equ 80*25                   ;screen size (80x25 or 40x25)
;
screen   segment at 0B800h                ;segment address B800
scrnmap dw screensize dup(?)              ;length of screen
screen   ends
```

```
;
stack    segment para stack        ;segment for the stack
         dw 128 dup(?)             ;give the stack 256 bytes
stack    ends
;
code     segment                   ;segment for code
program  proc far                  ;procedure for return to DOS
         assume cs:code,ds:screen,ss:stack
         push ds                   ;for far return to DOS
         mov ax,0
         push ax
         mov ax,screen             ;set up screen segment in ES
         mov es,ax
;
         mov dx,flashes            ;Number of times to flash
loop0:   mov bx,1                  ;Where first attrib is stored
loop1:   mov cx,screensize         ;Length of screen area
         mov ah,es:[bx]            ;get current attribute
         add ah,16                 ;increment backround color
         jno no_reset              ;affect blinking (sign bit?)
         mov ah,es:[bx]            ;get attribute again
         and ah,10001111b          ;zero backround color bits
no_reset:
         mov es:[bx],ah            ;store attribute
         add bx,2                  ;point to next attribute
         loop loop1                ;loop until CX is zero
         dec dx                    ;done all flashes?
```

```
        jne loop0          ;if we have not, flash again

        ret                ;return to DOS
program endp               ;procedure complete
code    ends               ;code segment complete
        end                ;program complete
```

Program 5-3. Flash_M.BAS

```
100 ' FLASH_M.BAS
110 '
130 '
140 DEFINT A-Z
150 '
160 'Constants definition
170 FLASHES = 80                      'numbe
    r of times to flash
180 SCREENSIZE = 80*25                'size
    of the screen
190 NORMAL = 7                        'norma
    l attribute
200 REVERSE = 112                     'rever
    se attribute
210 '
220 DEF SEG = &HB000 'screen starts at B000:00
    00
```

```
230 '       FLASHES
240 DX =    FLASHES
            MOV DX,FLASHES
250 BX =    1                                      'LOOP0
            MOV BX,1
260 CX =    SCREENSIZE
            MOV CX,SCREENSIZE
270 AH =    NORMAL                                 'LOOP1
            MOV AH,NORMAL
280 ZF =    (AH = PEEK(BX))
            CMP AH,ES:[BX]
290 IF NOT ZF THEN 310
            JNE NOCHANGE
300 AH =    REVERSE
            MOV AH,REVERSE
310 POKE BX,AH                                     'NOCHA
       NGE: MOV ES:[BX],AH
320 BX =    BX + 2
            ADD BX,2
330 CX =    CX - 1:IF NOT CX = 0 THEN 270
            LOOP LOOP1
340 DX =    DX - 1:ZF = (DX = 0)
            DEC DX
350 IF NOT ZF THEN 250
            JNE LOOP0
360 END
            RET
```

Program 5-4. Flash_C.BAS

```
100 ' FLASH_C.BAS
210 '
220 '
230 '
240 DEFINT A-Z
250 '
260 ' constants definition
270 FLASHES = 80
280 SCREENSIZE = 80*25
    '40*25 for 40x25 screen
290 '
300 DEF SEG = &HB800
310 '
320 DX = FLASHES
        MOV DX,FLASHES
330 BX = 1
        MOV BX,1
340 CX = SCREENSIZE
        MOV CX,SCREENSIZE
350 AH = PEEK(BX)
        MOV AH,ES:[BX]
360 SF = AH AND 128:AH = AH + 16
        ADD AH,16
370 OF = (SF XOR (AH AND 128)) > 0:IF NOT OF T
    HEN 400'JNO
```

```
380 AH = PEEK(BX)
  , MOV AH,ES:[BX]
390 AH = AH AND &H8F
  , AND AH,10001111B
400 POKE BX,AH
  , MOV ES:[BX],AH
410 BX = BX + 2
  , ADD BX,2
420 CX = CX - 1:IF NOT CX = 0 THEN 350
  , LOOP LOOP
430 DX = DX - 1
  , DEC DX
440 IF NOT DX = 0 THEN 330
  , JNZ
450 END
```

6
Subroutines and the Stack

The stack is quite possibly one of the most useful and dynamic storage methods available to a computer. Many large computers rely solely on stacks for data manipulation. In an effort to clarify a stack's design, many analogies have been applied to its operation. Writers have called on everything from dishes at a coffee shop to a programmer's cluttered desk.

Here we will use the analogy of cafeteria trays. The last tray put on the stack is the first tray to come off. This makes the pile of trays a *last in, first out* storage system, or LIFO for short. The computer's *stack* can be thought of as this pile of trays. The computer puts trays down one by one, and when it needs them again, it takes them back. Notice that a stack reverses the order of the trays.

Computer programmers have given names to the processes of putting something onto the stack and of taking it back. The putting on is called PUSHing data onto the stack, and the taking back, POPping. The 8088 has a variety of PUSH and POP operations.

Implementing the Stack

Two registers are used to manage the stack, the SP (Stack Pointer) and the SS (Stack Segment). SP always points to the last piece of data PUSHed onto the stack. It starts at the highest possible stack location and works its way down as information is added to the stack. SP acts as an offset from the base of the segment pointed to by the SS register (Figure 6-1). (See Chapter 2 if you are unfamiliar with segment:offset addressing.)

Figure 6-1. SP Offset from SS

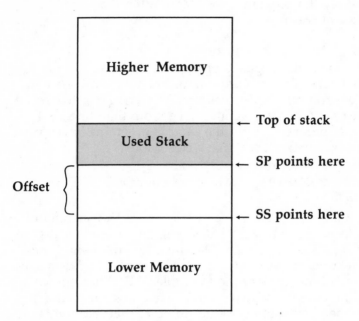

The microprocessor (the 8088) handles the stack as words, not as bytes. Only words can be PUSHed onto and POPped off the stack. In a PUSH operation, the 8088 decrements SP by two and stores the word at the memory location pointed to by SS:SP. When the word needs to be POPped back, the 8088 retrieves the word pointed to by SS:SP and increments SP by two. Generally, it is not very important to know the mechanics of the stack; however, some types of programming require a thorough understanding of stack manipulations (especially when combining assembly language with Pascal or BASIC).

The maximum length of a stack is 64K (the addressing limit of the SP register). For most machine language programs, a stack of 256 bytes is sufficient. The DOS manual recommends that you reserve at least 128 bytes beyond your requirements if you use DOS functions (such as character print). If the stack is too small, the results are unpredictable. The problem is that the computer starts to store the PUSHed data in memory that was not reserved for the stack. This memory may have been reserved for something else, probably data, possibly the program itself. More often than not, the computer will crash.

Declaring the Stack Segment

Almost all machine language programs require you to declare a stack segment. The only exceptions are device drivers and .COM files. You must specifically tell the assembler to declare a stack segment, but you cannot have more than one stack segment per program. All of the sample programs have defined stack segments. Let's take a closer look.

```
stack   SEGMENT STACK
        DW xxx DUP (?)       ;where xxx can be any number
stack   ENDS
```

The name of the stack segment is *stack*. The operand of the pseudo-op SEGMENT, STACK, tells the assembler that we are defining a stack segment. DW should be used since the stack is defined as word-sized data. The *xxx* DUP (?) is a special command that says to the assembler, "DUPlicate what's between the parentheses *xxx* times." The question mark (?) tells the assembler that the value stored at that location is undefined. The xxx can be any number which does not exceed the maximum stack length. The stack segment can be up to 65,536 bytes long (or 32,768 words). The stack ENDS ends the stack segment definition. In the sample programs we have used:

```
stack   SEGMENT STACK
        DW 128 DUP(?)
stack   ENDS
```

Here, we have defined the stack to be 128 words (256 bytes) long.

Now you know how a stack works and how it's defined. Its use can be very powerful and convenient.

Subroutines

First off, you might ask, "What is a subroutine?" This is difficult to answer, for it depends on your point of view. In a sense, DOS considers all programs subroutines to itself, yet parts of DOS can act as subroutines to your programs. However, it is possible to generalize. A subroutine is often a short program which does one task. DOS, for example, includes subroutines which print text to the screen and control disk files. These subroutines cannot execute alone. They need a program to call them and give them information to work on. You can think of these subroutines as helpers. They make the task of programming easier and less time-consuming.

Subroutines are also used to break large programs into smaller, more manageable sections. In such a program, each subroutine handles a specific task and the main routine calls each subroutine as it is needed. Breaking a large program into smaller parts makes it easier to find bugs because each subroutine is responsible for a specific task. If something is not working correctly, you know which routine is to blame.

It is often useful to include a comment header at the beginning of your subroutines. The header should state the routine's name and purpose. It should also indicate which registers are preserved or which are destroyed. This way, you can easily determine which registers are being altered and which are maintained. Although it is nice to write subroutines which alter no registers, this is often unnecessary. For example, if your main routine does not use SI and DI, the program's subroutines can use them freely without preserving them. If you use these subroutines in another program which uses SI and DI, however, the subroutines will need to preserve those registers for your new program to work correctly.

CALL and RET. The 8088 implements subroutines with two instructions, CALL and RET. There are four types of CALLs and four types of RETs. Fortunately, the assembler selects the correct commands for us.

The CALL instruction is the machine language equivalent of BASIC's GOSUB command. As mentioned above, there are four different CALL commands. They all have the same general format:

CALL *operand*

where the operand is either a label (direct CALL) or an addressed memory location (indirect CALL).

The actual process of CALLing a subroutine is the same in all cases. When the 8088 executes a CALL instruction, it pushes the current position within the program on the stack, and jumps to the specified routine. At the end of the routine, a RET undoes the CALL. The computer pops the stack to retrieve its previous program position and resume execution where it left off. As routines call other routines, the computer is said to be going into deeper subroutine levels (see Figure 6-2). As each routine comes to an end, the RET command pops the computer up one level. The CALL and RET instructions affect none of the flags and only the SP, IP, and possibly CS registers.

Figure 6-2. Subroutine Levels

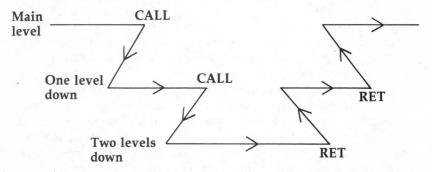

The *near CALL*, or a *Direct Intra Segment* CALL, is much like a near JMP, in that the operand is a 16-bit displacement to the called label. The actual calling mechanism works this way: The IP (Instruction Pointer) register is pushed onto the stack, then the new IP is calculated by adding a displacement to the original IP. Program execution continues at this new position. Since this instruction alters only the IP, you cannot move from one segment to another.

The operand of a near CALL is a label. It must have a near attribute. Generally, this refers to the names of near procedures (those procedures defined with the PROC NEAR command). For more information about the PROC command, see Chapter 14.

Far CALLs, or *Inter Segment Direct* CALLs, are very much like far JMPs. The operand of a far CALL is a double word. Note that this CALL is absolute, not relative. Far CALLs push both the CS (Code Segment) and IP onto the stack. The contents of the CS register are pushed first.

With a far CALL it is possible to CALL a subroutine in a different code segment: The operand of a far CALL must have a far attribute; in other words, it must be the name of a far procedure. Far procedures are defined with the PROC FAR pseudo-op. See Chapter 14 for more details on the PROC pseudo-op.

Indirect CALLs are similar to indirect JMPs. With indirect CALLs, the address of the subroutine is not coded with the instruction, but is held in a general register or a data table. There are two indirect CALLs, one for *Intra Segment* CALLs and another for *Inter Segment* CALLs. The indirect Intra Segment CALL is much like a near CALL since it pushes only IP onto the stack. Indirect Inter Segment CALLs push both CS and IP onto the stack. Advanced machine language programmers can use indirect CALLs just as BASIC programmers use the ON/GOSUB construction.

There are basically two kinds of CALLs, near CALLs, which push only IP onto the stack, and far CALLs which push both CS and IP. As you may suspect, there are two kinds of RETurns, one for near CALLs, and another for far CALLs. A variation of the standard RET will be discussed with parameter passing.

The near RET instruction, also called an *Intra Segment RETurn*, pops IP off the stack and thus terminates a near subroutine. A far RET (also called an *Inter Segment RETurn*, or a long RETurn) pops both CS and IP.

It is important that subroutines accessed with near CALLs end with near RETs, and that routines called with far CALLs end with far RETs. Imagine the chaos if a far RET were executed after a near CALL. The IP register would be restored correctly, but the CS register would take the value of whatever was PUSHed onto the stack before the near CALL. The microprocessor would begin executing at some random address in memory. This would almost definitely crash the computer. Fortunately, the assembler takes care of this detail for us. RETs in PROC FAR-ENDP structures are made far RETs, and RETs in a PROC NEAR-ENDP structure, near RETs.

Programs Are Far Procedures

You may now be wondering why all programs are defined as far procedures. Clearly, it's to force the assembler to make the RET at the end of the program a far RET; but why? Notice that the first instructions in every program are to push the DS (the data segment) register and then a zero (via AX) onto the stack. The reason for this can be explained as follows. When

DOS transfers control of the computer to an .EXE file, it passes some important information. DS and ES hold the base of the program segment prefix. This prefix holds some critical data for DOS while the program is executing.

To return to DOS, IP must be set to zero and CS to the base of the program segment prefix. Since neither CS or IP can be the destination of a MOV operation, the simplest way to change them both is with a FAR RET operation.

The sequence

PUSH DS
MOV AX,0
PUSH AX

simulates a far CALL to our program. When the far RET is performed, the microprocessor pops zero into IP and the base of the program segment prefix into CS. It is also possible to use an inter segment indirect JMP, but this is more complex and requires more programming.

Our subroutines should all be near procedures. For this reason, any program which includes its own subroutines must be defined in at least two parts. One, the PROC FAR, is used to hold the main program. The other, one or more PROC NEARs, is used to hold the subroutines.

Using Subroutines

Before you can use subroutines effectively, there are some considerations that need to be examined. For example, how do you pass information from the main program to the subroutine and from the subroutine back to the main program? How do you write subroutines so that they do not affect any registers?

A subroutine must often use registers to perform its operations. In doing so, the original values contained in the registers are destroyed. But suppose the program calling the subroutine stored some important value in an affected register? In addition, some subroutines require that the registers be set to certain values before they are called (DECIMAL_OUT from "Primes," for example, requires that AX be set to the number to print). The original values of the registers must be stored, either by the calling program or by the subroutine. You could store the values in memory locations, but then you would have to declare memory positions for the registers in the data segment. The simplest method is to PUSH the values of the affected registers onto the stack, and POP them off afterwards.

PUSH. The format of the PUSH instruction is shown below. The operand can be any register or memory location. It cannot be an immediate value.

PUSH *operand*

Here are some examples of legal PUSH instructions:

PUSH CS
PUSH AX
PUSH SI
PUSH [BX+3]

Note that the 8088 can push only words onto the stack. No provision is made for pushing bytes.

POP. The POP instruction takes an identical format. Again, there is no provision for popping byte quantities from the stack. Remember also that the stack returns values backwards. If you use

PUSH AX
PUSH BX
PUSH DX

you have to use

POP DX
POP BX
POP AX

to restore the registers correctly. To PUSH all of the registers, you have to use something like

PUSH AX
PUSH BX
PUSH CX
PUSH DX
PUSH SI
PUSH DI
PUSH BP
PUSH DS
PUSH ES

All of the registers are pushed except SS, CS, SP, and IP, since these must remain the same for the subroutine to work. To restore all of the registers, you would use:

POP ES
POP DS
POP BP
POP DI
POP SI
POP DX
POP CX
POP BX
POP AX

It is not necessary to POP a value back into the register that PUSHed it. You could (if you found it necessary) transfer a value via the stack as below.

(calculate a value in AX)
PUSH AX
(do some program)
POP BX
(and use the value)

If you look carefully at the DECIMAL—OUT routine in the sample program Primes, you will find that it uses this method to move a value from DX to AX. Often you will see programs setting the segment registers via the stack. For example to MOV DS,CS (an illegal operation), you could use

PUSH CS
POP DS

PUSHF and POPF. There are two specialized PUSH and POP instructions. PUSHF pushes the flags register onto the stack, and POPF pops it back. Although this may not be a commonly used instruction, it is the only way you can store the flags.

PUSHF and POPF are often used to change or examine the status of the flags. There is no 8088 instruction to move the entire flags register into another register. The only way to examine all of the 8088's flags is to PUSHF and POP the flags word into another register as below.

PUSHF   ;to get the flags
POP AX   ;AX now holds the flags register

To move a value from a register to the flags, you could use something like

PUSH AX   ;AX holds the new flag values
POPF   ;sets the flags register

The flags register can be broken down into bits as in Figure 6-3.

Figure 6-3. The Flags Register

bit 15   **bit 0**

-	-	-	-	O	D	I	T	S	Z	-	A	-	P	-	C

The following symbols are used: –, unused bit; A, Auxiliary Carry flag (AF); C, Carry flag (CF); D, Direction flag (DF); I, Interrupt enable/disable flag (IF); O, Overflow flag (OF); P, Parity flag (PF); S, Sign flag (SF); T, Trap mode (single step) flag (TF); Z, Zero flag (ZF).

Note that, using this technique, you can set several flags (CF, DF, IF, etc.) at the same time. Generally, however, you will want to set only the trap flag using this method. See Chapter 11 for an example of this technique.

Parameter Passing

Subroutines often need to receive a value from the main routine. In addition, the subroutine sometimes needs to return a value or indicate an error condition. There are four ways that a value or condition can be passed from the main program to the subroutine or vice versa. Information can be passed via a register, a memory location, the flags, or the stack. All four have their own advantages and disadvantages.

Using registers. Passing parameters via registers is by far the simplest approach. You load a register with the value that you want to pass and call the routine. For example, Primes passes a value in AX to the DECIMAL_OUT routine. Although this approach is simple, it might become difficult to remember which routines take which registers. To alleviate this problem, it is often convenient to add a list of the parameter-passing registers to the comment header of the subroutine. This way you know which registers need to be filled with what values.

Flags. Passing parameters via the flags is also very convenient. Although you cannot pass a specific value, you can pass a condition. The most convenient flag to use is the carry flag (CF). There are three instructions that can be used to assign a value to the carry flag, CLC, STC, and CMC. CLC (CLear Carry) makes the carry flag zero. STC (SeT Carry) makes the carry flag one. CMC (CoMplement Carry) NOTs the carry: If it is zero, it is made one; if it is one, it is made zero.

Passing information via the carry flag is most convenient when the subroutine must return a condition to the calling program. Many DOS functions set the carry flag on return to indicate that an error has occurred. Another register holds the error number. If the carry flag is clear, there is no error. You could do something like this with your subroutines. If the subroutine needs to indicate an error condition, it could set the carry. The calling program needs only to perform a JC or JNC to determine if an error was encountered. Remember that none of the CALLs or RETs themselves affect any of the flags.

Memory locations. If you would like to pass a large number of values, it is most convenient to use memory locations. Since it's impossible to pass a table or a string from a register to a subroutine, the most common technique is to pass the address of the data in one of the registers (usually BX). This allows the subroutine to maintain its independence from the main program, while you pass a table or string as a parameter. In the comment header of the routine you should include a description of the data table. This way, you know how to format the table when you use the routine in another program.

Occasionally, it is convenient to pass just a few parameters via memory locations, especially when the parameters are already stored in memory. Such is the case with OUTPUT from Primes. The OUTPUT subroutine could have been written to receive the parameters in different registers; however, OUTPUT was not meant to be a general-purpose subroutine, so it could rely on the Primes structure. DECIMAL_OUT, however, which is called by OUTPUT, is a general-purpose routine; it can be used anytime we want to print a binary number in decimal.

Using the stack. The last method of transferring values from the main program to the subroutine is via the stack. This method of passing parameters is probably the most complex, but it does offer some advantages over the other two systems.

The basic principle is easy to understand: Push all of the parameters you want to pass onto the stack before you call the subroutine. Unfortunately, the routine which is called cannot simply pop the values off the stack because the return address is now on top of the stack. You could pop the return address off the stack, pop the values, then push the return address back onto the stack (as below), but there is a far more elegant approach.

```
CALLER    PUSH PARAM_ONE    ;store parameter one
          PUSH PARAM_TWO    ;store parameter two
          CALL ROUTINE      ;call the routine
          (more code)       ;finish the program

                .
                .
                .

ROUTINE   PROC NEAR
          POP AX            ;get return address
          POP SI            ;get parameter two
          POP DI            ;get parameter one
          PUSH AX           ;restore return address
          (do whatever)     ;use the parameters
          RET               ;return to caller
ROUTINE   ENDP
```

The BP (Base Pointer) register has, up to now, been unexplained. This register is used to address data in the stack. In its default addressing scheme, it acts as an offset into the stack segment (the segment pointed to by SS), just as [BX] can be used to address memory in the data segment (the segment pointed to by DS). To read values from the stack, we move the SP (stack pointer) register into BP, then use BP as an offset into the stack (see Figure 6-4). BP must be adjusted to point to the correct data, however.

Figure 6-4. Using BP to Address Data on the Stack

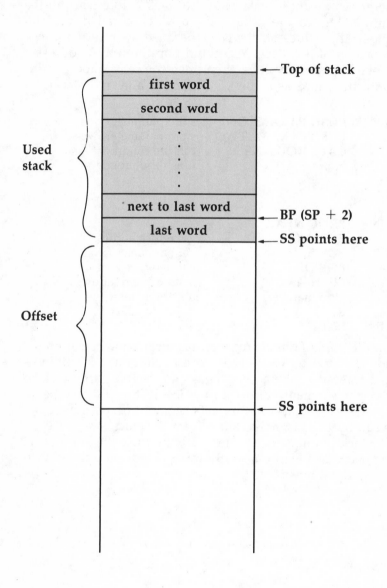

As you can see from Figure 6-4, after moving SP into BP we must add two to BP to address the last word stored on the stack. Remember, the stack grows downward, from higher memory locations to lower ones. For each additional word, we must increment BP by two (if the addressing modes have you confused, be patient; they are all explained in the next chapter). Now examine the code below:

CALLER	PUSH PARAM_ONE	;store parameter one
	PUSH PARAM_TWO	;store parameter two
	CALL ROUTINE	;call the routine
	(more program)	;finish up

.
.
.

ROUTINE	MOV BP,SP	;set BP
	MOV SI,[BP+2]	;get parameter two
	MOV DI,[BP+4]	;get parameter one
	(do whatever)	;use the parameters
	RET 4	;return to caller

In this example, rather than pop the parameters off the stack, we use BP as a pointer, and copy the parameters into SI and DI for processing. SP does not change, so the stack (including the parameters) remains unaltered.

Note the RET 4 at the end of this subroutine. Routines which are passed parameters via the stack need some way of removing them. The calling program could pop them off the stack, but this lacks elegance. Instead, Intel has provided us with a command which automatically pops parameters from the stack when we return from a subroutine. This command, RET *n*, comes in two forms. The first is an *Intra Segment and Add Immediate to Stack Pointer* RET instruction. In other words, it is a near RET which also pops off the number of bytes specified in the operand

RET *n*

where *n* is a 16-bit displacement.

This kind of near RET pops IP off the stack and adds the displacement to the stack pointer. For example, RET 2 would return from the subroutine and pop two bytes (or one word) off the stack. RET 16 would return and pop 16 bytes (or eight words) off the stack.

The second form of the RET *n* command works like the first, but is used to return from far procedures rather than near procedures. The label *Inter Segment and Add Immediate to Stack Pointer* identifies this as a long RETurn.

Many compiled and interpreted languages (such as Pascal and BASIC) use the stack to pass parameters. BASIC also uses this method when machine language subroutines are called with USR or CALL statements (see Chapter 10).

Bear in mind that it is also possible to use the stack to return values to a calling routine. The calling routine would then pop the returned values off the stack (in this case, RET n might not be used). Note, however, that the calling routine must make room on the stack for the returned values if you want to avoid popping and pushing the return address.

You might be wondering what advantages this system offers over the other methods of passing parameters. The greatest benefit comes in writing recursive routines, routines which can call themselves. BASIC programmers will be completely unfamiliar with this idea, since BASIC subroutines (unless very cleverly written) cannot call themselves. In Pascal or Logo, however, this is possible. Recursive routines are not important to beginning machine language programmers, but they are very powerful, and particularly useful when you need to analyze a large number of possibilities. The most common example of a recursive routine finds the factorial of a number (*X!*, the product of all the numbers from 1 to X).

Decimal Output

Now that you understand the stack and subroutines, look at the DECIMAL_OUT routine in the program PRIMES.ASM from Chapter 4. Before we get into the actual code, let's consider how we can convert a binary number into decimal. The method used in DECIMAL_OUT is to repeatedly divide the number to be printed by 10. This can be made clear with an example.

Suppose we start with the number 567. After the first division by 10, the quotient will be 56, and the remainder 7. Note that the least significant digit of 567 (the one's digit) is the remainder. Now, divide by 10 again: The remainder will be 6 (the ten's digit of the original number), and the quotient 5. It's clear what is going on. When we divide by 10 again, the quotient is 0, and the remainder 5. The entire number has been converted. The one drawback to this system is that the digits are converted from the least significant to the most, but we must print the numbers starting from the most significant to the least. We can use the stack to reverse the order of the digits.

The comment header at the beginning of this subroutine says that it is passed the number to print in AX, and that CX, AX, and DX are destroyed. In the first instruction of the routine, CX is set to zero. CX is used to count the number of digits that must be printed. Then CX is incremented by one. This means that we will always print at least one digit. DX is set to zero in preparation for the DIV by BASE. BASE is a variable which holds the base of the printed number. If we make BASE ten, the number will be printed in decimal; if BASE holds eight, the number will be printed in octal (base 8). Next we push DX onto the stack. Remember that DX holds the remainder of the division, the digit that we want to print. Then we check AX (the quotient) to see if it's zero. If AX is zero, the entire number has been converted, and we go to the part of the routine which actually prints the number.

The printing part of the routine (labeled PRINT_DIGITS) POPs the digits off the stack one by one, adds the ASCII value of zero (to convert a number from 0 to 9 to a character from 0 to 9), and calls the CHARACTER_OUT routine. Note that CX holds the number of digits which were pushed onto the stack, so the LOOP instruction will repeat until all of the digits have been printed.

You can use this routine in your programs when you need to print a binary number in decimal or some other base. Note that you cannot use this routine to print a number in hex because the characters A through F do not follow character 9 in the ASCII character set. See Chapter 7 for a routine to print numbers in hex.

A Few Points to Remember
When you are using the stack and writing subroutines it is important to keep the following in mind:

• All PUSHes should have corresponding POPs (RET n, or an adjustment of the SP, such as ADD SP,n, can be substituted). In other words, you don't want to leave extra values on the stack and you don't want to POP more values off the stack than you put on.

• The computer uses the same stack for CALL/RET and
PUSH/POP. If you leave extra values on the stack, the computer will use these values as the return address when it
leaves the subroutine. If you POP too many values off the
stack, you will lose one level of subroutines. Although you
can use this to bypass one level of RETurns by POPping the
return address off the stack, this style of programming is
risky and needlessly complex.
• It is not necessary to POP a value into the register that
PUSHed the value.

Programs which have stack trouble often refuse to stop
running (they seem to run fine, but then start executing over
again when they should stop), or they run for a while and
mysteriously crash the computer. If you seem to have a persis-
tent but elusive problem, check stack manipulations carefully.
Be particularly wary of PUSHing a register and jumping
around its POP. Nothing can cause more headaches than a
poorly managed stack.

7

Addressing Modes

At first glance, the great variety of addressing modes available to the 8088 machine language programmer can be mind-boggling. To complicate matters further, there are many ways to request the same addressing mode of the assembler. You will find, however, that the seemingly complex address modes are quite straightforward.

There are six addressing modes available to the 8088. The purpose of the different modes is to give the programmer a variety of ways to determine an effective address, the address of the memory location which is going to be examined.

An *effective address* has two components, a segment address and an offset. The *segment* address is stored in one of the four segment registers (CS, DS, ES, or SS). Remember, these registers hold the addresses of your program's code segment, data segment, extra segment, and stack segment. The offset portion of the effective address can be a constant value, the value of a register, the sum of a register and a constant value, the sum of two registers, or the sum of two registers and a constant value.

For all of the addressing modes, the segment address marks the beginning of the segment, and the offset address points to a location within the segment, relative to the beginning.

Direct Mode Addressing

The first and simplest of the six addressing modes is *direct mode addressing*. In this addressing mode, the offset is a constant value. This constant is usually the address of a variable which is calculated by the assembler and is relative to the beginning (the base) of the segment it's defined in. For example, if the data segment were defined as

```
DATA        SEGMENT
SOME_DATA   DW 933,9265
MORE_DATA   DW 5543,839
DATA        ENDS
```

103

the offset address of SOME_DATA would be calculated as 0. SOME_DATA is the first variable defined, thus its address is at the base of the segment DATA. On the other hand, the offset address of the second variable, MORE_DATA, is 4 because MORE_DATA begins four bytes after the base of the segment DATA (the pseudo-op DW defines words, which are two bytes long).

To use direct mode addressing, simply use the name of a variable. For example, to move the value of SOME_DATA into AX, you could

MOV AX,SOME_DATA

Remember that SOME_DATA itself is a symbol that represents an address in memory. The above operation moves the word pointed to by SOME_DATA into AX. In other words, it is something like the BASIC

AX = PEEK(SOME_DATA)

If you want to move the actual address of SOME_DATA into AX (perform AX = SOME_DATA), you have to use

MOV AX,OFFSET SOME_DATA

The OFFSET command tells the assembler that you want AX to hold the address of SOME_DATA, not the word SOME_DATA points to.

For tables of data, it is sometimes useful to use this format:

MOV AX,SOME_DATA[0]

where [0] is a displacement into the SOME_DATA table. Be careful; this is not like a BASIC array. In machine language the number between the brackets always refers to bytes. Since SOME_DATA is made up of words, use

MOV AX,SOME_DATA[2]

to access the second word (9265) of the SOME_DATA table. If you prefer, you can also use

MOV AX,SOME_DATA+2

where the constant 2 is clearly added to the address of SOME_DATA.

For the sake of clarity, the above examples use the instruction MOV, and show different addressing modes only in the source operand. The same rules apply to any instruction which accepts addressing modes; and various addressing modes can be used in the destination operand as well as the source.

Register Indirect Mode Addressing

Only four of the registers can be used in register indirect addressing: SI, DI, BX, and BP (source index, destination index, base, and base pointer). In *register indirect mode* addressing, the value contained in the register is used as the offset address of the data. You must set the register to point to the data you want to access.

Here are examples of this addressing mode, using each of the four possible registers:

MOV AX,[SI]
MOV AX,[DI]
MOV AX,[BX]
MOV AX,[BP]

Of course, the destination operand can also use register indirect addressing:

ADD [BX],AX
MOV [DI],DL
SUB [BP],AH

It is important to remember that the 8088 cannot perform "memory to memory" operations; thus the following commands are illegal:

MOV [BX],[BP]
MOV SOME_DATA,[BX]

Programmers often use register indirect mode addressing when they must access a one-dimensional array or table of values. The following discussion provides examples of table addressing.

Based Mode and Indexed Mode Addressing

Based mode addressing and *indexed mode addressing* are identical in concept; the only difference is the register used. Based mode addressing uses one of the base registers (BX or BP), while indexed mode addressing uses one of the index registers (SI or DI). The basic principle of based mode/index mode addressing is to add a constant to the contents of the register. The sum becomes the offset portion of the *effective address*.

The acceptable forms of based mode/indexed mode addressing are numerous. The basic format is

MOV CX,[BX]+3

Another common format is

MOV CX,[BX+3]

Both of these take the value of BX, add 3, and use the sum as the address of the data. The different formats are only for the convenience of the programmer. The assembler doesn't care which format you use. The constant does not have to be a positive number; the command

MOV CL,[BX-1]

is quite acceptable, and moves the byte below BX to the CL register.

The constant can also be the name of a variable. Consider the following data segment:

DATA   SEGMENT
BYTE_DATA   DB 1,3,3,7,5,2,9,4,9
WORD_DATA   DW 848,664,2258,753,209
DATA   ENDS

We can use either

MOV AL,BYTE_DATA[BX]

or

MOV AL,[BYTE_DATA+BX]

to get the BX byte in the BYTE_DATA table. For example, if BX holds 3, AL will hold the fourth byte of BYTE_DATA, or the number 7.

Word-sized data presents a slight problem because all addressing is based on bytes, not words. We can use

MOV AX,WORD_DATA[BX]

to address the table WORD_DATA, but BX needs to hold 0 to get the first word, 2 to get the second, 4 to get the third, etc. After executing

MOV BX,6
MOV AX,WORD_DATA[BX]

AX holds 753.

Notice the similarity between based mode/index mode addressing and register indirect mode addressing. In register indirect mode addressing, the value of a register alone is used as the address of the data. With based mode/indexed mode addressing, the value of a register is added to a constant, and the sum is used as the address of the data. As with register indirect addressing, based mode/indexed mode addressing is very useful in accessing a table or a one-dimensional array of values.

Based Indexed Mode Addressing

You just saw how to form an address by adding a constant to a register. You can also form an address by combining the contents of two registers. With *based indexed addressing* the contents of a base register (BX or BP) are added to the contents of an index register (SI or DI). The resulting sum is used as the address of the data. There are only four possible combinations of these registers: BP + SI, BP + DI, BX + SI, or BX + DI. However, each combination can be expressed in four alternate forms. The assembler interprets these four expressions as identical:

MOV AX,[BP][SI]
MOV AX,[SI][BP]
MOV AX,[BP+SI]
MOV AX,[SI+BP]

The most common use for this kind of addressing is in accessing a two-dimensional array (an array with two subscripts). For example, the base register could hold the address of the beginning of a row, while the index register could hold the number of the column we are trying to access. In Figure 7-1, BX holds the address of the row, and SI holds the number of the column we are trying to address.

Based Indexed Mode with Displacement Addressing

The last addressing mode available to the machine language programmer is called *based indexed mode with displacement addressing*. This addressing mode is simply a combination of the last two addressing modes. First the contents of two registers are combined; then a constant is added to the sum of the registers to form the *effective address*.

Figure 7-1. Two-Dimensional Table Access Using Based Indexed Addressing.

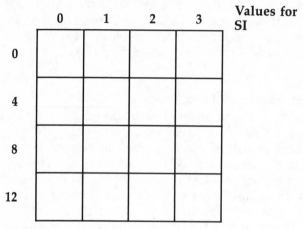

The assembler has a variety of possible formats for based indexed mode with displacement addressing:

MOV AX,[BX+DI+12]   ;the three can appear in any order
MOV AX,[BX+12+DI]
MOV AX,[12+DI+BX]   ;etc.
MOV AX,[DI+12][BX]   ;or broken up in a variety of ways
MOV AX,[BX+12][DI]
MOV AX,8+[BX][DI]+4   ;the constant can be in two parts
MOV AX,12+[BX][DI]   ;or just in the beginning

and they go on and on. To the assembler, all of these instructions are identical.

Often, the value of the constant is the address of a variable:

MOV AX,ANY_DATA[BP][DI]
MOV AX,[ANY_DATA+BP+DI]

If you like, you can add another constant (beyond the address of the variable):

MOV AX,ANY_DATA[BX][SI]+14

As with based indexed addressing, based indexed with displacement addressing can be useful when accessing a two-dimensional array.

The names of the different addressing modes we have given here might be called the official Intel names. It is far more important to understand how they work than to memorize the names. Table 7-1 at the end of the chapter lists all of the addressing modes and their possible register combinations. Note that the format of the operand is the one used by DEBUG.

Eliminating Ambiguity: The PTR Instruction

Remember that any of the addressing modes described above can be used as the source or the destination operand of an instruction (but not both at the same time). Remember also that the source can be an immediate value, and that a register can act as either the source or the destination. When one operand is an immediate value, the size of the operation is sometimes ambiguous. For example, in

CMP [BX],12H

the assembler has no way of knowing if [BX] points to a word or a byte. If you try this, the assembler will respond with error 35 (Operand must have size). Note that the error for

CMP [BX],1234H

is different. If you try this, you will get error 50 (Value is out of range), because the word 1234H is too large for the expected use (comparison with the byte-sized memory location addressed by [BX]).

When the size of an operation is ambiguous, the PTR instruction is used to clarify the instruction. Our first statement above must be replaced with

CMP BYTE PTR [BX],12H

if [BX] points to a byte, or with

CMP WORD PTR [BX],12H

if [BX] points to a word. However, the assembler can make certain assumptions. If we define a variable in our data segment as

MORE_INFO DW 5142,3387,9808

the instruction

CMP MORE_INFO[SI],43H

is not ambiguous. MORE_INFO is defined as word data, so

the assembler assumes that [SI] points to a word. If, however, you want to compare 43H to the byte pointed to by [SI], you can override the assembler's assumption with

CMP BYTE PTR MORE_INFO[SI],43H

There is another method which is discussed in Chapter 15.

LDS/LES and the DD Pseudo-op

There are two very specialized instructions that are used to load the DS and ES segment registers with values, LDS (Load Data Segment) and LES (Load Extra Segment). The format for these instructions is

LDS *destination,source*
LES *destination,source*

where *destination* is any general register and the *source* is a memory location addressed by one of the methods described above. The instruction moves the word pointed to by the source into the destination register. The following (higher addressed) word is moved into DS (if LDS is used), or ES (if LES is used). Here are some examples:

LDS SI,DOUBLE_WORD_DATA[BX][DI]+2
LES DI,DWORD PTR [BP][DI]
LES BX,DWORD PTR [BX]
LDS BP,DWORD PTR [BX]+4

If you do not specify DWORD PTR, the assembler will give you error 57 (Illegal size for item). The addressed memory location must be defined with the DD (Define Double word) pseudo-op. The operands of the DD pseudo-op can be a label or a constant value. See the examples below.

DOUBLE_WORD_DATA   DD FAR_LABEL,FAR_PROC ;FAR labels
                         DD 1343234,432343   ;constants

LDS and LES can be useful if your program has more than one data segment. Remember to include an ASSUME statement when DS or ES is changed.

Segment Overrides

All memory access is performed using an offset into a segment. The segments are defined by the four segment registers. Machine language programs are addressed using the IP as an offset into the segment defined by the CS register. The stack is addressed using the SP register as an offset into the segment defined by the SS register. Most data is addressed using an offset into the segment defined by the DS register. All of the addressing modes described above are offset into the data segment, except when BP is involved. When BP is used, the offset is added to the SS, not the DS register. In other words, BP is generally used to access the stack segment.

However, it is not mandatory to use DS or SS. You can tell the 8088 which segment register to use for addressing data with a segment override command. A *segment override* command is sometimes called a *segment prefix* command, or just a SEG command. The segment override tells the 8088 to use a specific segment register when it addresses memory. There are four segment override commands, one for each segment register:

CS:
SS:
DS:
ES:

The segment override is often included with the addressing mode. For example, if the BP register is used to address data in the data segment rather than the stack segment, you can use something like

MOV AX,DS:[BP]
MOV AX,DS:[BP+DI]

If the PTR command is used, it should appear before any segment overrides, as in

MOV BYTE PTR ES:[BX],0
CMP WORD PTR CS:[DI],15H

Bear in mind that the selection of the segment is generally automatic. The assembler uses the ASSUME pseudo-op to determine which segment register is used to address specific data. Consider the following data segment declarations:

DATA1   SEGMENT
FIRST   DW 1,2,3,4
SOME   DB 'MORE DATA'
DATA1   ENDS

DATA2   SEGMENT
SECOND   DW 0AH,0BH,0CH,0DH
THIRD   DB 'RUNNING OUT OF IDEAS'
DATA2   ENDS

and the ASSUME:

ASSUME ES:DATA1,DS:DATA2

Now, whenever FIRST or SOME is accessed, the ES register will be used as the segment register. All instructions involving the FIRST or SOME labels will have an extra segment override. Any access to DATA2 uses the DS register. For example:

MOV AX,FIRST[BP]   ;even though BP usually uses SS

If you prefer, you can also use:

MOV AX,ES:[BP]
MOV AX,DATA1:[BP]

All three of these examples use ES as the segment register. The following

MOV AX,SECOND[BP]   ;BP is now using DS as segment register
MOV AX,DS:[BP]
MOV AX,DATA2:[BP]

use DS rather than ES. Specifying a label name, a segment name, or a segment register tells the assembler which segment register to use. However, in

MOV BP,OFFSET SOME
MOV AX,[BP]

MOV AX,[BP] is ambiguous. The assembler has no way of knowing if you want to use DS, ES, or SS as the segment register; thus the offset held in [BP] might point to an undesired location. You must specifically tell the assembler which segment register to use:

MOV BP,OFFSET SOME
MOV AX,ES:[BP]

If you do not specify a segment register, the assembler will assume the default segment. The default segment register is DS unless BP is involved, in which case the default is SS. Again, the segment assignment is generally automatic, but you must be certain that you are communicating your ideas to the assembler correctly, to avoid unpleasant surprises.

There are many uses for segment overrides. Anytime the BP register is used to access data in the data segment, an override is used. However, there are times when you might want to use BX or DI to access the stack segment, or perhaps use BP and SI to address something in the ES (Extra Segment). You can even store data in the code segment and use the segment

override to access the data properly (see "Hexconv," the
sample program at the end of this chapter).

Special Consideration of the Segment Registers

The segment registers cannot be used as operands in *any*
instructions except MOV, PUSH, and POP. In other words,
the segment registers cannot be used in operations such as
ADD or SUB.

When the segment registers are the destination of the
MOV instruction, the source operand cannot be an immediate
value. The source can be any other register (except another
segment register) or an addressed memory location. Perhaps
this was designed for our safety. We wouldn't want a program
to haphazardly change the values of a segment register.

Specialized Addressing

There are three rather specialized but useful instructions that
are related to memory addressing. These are LEA (Load Effective Address), XCHG (eXCHanGe), and XLAT (translate).

LEA. The *Load Effective Address* instruction calculates an
address and moves the calculated address into the specified
register. LEA takes the general format

LEA *destination,source*

where the *destination* can be any general word-sized register,
and the *source* is any addressed memory location. Remember
that the address, not the value contained in the addressed
memory location, is moved into the destination register. For
example:

LEA BX,[SI][BP]+10

moves the quantity SI + BP + 10 into BX. It does *not* move
the word pointed to by SI + BP + 10 into BX. The purpose of
this instruction is to allow offsets to be subscripted with registers. This is not permitted with the standard MOV instruction. For example,

MOV BX,OFFSET SOME_DATA[BX]

is illegal; you must use instead

LEA BX,SOME_DATA[BX]   ;get the offset
MOV BX,[BX]   ;load the data in BX

You can also use LEA if more than two subscripting variables are required. You might use something like

LEA BX,MORE_DATA[BX][DI]
MOV AX,[BX][SI]

if what you really wanted was MORE_DATA[BX+DI+SI], a nonexistent addressing mode. In this case, the LEA instruction replaces the rather awkward

ADD BX,DI
MOV AX,MORE_DATA[BX][SI]

which is somewhat unclear.

You can also use LEA if you need to temporarily adjust an offset. For example, you might write a program which needs to address the memory around SI–16, in which case, it would be to your advantage to use:

LEA DI,[SI–16]

and use DI for SI–16. This simplifies the code and may make it easier to understand and follow.

XCHG. The exchange operation is much like the SWAP operation in BASIC. XCHG takes the format

XCHG *destination,source*

and switches the contents of the source and destination. The source and destination can be any general byte or word register, or any addressed memory location. You cannot XCHG two memory locations, so one operand of XCHG must always be a register. No flags are affected by XCHG.

Remember that this operation is more complex than MOV. MOV copies a value from the source to the destination, without destroying the contents of the source. XCHG switches the two; what was in the destination is now in the source, and what was in the source is now in the destination.

XLAT. XLAT takes the general form

XLAT *source-table*

It is a one-byte instruction used to retrieve single bytes from a table of data. The *source-table* operand is only for the assembler. When you use DEBUG, XLAT will appear alone on a line. XLAT "translates" a byte through a table lookup procedure. The BX register must hold the address of the table, and AL the byte which is being translated. AL is used as an offset into the table, and the byte which is addressed is loaded into

AL. The old AL is lost. The closest approximation of XLAT's addressing is

MOV AL,[BX][AL]   ;this is illegal, you must use XLAT

The source-table must be defined as a byte table; otherwise, an error from the assembler will result. Using XLAT is rather cumbersome, but straightforward.

MOV AL,BYTE_TO_BE_TRANSLATED   ;set byte to translate
MOV BX,OFFSET TABLE_NAME   ;set base of table
XLAT TABLE_NAME   ;do translation

You can use LEA BX,TABLE_NAME, rather than MOV BX,OFFSET TABLE_NAME if you so desire. When this code fragment is executed, AL will hold the translated value. Note that XLAT affects none of the flags.

XLAT will only translate byte-sized quantities. Because of this limitation, the length of the translation table is limited to 256 bytes. You do not need to create a table which is 256 bytes long; however, neither the 8088 nor the assembler makes any boundary checks on access to the table. Boundary checks are the responsibility of the programmer. The sample program Hexconv uses XLAT with a short 16-byte table.

Using XLAT

Our sample program for this chapter uses the XLAT instruction in the process of converting a binary word into ASCII hex digits. The number is printed on the screen. The routine is given the number to print in AX.

WORD_OUT begins by saving the registers which it uses. CH is used to count the number of hex digits that we must convert, and CL is set to the number of rotates to perform (ROL will be explained in the next chapter). Next, AX is stored. We extract the lowest nybble (the nybble to convert) by ANDing it with 15, set the base of the ASCII table (notice that the table is in the code segment, not the data segment), and perform XLAT. AL, which held a number from 0 to 15, now holds an ASCII digit. We print the digit, recover AX, and check to see if all of the nybbles have been converted. If they have, we restore all the stored registers, and return to the calling program.

The sample calling program is not very complex; it just sends WORD_OUT all of the numbers from 0 to FFFFH. If CX is 0 after the INC CX command, then we have gone through all of the numbers and CX has cycled back to 0. The program can be stopped at any time by pressing Ctrl-Break (or Fn-Break on the PCjr).

WORD_OUT can be used in any of your programs which need to output hex numbers—simply extract the routine from this program and insert it into yours. Likewise, you can extract the DECIMAL_OUT routine from the "Primes" program if you need to print numbers in decimal. When you do so, don't forget to copy the routine CHARACTER_OUT as well.

Table 7-1. Table of Addressing Modes and Possible Register Arrangements

Addressing Mode	Possible arrangements
Direct	(label)
	displacement
Register Indirect	[BX]
	[BP]
	[SI]
	[DI]
Based	[BX+n]
	[BP+n]
Indexed	[SI+n]
	[DI+n]
Based Indexed	[BX+SI]
	[BX+DI]
	[BP+SI]
	[BP+DI]
Based Indexed with Displacement	[BX+SI+n]
	[BX+DI+n]
	[BP+SI+n]
	[BP+DI+n]

n represents a signed 8- or 16-bit displacement

Program 7-1. Hex to ASCII Conversion Using XLAT

```
; HEXCONV.ASM
;
; This program outputs the hex numbers
; from 0000H to FFFFH.
;
;
        page    ,96
;
cr      equ 13                      ;carriage return
lf      equ 10                      ;line feed
;
stack   segment stack
        dw 128 dup(?)               ;stack
stack   ends
;
code    segment
program proc far
        assume cs:code
        push ds
        mov ax,0
        push ax
;
        mov cx,0                    ;zero counter
another:
        mov ax,cx                   ;output the counter
```

117

```
            call word_out
            mov dl,cr        ;print a carriage return
            mov ah,2
            int 21H
            mov dl,lf        ;print a line feed
            mov ah,2
            int 21H
            inc cx           ;do the next digit
            jnz another      ;cycled back to zero?
            ret              ;yes, so return to DOS
program endp
;
; Output word as hex ASCII
; value passed in AX
; only AX affected
;
hexconv proc near
asciinums db '0123456789ABCDEF'
word_out:
            push cx          ;save CX
            push bx          ;save BX
            push dx          ;save DX
            mov ch,4         ;set number of nybbles to print
loop1:      mov cl,4         ;set ROL counter
            rol ax,cl        ;ROL AX four times
            push ax          ;save AX
            and al,0fH       ;get a single nybble
```

```
        mov bx,offset code:asciinums   ;set base of table
        xlat asciinums                 ;do translation
        mov dl,al                      ;print the digit
        mov ah,2
        int 21H
        pop ax                         ;recover number
        dec ch                         ;check counter
        jnz loop1
        pop dx                         ;recover DX
        pop bx                         ;recover BX
        pop cx                         ;recover CX
        ret                            ;return to caller

hexconv endp
code    ends
        end
```

2
Advanced Programming

8
Advanced Arithmetic

As you become a more proficient programmer, you may find that 16 bits is not enough room to store all of your data. After all, limiting your calculations to the numbers from −32,768 to 32,767 (or 0 to 65,535 for unsigned numbers) can be constricting. In this section you will learn how 16-bit words can be chained together into 32-bit (or even 64-bit) quantities.

Adding Multiword Numbers

To understand how the computer can add two multiword numbers together, consider how we add two multidigit numbers. For example, when adding the numbers 17 and 25, first add the one's digits: 7 plus 5 equals 12. The ten's part of our partial sum is the carry into the next digit. In other words, we have to carry a 1 into the next (more significant) digit. When adding the ten's digits together, remember to include the carry. Summing up, the 1, the 2, and the extra 1 from the carry make 4. Remember, this is four 10's. Our complete sum is 42. In our example, we carried from one digit to the next. The 8088 uses the carry flag to carry from one word (or byte) to the next.

When the microprocessor performs an ADD, however, it does not take the carry flag into account. A second addition instruction, ADC (ADd with Carry), is used when the state of the carry flag must be considered. In all other respects, such as possible operands and resulting flags, ADC is identical to ADD. Using ADD with ADC, we can chain bytes or words together into very large numbers.

For example, to add a 32-bit number stored in AX:DX (AX holds the least significant word, and DX the more significant word) to another in BX:CX (BX holds the least significant word), you could use the following code (this stores the result in BX:CX):

ADD BX,AX ;add the less significant words together...
ADC CX,DX ;...and the more significant words

Note that you must start with the least significant and proceed
to the most significant word.

If you need even larger numbers (say 64-bit words), you
can use a loop to add them together. Consider this example
(for MASM only):

```
[in your data segment]
NUMBER_ONE      DQ 1348176354    ;define a 64-bit word
NUMBER_TWO      DQ 7564627653    ;define another
SUM             DQ ?             ;undetermined value for sum
[in your code segment]
                MOV CX,4         ;number of words to add
                                 ;together
                MOV BX,0         ;point to least significant word
                CLC              ;so first ADC is like an ADD
L1:             MOV AX,WORD PTR NUMBER_ONE[BX]
                                 ;add the two...
                ADC AX,WORD PTR NUMBER_TWO[BX]
                                 ;...corresponding...
                MOV WORD PTR SUM[BX],AX
                                 ;...words together
                INC BX           ;point to next significant word
                INC BX
                LOOP L1          ;finish them all
```

The DQ pseudo-op defines a 64-bit word (see Chapter 14 for
more details). Two INC BX instructions are used to add two to
BX. The ADD instruction cannot be used because it changes
the state of the carry flag; INC and DEC do not affect the
carry flag. Also notice that the carry flag was cleared (CLC)
before entering the loop. If the carry is clear, ADC is just like
ADD.

Subtracting Multiword Numbers
Subtracting two multiword numbers is just as simple as adding them. In subtraction, however, the carry flag is used to indicate a *borrow* into the highest bit rather than a carry.

Consider how we subtract two multidigit numbers. To
subtract 27 from 50, first subtract the ones. 7 cannot be subtracted from 0, so we borrow a 10 from the next higher digit;
10 minus 7 equals 3. When subtracting the ten's place, 1 must
be taken for the 10 borrowed earlier. Thus, 5 minus 2, minus
another 1 for the borrow, leaves 2. Remember, this is two
10's. The difference is 23. The 8088 uses the carry flag to indicate a borrow from one word (or byte) to the next.

When we use the SUB instruction, however, the microprocessor does not consider the state of the carry flag when it subtracts. You must use the SBB (SuBtract with Borrow) operation if you want the microprocessor to take the state of the carry flag into account. If the carry flag is set (indicating there was a borrow), SBB decrements the resulting difference by one to take care of the borrow. SUB and SBB are identical in terms of how they set the flags and the operands they take. If the carry flag is clear (indicating no borrow), SBB is just like SUB. We can subtract two multiword values using SUB with SBB.

For example, if we want to subtract two 32-bit words, one stored in AX:DX, the other in BX:CX (AX and BX hold the least significant word; the result is stored in BX:CX), we can use:

SUB BX,AX   ;subtract the least significant words...
SBB CX,DX   ;...and the more significant words

As with multiword addition, you must begin subtracting with the least significant word and proceed to the most significant. If you need larger numbers, say 64-bit quantities, you can use a loop structure as shown above in the 64-bit word addition; just change all of the ADCs to SBBs.

Comparing Multiword Numbers

When dealing with multiword numbers it is often convenient to compare them with other multiword numbers. The techniques are quite easy to understand. Consider how you would compare two multidigit numbers. Suppose you were asked which is larger, 52 or 27. Clearly, 52 is larger. All you had to do was look at the ten's digit (the most significant digit); you didn't need to look at the one's digit to know that 52 is larger than 27. Now, suppose you were asked how to compare 29 and 22. This time, the ten's digits are the same; you have to inspect the one's place to determine which is larger.

The same techniques are used in programs that compare two multiword numbers. Start by comparing the most significant words. If they are the same, check the next less significant words. Clearly, if all of the words are the same, the two numbers are equal. The following code can be used to compare two double words; one is stored in AX:DX and the other in BX:CX:

```
              CMP DX,CX
              JNE DO_CONDITIONAL
              CMP AX,BX
DO_CONDITIONAL:  JA AX_DX_ABOVE_BX_CX
```

Converting Between Formats

When your program uses many different number sizes (bytes, words, and double words), it often becomes necessary to convert between them. To convert unsigned numbers, you simply put a zero into the more significant part of the number (whether byte or word). For example, you would use MOV AH,0 to convert an unsigned byte in AL into an unsigned word in AX.

For converting signed numbers, the 8088 provides two instructions, one to convert a byte to a word (CBW) and another to convert a word into a double word (CWD). Neither CBW (Convert Byte to Word) nor CWD (Convert Word to Double word) takes an operand. CBW converts the byte in AL into a word in AX. CWD converts the word in AX into a double word stored in AX and DX (DX holds the more significant word). Because their effect is to extend from smaller to larger sizes, CBW and CWD are also known as *sign extend* instructions. These operations are most often used before signed division, when a signed word is divided by another signed word, or a signed byte is divided by another signed byte. For example, to divide a signed word in AX by another signed word in BX:

CWD   ;sign extend AX into DX
IDIV BX   ;divide AX:DX by the signed word in BX

You can use the techniques discussed above to perform many elaborate mathematical operations. By chaining bytes or words together, you can represent extremely large numbers. However, there are other ways of representing numbers within the 8088 microprocessor.

Binary-Coded Decimal (BCD)

The 8088 provides three methods of storing numeric data. We have already discussed pure binary. The other two systems are powerful extensions of the binary system.

The basic principle of these "new" numeric data storage techniques revolves around the idea of binary-coded decimal

(BCD) numbers. In Chapter 2 you learned that computers store all of their numbers in binary. While this is convenient for the computer, humans generally find it difficult to understand, and even more difficult to convert to decimal. To assist the programmer, the 8088 has been designed to use BCD as well as pure binary. In BCD, each decimal digit is stored as a four-bit binary number. Look, for example, at Figure 8-1.

Figure 8-1. BCD, Hex, and Binary

Binary	Hex	BCD
0000	0	0
0001	1	1
0010	2	2
0011	3	3
.		
.		
.		
1000	8	8
1001	9	9
1010	A	undefined
1011	B	undefined
.		
.		

etc.

Notice that only the hex digits 0 to 9 are defined in BCD. The hex digits A to F are undefined, and represent no value in BCD. This type of numeric storage is convenient because it is very easy to convert a BCD number into ASCII decimal. Each four-bit number represents one decimal digit.

The 8088 uses the BCD storage technique in two ways, *packed* and *unpacked*. In unpacked storage, each digit is given an entire byte, the upper nybble is unused. IBM and Intel refer to this kind of numeric storage as ASCII. Using this method, you can store the numbers from 0 to 9 in one byte. This is far less than is possible using binary (0 to 255), but it is extremely easy to convert unpacked BCD into conventional ASCII (just add 48, the ASCII code for the zero character, to the number).

Defining unpacked BCD data in a program is fairly simple. Since only the digits from 0 to 9 are valid, the simplest method is to use the DB pseudo-op.

UNPACKED_DATA   DB 5,3,1   ;defines 135

Unpacked BCD digits are best defined starting from the least significant digit and ending with the most significant. Unfortunately, it is somewhat confusing because the numbers must be read backwards.

You can also use the DW command, as in:

UNPACKED_WORD_DATA
DW 0301h   ;defines 31 (unpacked)

Remember that the assembler automatically places the less significant byte of a word first, so the order of the digits will be correct if you use DW.

In packed BCD data, both the upper and lower nybbles are used to hold decimal digits—two BCD digits per byte. This kind of number storage is referred to as *decimal* in IBM and Intel literature. Packed BCD number storage allows you to store the numbers from 0 to 99 in a single byte. This is more than unpacked BCD storage, but it is also more difficult to convert packed BCD numbers into ASCII for output. The methods for this are outlined in the discussion on bit shifting later in this chapter.

There are two data-defining pseudo-ops you can use to define packed BCD data. DB can be used as follows:

PACKED_BCD_DATA   DB 12h,43h   ;defines 1243 or 4312

With packed BCD numbers, it is more conventional to have the less significant byte follow the more significant. Note that this is the opposite to unpacked BCD numbers.

The DT pseudo-op is designed specifically to define packed BCD data. Note that this command is not available with ASM, the *Small Assembler*. DT (for Define Ten bytes) will define 18 BCD digits. The first byte is used to hold the sign (00H is positive, 80H is negative); the other nine, the data. The data is stored as most significant first; the last byte holds the least significant digits. For example:

LARGE_DATA   DT 7893146

becomes

00 00 00 00 00 00 07 89 31 46

A negative number, defined with

NEGATIVE_EXAMPLE   DT -125368953553

would assemble as:

80 00 00 00 12 53 68 95 35 53

If you use this command, you will have to write special addition and subtraction routines which handle the sign of the number. It was actually designed to be used with the 8087 Numeric Data Processor. Note that you can define only 18 digits; defining more results in a 29:Division by 0 or overflow error from the assembler.

Using BCD Math

Unlike some microprocessors (such as the 6502), the 8088 does not have decimal or ASCII math modes. Instead, an adjustment instruction is needed before or after each arithmetic operation (ADD, SUB, MUL, DIV, etc.). Note that it is the responsibility of the programmer to call these instructions. There is no way to make the microprocessor perform all of the mathematical operations in a BCD mode. There are six adjustment instructions available; four pertain to ASCII math, and two to decimal math.

AAA (ASCII Adjust for Addition). The AAA instruction performs an ASCII adjustment on the result of an addition. The instruction takes no operands and always adjusts the AL register. Only the lower nybble of AL is considered. If the BCD digit held in AL is valid, the upper nybble is cleared, as are CF and AF. If the BCD digit held in AL is not valid (it is hex A to F), the digit is adjusted to a valid digit, AH is incremented by one (to handle the carry), CF and AF are set (to indicate a carry), and the upper nybble of AL is cleared.

For example, you would use

```
ADD AL,BL
AAA
```

if you are adding two valid unpacked BCD numbers stored in AL and BL. If the sum of AL and BL is 9 or less, AAA appears to do nothing. If the resulting sum is greater than 9, AAA adjusts the sum by adding 6 (AA becomes 0, BH becomes 1, etc.), AH is incremented by 1, and CF and AF are set. To chain many unpacked BCD additions together you could use:

```
[in the data segment]
SMALL_1     DB 4,0        ;4 (least significant digit first)
SMALL_2     DB 7,0        ;7 as unpacked BCD data
SMALL_SUM   DB ?,?        ;undefined variable to hold sum
[in the code segment]
MOV AX,WORD PTR SMALL_1   ;add the two numbers together
ADD AX,WORD PTR SMALL_2
```

```
AAA                          ;ASCII adjust lower digit
MOV SMALL_SUM[0],AL          ;store adjusted digit
MOV AL,AH                    ;adjust the other digit
AAA
MOV SMALL_SUM[1],AL          ;store adjusted higher digit
```

Notice that 16-bit addition is used. The way the numbers are added is unimportant. It is easier to add the numbers together first, and then adjust the sum. Any carry resulting from AAA is handled automatically because the next higher digit is already stored in AH. When AAA performs a carry (if the digit is not valid), it increments the AH by one. AH is moved into AL and then adjusted itself. Any carry resulting from this second adjustment indicates an overflow situation, and another byte is needed to hold the sum.

This method is fine for small BCD numbers, but using it with larger numbers would require a great deal of code. A loop is more efficient, as the example below demonstrates.

[in the data segment]

ONE_NUMBER	DB 2,5,1,2,5,0	;52152 in unpacked form
TWO_NUMBER	DB 0,4,6,8,0,0	;8640 in unpacked form
SUM	DB 6 DUP(?)	;undefined sum of two numbers

[and as your code]

```
        MOV CX,6                    ;number of digits to
                                    add together
        MOV BX,0                    ;point to the least
                                    significant digit
        CLC                         ;simulate "ADD" for
                                    first ADC
L1:     MOV AL,ONE_NUMBER[BX]       ;put one digit in AL
        ADC AL,TWO_NUMBER[BX]       ;add other digit to it
        MOV SUM[BX],AL              ;store the sum
        INC BX                      ;point to next higher
                                    digit
        LOOP L1                     ;do all of the digits

        MOV CX,6                    ;number of digits
        MOV BX,0                    ;point to least signifi-
                                    cant digit
        MOV AL,SUM[BX]              ;get least significant
                                    digit of sum
L2:     MOV AH,SUM[BX+1]            ;put next higher digit
                                    in AH
        AAA                         ;perform ASCII
                                    adjust
```

MOV SUM[BX],AL	;store the adjusted sum
MOV AL,AH	;move next digit into AL
INC BX	;point to next higher digit
LOOP L2	;do all of the digits

This code performs the same operations as the previous example, only this time the operations are performed in a loop rather than in a straight line. Note that the entire number is added together first, then the entire sum is adjusted. This is only one illustration of how the AAA instruction can be used to sum and adjust multidigit numbers.

AAS (ASCII Adjust for Subtraction). This instruction is the subtraction equivalent of AAA. Like AAA, AAS does not take an operand; it always performs an ASCII adjustment on the AL register. If the unpacked BCD digit in AL is legal, AAS clears the upper nybble of AL and clears CF and AF. If the digit is not legal, AAS sets CF and AF, clears the upper nybble of AL, and decrements AH by 1.

Illegal digits are always the result of an ASCII subtraction when the result is negative. AAS is designed to cope with the problem of negative BCD numbers. In Chapter 4, we used the analogy of a counter on a tape player to explain negative binary numbers. We said that 999 was like −1 (999 is one count behind 0). A similar method is used to store negative numbers in BCD.

Using AAS is just as simple as using AAA. For single-digit applications, you could use code similar to the following if you wanted to subtract an unpacked BCD digit in BL from one in AL:

```
SUB AL,BL
AAS
```

For larger quantities, you will have to chain AAS instructions together, as we chained AAA instructions together in the previous section. For very large quantities, it is convenient to use loops as we did above. Of course, for subtraction you would substitute SUB for ADD, SBB for ADC, and AAS for AAA.

AAM (ASCII Adjust for Multiplication). AAM is used to convert the result of a multiplication into two valid BCD digits. This only applies to AL, so it is used after an eight-bit multiplication. After AAM is performed, the lower digit of the product is stored in AL, and the upper digit in AH. The previous contents of AH are lost. Using AAM is very straightforward; for example, to multiply an unpacked BCD digit in AL by another in BL, use

MUL BL   ;one of the operands for MUL is always AL
AAM

AAM will take the product of the MUL instruction and convert it into two valid BCD digits; the least significant in AL, and the more significant in AH. For BCD multiplication, you must always use MUL, never IMUL. You can chain MULs together (like you can chain ADDs and SUBs), but the techniques are rather difficult.

AAM can also be used anytime you would like to convert a binary number from 0 to 99 into two unpacked BCD numbers, for a simple decimal output routine for example. An output routine such as this is shown below. If AL does not contain a binary number from 0 to 99, AAM returns invalid BCD digits; no flags are set to indicate any kind of error.

```
AAM               ;AL holds the number to print
ADD AX,'00'       ;add ASCII zero to both unpacked digits
PUSH AX           ;save AX
MOV AL,AH         ;output the more significant digit first
CALL BYTE_OUT     ;print character in AL
POP AX            ;retrieve AX
CALL BYTE_OUT     ;print the less significant digit
```

AAD (ASCII Adjust for Division). Unlike the other ASCII adjust instructions, AAD is used *before* the mathematical operation. AAD converts the two unpacked BCD digits stored in AL and AH (AL holds the least significant digit) into a binary number in AL. AH is set to 0. Using this instruction is no more complicated than any of the others. To divide two unpacked BCD numbers stored in AL and AH by another in BL, use

```
AAD      ;convert the two BCD digits into a binary number
DIV BL   ;divide AX by BL
AAM      ;convert the quotient (in AL) into a BCD number
```

Note that the above example destroys the remainder. If you are after the remainder, not the quotient, you will have to move AH (which holds the remainder after eight-bit division) into AL before performing the AAM command, as in:

```
AAD          ;convert the two BCD digits into binary
DIV BL       ;divide AX by BL
MOV AL,AH    ;move the remainder into AL for conversion
AAM          ;convert AL into valid BCD digits.
```

Chaining DIVs together is more difficult than chaining MULs, although it can be done.

AAD is much like a converse of AAM. While AAM converts a binary number into two unpacked BCD digits, AAD converts two unpacked BCD digits into a binary number. One might use AAD in a simple decimal input routine which accepts two ASCII digits, but requires a binary number for calculations. Note that AAD does not check the validity of the BCD digits before it performs the conversion. If the digits are not valid, AAD will return an erroneous binary number. No flags are set to indicate an error.

DAA (Decimal Adjust for Addition)

This instruction is similar to AAA above, but is used to adjust the result of a packed BCD addition. It takes no operands, but always adjusts the AL register. If the number is greater than 99, the carry is set, indicating that the next more significant byte needs to be incremented by one.

Unlike AAA, which increments AH when a carry is necessary, DAA does not affect the AH register. It is the programmer's responsibility to adjust the succeeding digits if the carry flag is set (the auxiliary carry flag is set only to indicate a carry out of the lower nybble).

You can use DAA just like AAA. For example, the following code adds the two packed BCD numbers stored in AL and BL:

```
ADD AL,BL
DAA
```

You can also chain decimal additions together, just as we chained ASCII additions together. For larger numbers (such as those defined with the DT pseudo-op), you would probably use loops to sum the numbers together:

```
[in the data segment]
    ONE_NUMBER      DT 346346524    ;using DT command
    TWO_NUMBER      DT 687987346
    SUM             DT ?            ;ten undefined bytes

[and as your code]
    MOV CX,9                        ;the number of bytes to add
```

```
        MOV BX,10                      ;point to the least significant
                                        digit
        CLC                            ;simulate ADD for first ADC
L1:     MOV AL,ONE_NUMBER[BX]          ;put one digit in AL
        ADC AL,TWO_NUMBER[BX]          ;add other digit to it
        MOV SUM[BX],AL                 ;store the sum
        DEC BX                         ;point to next higher digit
        LOOP L1                        ;do all of the digits
                                       ;on exit here, carry set in-
                                        dicates overflow
                                       ;

        MOV CX,9                       ;number of bytes to adjust
        MOV BX,10                      ;point to least significant digit
        MOV AL,SUM[BX]                 ;get least significant digit of
                                        sum
L2:     DAA                            ;perform decimal adjust
        MOV SUM[BX],AL                 ;store the adjusted sum
        DEC BX                         ;point to next higher digit
        MOV AL,SUM[BX]                 ;move next higher digit into
                                        AL
        ADC AL,0                       ;add in possible carry from
                                        DAA
        LOOP L2                        ;do all of the digits
```

Note that INC does not affect the state of the carry flag, and that DT defines the packed BCD numbers from the most significant byte to least significant in increasing memory locations.

DAS (Decimal Adjust for Subtraction)

DAS is similar to DAA, but is used after subtraction rather than after addition. The result of the subtraction must be stored in AL. The carry flag is set if the next higher byte needs to be adjusted because of a borrow. Like DAA, this instruction does not affect the AH register. The succeeding byte must be adjusted by the programmer. As with AAS, DAS adjusts the difference according to our tape counter analogy for negative numbers (see Chapter 4).

Use DAS just like AAS; to subtract a packed BCD value in BL from one in AL, use

SUB AL,BL
DAS

Again, longer numbers can be subtracted just as they can be added. For very long packed BCD values, you will want to use loops, as we did above. Note that if you are using the DT format, you must check the sign byte and adjust the result and sign as necessary.

Comparing BCD Numbers

Comparing BCD numbers is as easy as comparing normal binary numbers. There is no need to adjust anything. Just use the CMP instruction as you always have. Note that you must start comparing with the most significant byte first, as described in the section on multiword math in this chapter.

Boolean Arithmetic

Boolean arithmetic refers to the logic operators. High-level language users will be most familiar with these commands in reference to conditional statements. We have all used expressions like

IF A>15 AND C=7 THEN . . .

or

IF J<3 OR K=2 THEN . . .

and, less frequently,

IF NOT L=4 THEN . . .

AND, OR and NOT are three of the various Boolean mathematical functions. When used in conditional statements, they serve as logic operators. Programmers who use the BASIC graphics GET and PUT commands should also be familiar with these operations. With the graphics commands (as in machine language), however, their bit-oriented nature is more apparent.

The 8088 has four Boolean arithmetic commands, AND, OR, XOR, and NOT. The Boolean operators have the general format shown below. The *operator* is one of the four Boolean arithmetic commands. The *function* is the operation performed by the operator. Any *source* or *destination* combination legal with commands such as ADD or SUB is legal with the Boolean operators. Note that the operator NOT has only one operand which acts as both the source and the destination. The Boolean commands can perform their operations on either bytes or words.

OPERATOR *destination,source*

destination = source FUNCTION destination

AND. We all understand the logical significance of the English word *and*. In the statement "Send Jack and Jill to the well," it is clear that both Jack and Jill are supposed to go to the well. In high-level languages, the AND operator serves a similar purpose. It is generally used to link two logical statements together. When both of the logical statements are true, the entire statement is true. In machine language, AND is a little different.

The AND operation inspects each bit of its two operands and sets the destination as follows:

0 AND 0 = 0
0 AND 1 = 0
1 AND 0 = 0
1 AND 1 = 1

In other words, a bit will be set in the destination only if it is set in both the source and the destination. For example, if we start with

11110000B and 11010111B

after ANDing these two numbers together, we obtain the result

```
    11110000B
AND 11010111B
    11010000B
```

Every time the corresponding bits are both 1, the result is a 1. If a 1 and a 0 line up together, then the resulting bit is 0.

The AND operator can also be used to *mask off* unwanted portions of a number. For example, we can isolate the lower nybble of a BCD packed byte (held in BL) using the instruction:

AND BL,0FH   ;(0FH=00001111B)

This operation tells the microprocessor to AND the contents of BL with 0FH, and store the result in BL. For example, if BL holds 01010011B,

```
    01010011B  contents of BL
AND 00001111B
    00000011B
```

The upper nybble of BL has been masked off. This is useful when you only want to deal with part of a number. For instance, the sample program in the last chapter used AND to extract the low nybble from a number.

You can also use this operation to isolate a single bit; you simply AND the number you are inspecting with the appropriate mask byte.

For example, if you want to isolate bit 5 (the bit representing the decimal value 32), you would use:

AND destination,32   ;(32D=00100000B)

This might prove useful in graphics applications.

Inspecting bits in this way proves so useful that Intel engineers provided the 8088 with another AND instruction called TEST. TEST is identical to AND in all respects, except that the result of the AND is not stored. For example, if you use

TEST destination,16

the flags will be set just as in the operation

AND destination,16

but the value of the destination will be unchanged. After such a TEST, you can JZ (Jump if Zero) or JNZ (Jump if Not Zero) to check for either a clear or set bit.

One often finds code such as

AND AX,AX

or

TEST AX,AX

This command is used to set the flags (PF, SF, or ZF) according to the value of AX. Note that the value of AX is unchanged.

OR. The OR operator is, in a sense, the converse of the AND operation. If we change our English example to read "Send Jack or Jill to the well," it takes on a new meaning. Now we are saying that either Jack or Jill (or both of them, making this OR inclusive) should go to the well.

The OR operation inspects the bits of the source and destination. The bits of the result are set according to the following rules:

0 OR 0 = 0
0 OR 1 = 1
1 OR 0 = 1
1 OR 1 = 1

If either (or both) of the bits is 1, the resulting bit is also 1.

Only when both of the bits are 0 is the result 0. For example, if we start with the numbers

01010100B and 11101010B

and OR them together, we obtain the result

    01010100B
OR <u>**11101010B**</u>
    11111110B

This operation has combined the two numbers (do not confuse this with *adding* them together). Whereas AND is used to separate two numbers, OR is used to put them together. For example, we could use OR to overlap two graphics images or to pack unpacked BCD digits (see the section on bit shifting in this chapter).

    Programmers sometimes use code such as

OR AX,AX

when they want to set the flags according to the value of AX. AX is not changed, but the SF, ZF, and PF flags are set appropriately.

    XOR. The Exclusive OR operation sets the bits of the result according to the following rules:

0 XOR 0 = 0
0 XOR 1 = 1
1 XOR 0 = 1
1 XOR 1 = 0

A bit in the result is set only if the two bits of the operands differ.

    XOR is used to invert specific bits. If we start with the two numbers

11110000B and 10010111B

in AL and BL respectively, and perform

XOR AL,BL

    11110000B
XOR <u>**10010111B**</u>
    01100111B

AL will hold 01100111B. XOR is very useful for graphics applications. (See Chapter 12 for a discussion of XOR in reference to computer graphics.)

    Programmers sometimes use code such as:

XOR AX,AX

when they want to zero a register. To zero a register with the MOV instruction requires more bytes than with XOR. If you need to make a program compact, you can use XOR *register,register* (or SUB *register,register*) when you need to zero a register. (IBM programmers do this in the ROM BIOS; it's a fairly common technique.)

NOT. The NOT instruction has the general format shown below. The source can be any general register, or an addressed memory location. NOT can be used on both bytes and words. After a NOT is performed, the result replaces the source value.

NOT *source*

NOT reverses the bits of the operand value. All of the 1's are made 0's, and all of the 0's are made 1's. In other words, it follows the rules

NOT 0 = 1
NOT 1 = 0

Generally, NOT is used to negate a number. The 8088 provides a negate instruction (NEG), but it can be used only on bytes or words. You cannot use NEG, for example, on a 32-bit number. To negate a 32-bit number, you must first NOT the two words and then add 1 to the result. The sample code below negates a 32-bit number stored in AX:DX (AX holds the least significant word).

```
NOT AX     ;take the ones complement of the number
NOT DX
ADD AX,1   ;add 1 to the result for twos complement
ADC DX,0
```

Shifting and Rotating

Bit *shifting* and *rotating* refers to the microprocessor's ability to move the bits in a number left or right. You can shift or rotate by a single bit or by a certain count. These instructions provide an easy way to multiply or divide a number by a power of 2 and for accessing different parts of a packed BCD number.

All of the bit-shifting instructions have the general format shown below. The *source* can be any general register or an addressed memory location. It can be either a byte or a word. The *count* is either the number 1 (perform the operation once), or the CL register (where CL holds the number of times to perform the shift operation).

OPERATION *source,count*

Shifts. There are four different shift operations, SHL (SHift Left), SAL (Shift Arithmetic Left), SHR (SHift Right), and SAR (Shift Arithmetic Right). They have the general format shown below. All of the shifts set the overflow flag, sign flag, zero flag, and parity flag accordingly. The *source* and *count* are explained above.

SHL *source,count*
SAL *source,count*
SHR *source,count*
SAR *source,count*

SHL and SAL are identical instructions. When a number is shifted to the left by one count, the most significant bit (the sign bit in a signed number) is moved into the carry flag, a 0 is moved into the least significant bit, and all of the other bits are moved one place to the left (see below). In other words, bit 7 (the most significant) is moved into the carry flag, bit 6 is moved into bit 7, bit 5 to bit 6, and so on. A 0 is moved into the least significant bit, bit 0.

This effectively multiplies the number by 2. For example, after the following code is performed

MOV AL,01101001B
SHL AL,1

AL will hold 11010010B, the overflow flag will be set (because the sign changed), and the carry flag will be clear (because bit 7 was a 0). If 11010010B is shifted left again, the result will be 10100100B, the overflow flag will be clear (because the sign did not change), and the carry flag will be set.

SHR is the counterpart to SHL. SHR shifts the source quantity to the right. When a number is shifted by one count to the right, the least significant bit is moved into the carry flag, a 0 is moved into the most significant bit, and all of the other bits are moved one place to the right (see below). This effectively divides the number by 2.

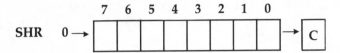

Since a 0 is moved into bit 7, the sign of the number is no longer meaningful. For this reason, SHR is reserved for unsigned numbers. If SHR is performed on 10010101B, the result will be 01001010B, and the carry flag and the overflow flag will be set (notice that the sign of the number changed).

SAR, the counterpart to SAL, is used to shift signed numbers to the right. When SAR is performed, the least significant bit is moved into the carry flag, the sign of the number is examined and moved into the second most significant bit; the other bits are moved once to the right. In other words, if the number is positive, SAR operates identically to SHR. If the number is negative, SAR moves a 1 (not a 0) into the most significant bit. This has the effect of preserving the sign of the source value.

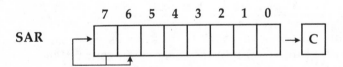

If SAR is performed on 11010101B (a negative number), the result is 11101010B. If, on the other hand, the source value is 00101011B (a positive number), the result is 00010101B.

SHL and SHR are used on unsigned numbers, while SAL and SAR are used for signed numbers. SAL and SHL are identical; there is no need to handle the sign bit specially when a number is shifted to the left. The SAL instruction was included only to complete the naming scheme. Note that DEBUG will not assemble SAL; you must use SHL.

For the right shifts, however, the sign bit must be handled specially. SAR retains the sign bit, while SHR does not. Note that whatever bit "fell off" the end of the number is held by the carry flag.

Rotates. There are four rotate instructions available on the 8088, ROR (ROtate Right), ROL (ROtate Left), RCR (Rotate through Carry, Right), and RCL (ROtate through Carry, Left). They take the general format shown below. Rotates set only the carry and overflow flags. The other arithmetic flags are not affected by these operations.

ROR *source,count*
ROL *source,count*
RCR *source,count*
RCL *source,count*

As stated before, the source can be a general register or any addressed memory location. The count can be either the value 1 or the CL register. If the count is the CL register, it must hold the number of rotates to perform.

ROL rotates the number to the left. The most significant bit is moved into the least significant bit and the carry flag. The other bits are shifted one position to the left (see below). For example, if the source value is 11001101B, the result of a ROL operation is 10011011B, and the carry flag is set.

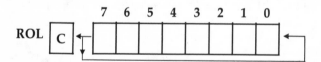

ROR is just the opposite of ROL. ROR takes the least significant bit and moves it into the most significant bit *and* into the carry flag. All of the other bits are shifted to the right one position (see below). If the source value is 10110101B, the result of a ROR is 11011010B, and the carry flag is set.

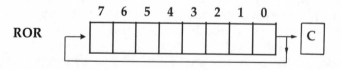

RCL moves everything to the left one bit. The most significant bit is moved into the carry flag, the contents of the carry flag is moved into the least significant bit, and the other bits are shifted to the left one position (see below). For example, if 00101001B is RCLed when the carry flag is set, the result is 01010011B, and the carry flag is clear.

RCR is similar to ROR; however, the carry flag is used as an additional bit. In a RCR operation, the least significant bit is moved into the carry flag, the contents of the carry flag is moved into the most significant bit, and the other bits are shifted one position to the right (see below). For example, if the source value is 10101001B and the carry flag is clear, RCR results in 01010100B, and the carry flag is set.

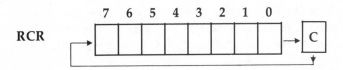

Using Bit Shifting and Rotating

You can use shifts to multiply or divide a number by a power of 2. For example,

SHL AX,1

multiplies the contents of the AX by 2. Performing the operation twice multiplies AX by 4; three times, by 8, etc. This type of multiplication is considerably faster than the corresponding MUL or IMUL instruction. You can, of course, use CL as the count for this operation. The code

MOV CL,3
SHL BX,CL

shifts BX three times, or multiplies the contents of BX by 8. The operation

SHR AX,1

divides the unsigned value in AX by 2. If AX holds a signed number, SAR should be used.

You can also use combinations of SHL and ADD instructions to multiply a number by other integers. For example,

```
MOV CX,AX    ;store AX in CX
SHL AX,2     ;multiply AX by 4
ADD AX,CX    ;add original AX to the product (multiply by 5)
SHL AX,1     ;multiply by 2 again
```

effectively multiplies AX by 10.

143

You can also combine rotates and shifts to shift numbers larger than 16 bits left and right. For example,

SHL low_word,1   ;shift the lower word once
RCL high_word,1   ;rotate lost bit into the higher word

shifts a two-word quantity once to the left. The SHL instruction sets the carry flag to the bit which "fell off" the end of the low word. The RCL moves that extra bit stored in the carry flag into the least significant bit of the high word. You can continue to chain RCLs if you need to shift a large number.

To shift a large number to the right, use

SHR high_word,1   ;shift the high word once
RCR low_word,1   ;rotate the lost bit into the lower word

If you are shifting a large signed quantity, remember to use SAR rather than SHR. Start with the highest word when you shift to the right, while you start with the lowest word when you shift to the left.

You can use shifts and rotates to relocate nybbles from one position in a number to another. The procedure HEXCONV, in the sample program at the end of the last chapter, uses this technique to determine the values of the different nybbles in order to print the correct digit. You can also use shifts and rotates to compact or separate (pack or unpack) BCD digits. If, for example, AH and AL hold unpacked BCD digits (AH is most significant), you can use something like

MOV CL,4   ;set shift count
SHL AH,CL   ;move digit in AH to the upper nybble
OR AL,AH   ;OR the two digits together

to pack the data into AL. You can reverse the procedure, and unpack the data, with the following code:

MOV AH,AL   ;move the digits into the other register
MOV CL,4   ;set the shift count
SHR AH,CL   ;move more significant digit into the lower nybble
AND AL,0FH   ;remove more significant digit from other register

The AND masks the extra digit from the AL register. AH now holds the more significant digit, and AL the lower.

You have been given some examples of the bit-shifting operations. All of the bit shifting and rotating instructions are diagrammed in Figure 8-2 below. As you have seen, shifting can be used to multiply and divide numbers by powers of 2. By combining bit shifts with other instructions, multiplying by other integers is possible. This is considerably faster than MUL or IMUL. You can also use these instructions to isolate different sections of a number, and to pack and unpack BCD data.

Figure 8-2. Bit Shifts and Rotates

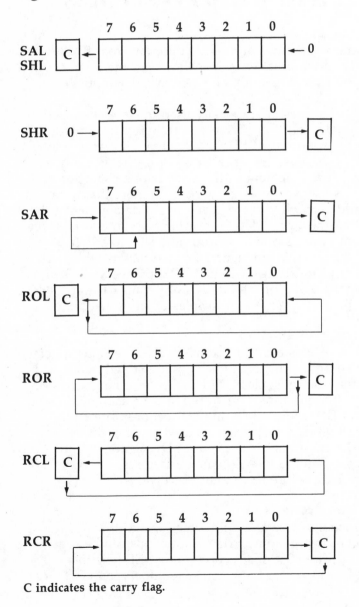

C indicates the carry flag.

9

String Instructions

Machine language strings are a little different from BASIC strings. There are a number of machine language instructions used to move, compare, scan, and otherwise manipulate strings.

In BASIC, strings are generally used to store characters. Remember, however, that characters are bytes. In fact, BASIC strings are really strings of bytes. A *string* is similar to a long table of bytes. In other words, a string in BASIC is really a kind of array. Each element in the array is one character in the string. Strings in machine language are no more than arrays of bytes. To add versatility to the string-handling abilities of the 8088, Intel has also provided for *word strings*. In a *word string*, each element of the string is a word, rather than a byte.

There are five machine language instructions which are used to manipulate strings: LODS, STOS, SCAS, MOVS, and CMPS. Before we get into the details of the instructions, let's examine some of the general principles of string handling.

The Direction Flag (DF)

Direction Flag, DF, is used to determine the directional operation of the string instructions. If strings are stored in succeeding addresses, you must clear DF before performing any string instructions. If your strings are stored in decreasing addresses, you must set DF before any string instructions. The CLD (CLear Direction flag) instruction is used to clear DF, while STD (SeT Direction flag) is used to set DF. Generally, however, strings are stored in succeeding addresses, so you will want to use CLD before any string instructions.

The REPeat Prefixes

String instructions have a feature which makes them different from the other instructions; string instructions can be repeated automatically. The 8088 instruction prefix REP tells the microprocessor to repeat the given string operation CX times.

For the code below:

MOV CX,100
REP LODS

LODS will be executed 100 times (LODS is explained below). There are two other REP instruction prefixes. The first, REPE/REPZ, repeats if the zero flag indicates a zero result. The other, REPNE/REPNZ, repeats if the zero flag indicates a nonzero result. Note that the check against the zero flag is an extension of the normal REP prefix.

The LODS Instruction

The LODS (LOaD String) instruction is used to access one byte or word of a string. There are actually two LODS instructions, one for bytes (LODSB) and another for words (LODSW). LODSB transfers the byte pointed to by SI to AL and adjusts SI to point to the next byte. LODSW transfers the word pointed to by SI to AX and adjusts SI to point to the next word. SI generally acts as an offset into the data segment; however, the segment can be changed with segment overrides (as described below).

LODS automatically adjusts SI to point to the next element in the string. This adjustment can be either positive (the string is stored in increasing addresses) or negative (it is stored in decreasing addresses). Remember that the direction flag tells the microprocessor which way the strings are stored. If the direction flag is clear (0), SI is incremented; if it is set, SI is decremented. In other words, after an STD, SI will be decremented each time LODS is used; after CLD, SI will be incremented each time LODS is used. Note that SI is adjusted (incremented or decremented) by 1 for LODSB and by 2 for LODSW.

The code below performs the same operation as LODSB when the direction flag is clear:

MOV AL,[SI]
INC SI

First, the byte pointed to by SI is moved into AL, then SI is incremented by 1.

The assembler accepts two formats for the LODS instruction. First, you can explicitly specify LODSB or LODSW. The other possibility is to use the format

LODS *operand*

147

where the *operand* is the name of the string being accessed. If the string is made up of bytes, the assembler will use LODSB; if, on the other hand, the string is made up of words, the assembler will use LODSW. Note that the LODS instruction itself does not take an operand. The operand is used solely by the assembler to determine the size of the operand and which segment register to use. If you do not have a specific operand, you must use the following format to override the segment register:

LODS *size* **PTR** *segment-register:*[SI]

The *size* is either byte or word (for LODSB and LODSW) and the *segment-register* is CS, DS, ES, or SS. If you do not specify a size (you just use LODS *segment-register:*[SI]), the assembler will assume you want LODSB.

LODS can be used when you need to sequentially access bytes or words in a table. LODS has the advantage that it automatically increments or decrements the pointer register. For example, you could use LODS to print a string one character at a time (the 0 byte indicates the end of the message):

```
[in the data segment]
MESSAGE DB 'This is a sample message',13,10,0
[in the code segment]
        MOV SI,OFFSET MESSAGE    ;get the address of the message
L1:     LODSB                    ;load one byte of the message
        CMP AL,0                 ;is it the end of the message?
        JE DONE                  ;yes, so we are done
        CALL PRINT_CHARACTER     ;print the character
        JMP L1                   ;get the next byte of the message
DONE:
```

Note that we are using the PRINT_CHARACTER routine from the program "Primes."

Also notice that SI is set to the address of the variable MESSAGE. The OFFSET command was discussed briefly in Chapter 7. OFFSET is used to determine the location of a variable. In this case, OFFSET will return the position of MESSAGE relative to the base of the segment it is in. Remember that OFFSET is an assembler command, not an 8088 command. The command MOV SI,OFFSET MESSAGE will be turned into an immediate MOV command, and the immediate value will be the address of MESSAGE relative to the base of the segment it's defined in.

The STOS Instruction

The STOS (STOre String) instruction is essentially the opposite of LODS. STOS is used to store a byte or a word in a string. Note that STOS uses ES:DI to address the string, not DS:SI. There is no way to override the segment assignment of STOS; you must always use ES.

As with LODS, there are two STOS instructions: STOSB (for byte strings) and STOSW (for word strings). STOSB stores AL in the memory address pointed to by ES:DI and adjusts DI to point to the next byte. STOSW stores AX in the memory address pointed to by ES:DI and adjusts DI to point to the next word.

The direction flag is used by STOS in the same way it is used by LODS. For STOSB, DI is incremented by one if DF is clear and is decremented by one if DF is set. For STOSW, DI is incremented or decremented (according to the state of DF) by two.

The STOS instruction can be repeated a certain number of times with the REP prefix. For example, you could use STOS with REP to fill a portion of memory. The following code fills the string TABLE with 100 ASCII spaces.

```
[in your extra segment]
TABLE   DB 100 DUP(?)                ;undefined table of 100 bytes
                                     ;

[in your code segment]
        CLD                          ;work upwards in memory
        MOV AL,' '                   ;space character in AL
        MOV CX,100                   ;number of times to repeat
        MOV DI,OFFSET TABLE          ;get the address of TABLE
        REP STOS TABLE               ;fill TABLE with spaces
```

The following code performs the same operation, but without the STOS and REP instructions:

```
        MOV CX,100                   ;number of times to loop
        MOV DI,OFFSET TABLE          ;get the address of TABLE
L1:     MOV BYTE PTR ES:[DI],' '     ;put a space in one byte of TABLE
        INC DI                       ;point to next byte in TABLE
        LOOP L1                      ;repeat the "fill"
```

Note that you can use REP prefixes with LODS as well, but doing so is rather pointless.

As with LODS, the assembler accepts two formats for

STOS. You can either explicitly specify STOSB or STOSW, or you can use the format

STOS *operand*

where the *operand* is the name of the string you are using. If the string is a string of words, the assembler will use STOSW; on the other hand, if the string is a string of bytes, the assembler will use STOSB.

The SCAS Instruction

The SCAS instruction (SCAn String) is used to search a string for a specific byte or word. As with STOS, SCAS always uses ES:DI to address the string. You cannot override the segment, so you must always use ES with SCAS.

There are two SCAS instructions, SCASB for bytes and SCASW for words. The SCASB instruction reads the byte pointed to by ES:DI and compares it with the byte in AL. In addition, DI is adjusted to point to the next byte in the string. The SCASW instruction reads the word pointed to by ES:DI, compares it with the word in AX, and adjusts DI to point to the next word in the string.

As with the other string instructions, DF is used to determine whether the pointer, DI in this case, should be incremented (if DF is clear) or decremented (if DF is set). In either case, DI is adjusted by one if SCASB is used, and by two, if SCASW is used.

After a SCAS operation, you can use any of the conditional jumps explained in Chapter 5. SCAS is the same as the following comparison:

CMP accumulator,ES:[DI]

Since SCAS is a decision-making instruction, it is often used with REPE or REPNE. You can use REPE and SCAS, for example, to find the first nonzero element in a table of words:

```
[in your extra segment]
WORDS DW 100 DUP (?)      ;undefined table of 100 bytes
                         ;

[in your code segment]
CLD                      ;work upwards
MOV CX,100               ;length of table
MOV AL,0                 ;looking for nonzero
MOV DI,OFFSET WORDS      ;get address of table
REPE SCAS WORDS          ;repeat until nonzero found
```

JCXZ ALL_ZEROS   ;if CX = 0 then table all zeros
[nonzero was found, and next element pointed to by ES:DI]

If a nonzero element is found, ES:DI will point to the word *after* the nonzero element. If you want to examine the nonzero element, you will have to adjust DI back one element.

The following code performs a similar operation, but does not use the SCAS instruction (note that, on return, DI is slightly different below):

```
    MOV CX,100            ;length of table
    MOV AL,0              ;looking for nonzero
    MOV DI,OFFSET WORDS   ;get address of table
L1: CMP AL,ES:[DI]        ;is element in table zero?
    JNE L2                ;element is not zero
    ADD DI,2             ;point to next element
    LOOP L1               ;do all 100 elements
    JMP ALL_ZEROS        ;table is all zeros
L2: [nonzero was found, and is pointed to by ES:DI]
```

As with the other string instructions, the assembler will accept two formats of the SCAS instruction. You can either specify SCASB or SCASW (for byte or word scans), or you can use the format

SCAS *operand*

where the *operand* is the name of the string you are scanning. If the string is made up of bytes, the assembler will use the SCASB operation. If the string is made up of words, it will use the SCASW instruction. Note that the operand is solely for use by the assembler. SCAS, as a machine language instruction, does not take an operand.

The MOVS Instruction

The MOVS (MOVe String) instruction and the CMPS (CoM-Pare String) instruction are probably the most complex of the five string instructions. MOVS is used to move a string from one place in memory to another. Again, there are really two MOVS instructions: MOVSB to move byte strings, and MOVSW to move word strings.

The MOVSB instruction moves the byte pointed to by DS:SI to the memory address pointed to by ES:DI. Both SI and DI are adjusted to point to the next byte according to DF. Remember that if DF is clear, string operations work up in memory (so for MOVSB, SI and DI are incremented by one),

and that if DF is set, string operations work down in memory
(for MOVSB, SI and DI are decremented by one). MOVSW
moves the word pointed to by DS:SI to the memory location
pointed to by ES:DI. DI and SI are adjusted to point to the
next word (SI and DI are incremented or decremented by two
depending on the state of DF). The segment register used to
address the destination must always be ES:DI. However, you
can change the segment register for the source with any of the
segment overrides as described below.

MOVS is often used with the REP prefix to move large
sections of memory from one place to another. The code

```
[in your data segment]
HERE                        DB 150 DUP(?)    ;150 undefined bytes
                                             ;
[in your extra segment]
THERE                       DB 150 DUP(?)    ;another 150 undefined bytes
[in your code segment]
CLD                                          ;work up
LEA SI,HERE                                  ;address of source string
LEA DI,THERE                                 ;address of destination string
MOV CX,150                                   ;length of string
REP MOVS THERE,HERE                          ;move the string
```

copies the byte string HERE to the byte string THERE. Note
that we can also use REPE or REPNE because MOVS does not
set the zero flag.

As with the other string instructions, the assembler will
accept two formats for MOVS. You can specify MOVSB or
MOVSW when you want to move byte or word strings, or you
can use the format

MOVS *destination,source*

where the *destination* is the string pointed to by ES:DI, and the
source is the string pointed to by DS:SI. Note that both the
source and destination strings must be either bytes or words.
If the operands are byte strings, the assembler will use
MOVSB. If the operands are word strings, it will use MOVSW.
If you do not have specific operands the assembler can use to
determine which segment register to use, you must use the
following format to override the segment register:

MOVS *size* **PTR [DI],** *size* **PTR** *segment-register*:**[SI]**

The *size* is either byte or word (for MOVSB and MOVSW),
and the *segment-register* is CS, DS, ES, or SS. Remember that
you *cannot* change the segment register for the destination,

only the source. Also note that if you do not specify a size with the PTR instruction, the assembler will assume you want MOVSB.

The CMPS Instruction

CMPS is used to compare two strings. As with the other string instructions, there are actually two CMPS instructions: CMPSB for bytes and CMPSW for words. CMPSB compares the byte pointed to by ES:DI with the byte pointed to by DS:SI, and adjusts SI and DI to point to the next byte. CMPSW compares the word pointed to by ES:DI with the word pointed to by DS:SI, and adjusts DI and SI to point to the next word. As with all string instructions, DF is used to determine whether SI and DI should be incremented or decremented. Note that you cannot change the segment used with the DI, you must always use ES with DI. You can, however, change the segment used with SI with one of the segment overrides. The techniques are the same as those used with the MOVS instruction. After a CMPS operation, you can use any of the conditional jumps explained in Chapter 5. CMPS is the same as

CMP DS:[SI],ES:[DI]

where SI points to the first operand, while DI points to the second.

REPE or REPNE prefixes are often used with this instruction. This allows you to compare two strings and stop when the two are the same, or are different. Note that this is not like SCAS, which looks for only one particular byte or word in a string. For example, the following code will compare two word strings until there is a difference between them:

```
[in the data segment]
ONE_STRING DW 20 DUP(?)
;
[in the extra segment]
OTHER_STRING DW 20 DUP(?)
[in the code segment]
CLD                                    ;work up in memory
MOV CX,20                              ;length of strings
MOV SI,OFFSET ONE_STRING              ;address of first string
MOV DI,OFFSET OTHER_STRING            ;address of second
REPE CMPS ONE_STRING,OTHER_STRING     ;compare the two
```

Note that after the CMPS, SI and DI will point to the word *after* they differ, not the word where they differ.

As with all of the other string instructions, CMPS can take two formats. You can specify CMPSB or CMPSW explicitly, or you can use the instruction

CMPS *operand_1,operand_2*

Operand_1 is the string pointed to by DS:SI, and *operand_2* is the string pointed to by ES:DI.

Note that MOVS and CMPS are the only two machine language instructions which perform memory-to-memory operations.

The repeat prefixes can be used with any of the string instructions. Also keep in mind that none of the string instructions (as machine language instructions) take any operands. The operands are specified only for the assembler, so that it can determine whether it should use the byte or word version of the instruction and which segment register to use.

Be careful using a REPeat prefix and a segment override with a string instruction. If an interrupt (see Chapter 11) occurs while the string instruction with a segment override is being repeated, the REPeat will not be completed. You must do two things to overcome this problem. CX must be zero at the end of the REPeated instruction and the interrupts must be disabled before the string instruction, and reenabled afterwards (using the CLI and STI instructions discussed in Chapter 11).

```
     CLI
R1:  REP MOVS WORD PTR [DI], WORD PTR ES:[SI]
     JCXZ R2
     DEC CX
     JMP R1
R2:  STI
```

Remember, this applies only if the string instruction is being repeated *and* there is a segment override. If the string instruction is not being repeated or if there is no segment override, there is no need to put in this special check (see the sample program from Chapter 10 for an example of this technique).

String Search Example

The sample program for this chapter is called "SORT.ASM." It alphabetically sorts a short list of character strings. The length and number of strings are specified by the constants STRING_LEN and NUMBER_STRINGS. In the example data (called NAMES), the length of each string is 16 characters, and there are 10 sample pieces of data. If you decide to change the length of the strings or the number of strings, remember to change these two constants at the beginning of the program.

The TEMP_STRING variable is used as a kind of string "accumulator." There are three messages which are also defined in the data segment. The first, UNSORTED_MES, begins with a carriage return and linefeed. This puts the cursor at the beginning of the next line of the screen. Note that there is a carriage return and a linefeed at the end of the string as well. The 0 is used to indicate the end of the string; it will not be printed. The second string, SORTED_MES, is similar. Note that we can use just linefeeds if we want to move to the next line of the screen. The last string defined in the data segment, CR_LF, is just a carriage return and a linefeed.

Next we defined the stack segment, as always. Following the stack declaration is the code segment. The first few instructions set up the FAR RETurn to DOS. DS and ES are set up as the data segment. Remember that some of the string instructions (MOVS and CMPS, for example) must use ES. The direction flag (DF) is cleared so that all string operations are performed going up in memory, not down. The rest of the main loop is well commented.

Notice how the PRINT_MES subroutine uses the LODSB instruction. Since the string is terminated by a zero byte, when AL holds 0, we know the entire string has been printed. The PRINT_MES routine calls CHARACTER_OUT. This is the same CHARACTER_OUT procedure that is used in the program in "PRIMES.ASM." The PRINT_STRINGS routine prints the data (in this case the names). If you like, you can have it print carriage returns between the strings (place the code to do this after the LOOP PRINT_ONE_STRING instruction).

The actual sorting routine comes next. The sort procedure searches the string for the lowest string (alphabetically) and exchanges it with the first element in the array. Then, it searches for the lowest string again (excluding the first one) and exchanges it with the second string. This goes on until the entire string has been sorted.

The routine SORT in SORT.ASM calls two other routines. The first, FIND_LEAST, searches for the lowest string. When the routine is called, BX must point to the first string to be checked, and DL must indicate which string it is (first, second, third, etc.). On return, BP points to the lowest string. The second, XCHG_STRINGS, exchanges the string pointed to by BP with the one pointed to by BX.

The program SORT.ASM is intended as a demonstration of the use of string instructions and is not very useful in its present form because you must reassemble it each time you need to sort new data. You must also reconfigure the program if your strings are a different length from the ones given here.

Program 9-1. SORT.ASM

```
; SORT.ASM
;
; This program sorts through a list of
; length strings.  The strings are
; made up of characters, although
; any byte sized data can be sorted.
;
        page ,96

string_len      equ 16           ;length of strings
number_strings  equ 10           ;number of strings
;
dseg    segment
names           db 'Koumrian T   '      ;data to be sorted
                db 'Berman J     '
                db 'Fenn P       '
                db 'Perry D      '
                db 'Sensabaugh J '
                db 'Sugiyama M   '
                db 'Clemens W    '
                db 'Rieffel E    '
                db 'Metcalf C    '
                db 'Hakansson A  '
temp_string     db string_len dup(?)    ;temporary string var
;
```

```
unsorted_mes    db      13,10,'Here are the strings before '
sorted_mes      db      'they are sorted:',13,10,0
                db      13,10,10,'And now the strings after '
                db      'the sort:',13,10,0
cr_lf           db      13,10,0                 ;cr-lf string
dseg    ends
;
sseg    segment stack                           ;stack segment
        dw 128 dup(?)
sseg    ends
;
cseg    segment
sort_names proc far
        assume cs:cseg,ds:dseg,es:dseg,ss:sseg
        push ds
        mov ax,0                                ;for far return to DOS
        push ax
        mov ax,dseg
        mov ds,ax                               ;set up DSEG in DS
        mov es,ax                               ;set up DSEG in ES
        cld                                     ;strings stored upward

        mov si,offset unsorted_mes              ;print first message
        call print_mes
        call print_strings                      ;print the strings
        call sort                               ;do the sorting
        mov si,offset sorted_mes                ;print second message
```

```
        call  print_mes              ;print strings again
        call  print_strings
        mov   si,offset cr_lf        ;print CR-LF
        call  print_mes
        ret                          ;return to DOS
sort_names endp
;
; print message pointed to by DS:SI
; message is terminated by a 0 byte
; assume no registers preserved
;
print_mes proc near
another_char:
        lodsb                        ;get byte of string
        cmp   al,0                   ;is it the end marker?
        je    done_print_mes         ;yes, finished printing
        call  character_out          ;print the character
        jmp   another_char           ;do another character
done_print_mes:
        ret                          ;return to caller
print_mes endp
;
; print a character passed in AL to screen
; only DL and AX affected.
;
character_out proc near
        mov   dl,al                  ;character to output
```

```
        mov ah,2                    ;output character
        int 21H                     ;print character
        ret
character_out endp
;
; print the names
; length of each name in string_len
; number of strings to print in number_strings
; assume all registers destroyed
;
print_strings proc near
        mov si,offset names         ;base of NAMES table
        mov dh,number_strings       ;number to print
print_next_string:
        mov cx,string_len           ;length of each string
print_one_string:
        lodsb                       ;get one byte
        call character_out          ;print the character
        loop print_one_string       ;do rest of string
        dec dh                      ;do other strings
        jnz print_next_string
        ret                         ;return to caller
print_strings endp
;
; do the actual sort of the strings
; uses "selection sort" algorithm (see text)
; assume all registers destroyed
```

```
;
sort    proc near
        mov bx,offset names        ;base of NAMES table
        mov di,0                   ;# strings already sorted
do_selection_again:
        call find_least            ;find lowest string
        call xchg_strings          ;put in lowest string
        add bx,string_len          ;point to next string
        inc di                     ;another string sorted
        cmp di,number_strings      ;sorted all?
        jbe do_selection_again     ;no, more to do
        ret                        ;return to caller
sort    endp
;
; find the least string
; BX pionts to first string to sort,
; DL is the string's number
; DX and BX preserved
; BP tells which string is least
;
find_least proc near
        push dx                    ;save DX and BX
        push bx
        mov bp,bx                  ;assume BX string least
        mov si,bx
        mov di,offset temp_string  ;move it into temp area
        mov cx,string_len
```

```
            rep movs temp_string,names

search_loop:
            cmp  dl,number_strings        ;checked all strings?
            je   found_least              ;yes, so found it
            mov  di,offset temp_string    ;check BX string...
            mov  si,bx                    ;...against temp area
            mov  cx,string_len
            repe cmps names,temp_string
            jcxz next_check               ;are they identical?
            ja   next_check               ;is BX strings greater?
            mov  bp,bx                    ;BP pionts to least string
            mov  di,offset temp_string    ;move new least to temp
            mov  si,bx
            mov  cx,string_len
            rep  movs temp_string,names

next_check:
            inc  dl                       ;check the next string
            add  bx,string_len
            jmp  search_loop

found_least:
            pop  bx                       ;recover BX and DX
            pop  dx
            ret                           ;return to caller

find_least endp

; exchange string BX with string BP
; only DX and CX preserved
```

```
;
xchg_strings proc near
        mov si,bp               ;move BP string to temp
        mov di,offset temp_string
        mov cx,string_len
        rep movs temp_string,names
        mov si,bx               ;move BX string to BP
        mov di,bp
        mov cx,string_len
        rep movs names,names
        mov si,offset temp_string ;mov temp to BX
        mov di,bx
        mov cx,string_len
        rep movs names,temp_string
        ret                     ;return to caller
xchg_strings endp
;
cseg    ends
        end                     ;end of program
```

10
Using Machine
Language with BASIC

Why, you may ask, would someone want to use machine language with BASIC? Machine language programs have the potential to do anything BASIC can manage, and to do it much faster. But it is often more convenient to use an existing BASIC feature, rather than invent a machine language routine to perform the same task. Thus, parts of your program (written in BASIC) can use BASIC's special features; parts of your program (in machine language) can execute with the necessary speed.

BASIC has many useful features. Here's a brief and incomplete list: full eight-byte floating-point number handling; easy manipulation of strings; an enormous variety of trigonometric and transcendental functions; easy-to-use disk files; simple text mode screen handling; extremely powerful graphics control, including DRAW, CIRCLE, PAINT, GET, PUT, WINDOW, and VIEW; easy control of joysticks and other peripherals; powerful PCjr music control; trapping of events (keystrokes, timers, joysticks, light pen, and more). The list goes on and on.

To make use of these features, the usual procedure is to write a program in BASIC which communicates with its machine language subroutine(s) by the CALL or USR statements. Theoretically, it is also possible to write an all machine language program that directly calls the subroutines in the BASIC interpreter ROM. However, BASIC is different on different members of the PC family, so this approach is not very feasible.

In this chapter, we will begin by discussing the difficult task of loading a machine language file into memory where it can actually run with BASIC. Then we shall explain how BASIC and machine language subroutines communicate with each other. The sample program included with this chapter is a routine called "Scroll," which allows you to scroll the current screen any distance to the right or left.

Pascal users, don't despair: Appendix F discusses the relatively simple task of using machine language with your Pascal programs.

Until now, loading a file has always been simple. In BASIC, you simply use the LOAD command; from DOS, you just type the name of the program, and DOS loads and executes it. But to use machine language with BASIC, it is necessary to be rather more devious than with normal DOS machine language programs. Don't worry too much, however; once a machine language program is installed properly in memory, BASIC's BSAVE and BLOAD commands are all that is needed to load and save it.

Where to Put the Program

One of the most difficult requirements for a machine language routine to be used with BASIC is that it must not get in BASIC's way. Almost any location within the BASIC work space is fair game to be clobbered without the programmer's knowledge. The BASIC work space typically starts at about the 26K mark on the PCjr, and around the 42K mark for the PC's BASIC.COM (the *work space* is what the default DEF SEG points to). BASIC takes over the entire 64K segment starting from that point, and uses it for

BASIC's own data area
COM buffers (for modem communication)
file buffers (for handling disk files)
your BASIC program
scalar data
array data
string data
stack space

Since the stack and string data grow down from the top of memory, and scalar and array data grow up from the bottom of memory, it's hard to find a place even relatively safe from BASIC.

There are two ways of getting your machine language routine in a safe place. First of all, BASIC provides some areas that are safe. If your program doesn't use the disk drives, the file buffers are safe places to put programs. See the BASIC

manual's appendix on "Technical Information and Tips." It's
also possible to DIMension an array and then place a machine
language routine in the space allocated for the array data. You
can find the addresses of file buffers and variables with
BASIC's VARPTR function. However, there is a difficulty with
this approach. Since your programs will be starting at some
unknown address within BASIC's data area, and not at offset
zero within a segment, the addresses within your program
(references to data and the like) will be wrong. You can avoid
this problem by not using variables in your program, but this
tends to be somewhat limiting. Simple programs can be used
in this way (and POKEd in from DATA statements, too), but
not programs of any complexity.

Another approach is more promising. Since BASIC has
such a firm grip on its work-area segment, the easiest place to
put a machine language subroutine is outside this segment.
This approach is easier, but there are a few complexities. First
of all, not all computers have extra space outside of the BASIC
work area; a 64K PC, for example, has no room left over once
BASIC has taken over. Second, the PCjr and the PC have their
BASIC work areas in different places in memory, making it
hard to establish a segment address that is outside BASIC's
work area on all computers.

As a rule, on 128K PCjrs, the best place to locate a machine language subroutine is at segment address 1700H (the
92K mark). This leaves 20K of unused memory between BASIC's
work area and the screen area (at segment address 1C00H). To
call a machine language routine at segment 1700H, use the
BASIC DEF SEG command:

DEF SEG = &H1700

and then use the CALL command.

If you have a PC with more than 96K of memory, any
segment address of 1C00H or above is okay, up to the limits
of your memory expansion. Use the DEF SEG command, as
above, to set the code segment to the right location.

If your computer has only 64K, don't worry. The BASIC
CLEAR command has a provision for freeing memory for machine language. Normally the CLEAR command is used to
clear out your variable area. However, optional parameters can
be specified to change the way BASIC handles its work area.
The particular format of the CLEAR command that we're concerned with is

CLEAR ,*maxsize*

The *maxsize* parameter tells BASIC how many bytes it can use for its work area. So, if you have a 64K PC, you can specify

CLEAR ,16384

leaving only 16K for your BASIC program. If you're using BASIC.COM (not BASICA), that should leave you all the room from segment address B00H to the top of your memory.

Another way to limit the size of BASIC's work area is by specifying a special parameter when you type BASIC from DOS. Normally BASIC takes as much memory as it can, up to a maximum of 64K, for its work area, but you can force it to start out with less memory with the following parameter:

BASIC /M:*maxsize*

This way, BASIC starts out with less memory, and you don't need to use the CLEAR command.

Program 10-1 is a short program that will tell you where you can start putting your machine language programs. The program is in machine language, and returns to the master BASIC program the segment address of BASIC's work area. By adding 1000H to that, we can find out where BASIC's 64K segment ends. If this program returns a value that's bigger than your available memory, you'll have to use CLEAR or the /M parameter to set up an area outside of BASIC. The machine language data statements in Program 10-1 are equivalent to this short machine language program. Later in the chapter, we'll explain how it works.

```
CSEG        SEGMENT CODE
PROGRAM     PROC FAR
            PUSH BP
            MOV BP,SP
            MOV SI,[BP+6]
            MOV [SI],DS
            POP BP
            RET 2
PROGRAM     ENDP
CSEG        ENDS
            END
```

For PCjr owners and PC owners with the color/graphics card, there's one other convenient spot to store programs. If your program uses the 80-column text screen, but doesn't change pages (see Chapter 12 for a discussion of pages), there's 12K of memory that can be used from segment address B900H up to BBFFH. Also, if your PC has both the mono-chrome and color/graphics boards, you can store machine language on one while using the other. But be careful when using this area: The SCREEN command can be used to wipe out all of graphics memory, and the 16K graphics modes will clear the color/graphics memory.

Loading the Program

Now we've established where to load programs. The next question is how we load them. The easiest way to accomplish this is with DEBUG. However, since we're loading our programs into unusual places (the top of memory instead of the bottom), we'll need a special machine language program to load the combined BASIC/machine language program wher-ever we want it to go. Program 10-2 should be typed in and used each time you load a program into BASIC for the first time (after that, you can use BASIC's BLOAD command).

Using EXELOAD. Once you've assembled and linked "EXELOAD.ASM" (Program 10-2), you're ready to begin bringing machine language programs into BASIC. We'll show you the technique to load a BASIC/machine language program, even though we haven't written any as yet. For now, we'll use the name "SCROLL.EXE" as our sample BASIC/machine language program, and the segment address 1C00H for our load address. To use EXELOAD, enter the following:

A>DEBUG EXELOAD.EXE
-N SCROLL.EXE   (use your filename here)
-E CS:12
091B:0012 00.00   **17.1C** (use your load address here)
-G

Program terminated normally
-Q

A>_

You have to use the N command to specify the name of your machine language program for BASIC, and set the segment address you want your program to load at with the E command. Once these two parameters are set, execute EXELOAD with the G command, then leave DEBUG with the Q command. It's also possible just to type

A>EXELOAD *filename*.**EXE**

if EXELOAD.ASM was assembled with the correct default segment load address. So, 128K PCjr users might assemble a version with MOV AX,1700H, while PC users with more than 96K could assemble theirs with MOV AX,1C00H.

If you have an expanded PCjr or a PC with more than 96K, you can just type BASIC (or BASICA). Otherwise, you'll have to specify the /M parameter. For example, if you have a 64K PC, you might want to specify

A>BASIC /M:32768

BSAVE and BLOAD. Finally, we're in BASIC, and our machine language program is still in memory where the EXELOAD program put it. At this point we should save the program in BASIC's own format, with the BSAVE command. The BSAVE command allows us to store machine language programs (or other data) on disk, and then retrieve them with the BLOAD command, thus avoiding the DEBUGing and EXELOADing. So you should enter

DEF SEG = &H1700

(using the address where you loaded your program in place of 1700 above). Then you save the program with the BSAVE command:

BSAVE "SCROLL.BSV",0,*length*

Choose any name for the file you like; a good extension for the file might be .BSV to indicate a BSAVEd file. The *length* of the file is approximately the same as the length of the .EXE file on your disk. However, if you're in doubt as to how much memory to save, always save more than the bare minimum.

The hassle is finished; from now on, to use your machine language program, all you have to do is enter

DEF SEG = &H *address*
BLOAD *"filename.ext"*,**0**

using the correct address and filename, and the machine language program will be loaded in. Make sure, however, that you always use the same segment address, since most programs can't be relocated to different locations in memory.

Parameter Passing

Now that you know how to load a program, you can learn how

to interface your machine language program with BASIC. Most machine language subroutines require parameters from the BASIC master program. For example, our scroll routine, discussed at the end of this chapter, must be told how far to scroll the screen. Of course, some machine language routines always perform the same task, and don't require any parameters, which simplifies the task of programming.

We'll begin our discussion with BASIC's CALL command. The other machine language command, USR, is more complex. The CALL command takes the format

CALL *variable[(variable[,variable]...)]*

This notation means that you can CALL without any parameters, with one, with two, or as many as you like. Since BASIC always uses a far CALL, your programs must end with a far RETurn, just like normal DOS programs; thus your program must be a far PROCedure.

If there are any parameters after the CALL statement, BASIC prepares to pass them by placing a special pointer for each variable on the stack before it calls your program. In this, it is much the same as the stack parameter-passing we discussed in Chapter 6. What is difficult, however, is that rather than placing the values of the variables on the stack, it places the *address* of the variables on the stack. Here's an example of this technique; this short program multiplies two variables together and leaves the result in a third:

```
CSEG       SEGMENT 'CODE'
ADDER      PROC FAR
           ASSUME CS:CSEG
                               ;
           PUSH BP             ;BP must be saved
           MOV BP,SP           ;BP points to stack area
           MOV SI,[BP+10]      ;SI points to first parameter
           MOV AX,[SI]         ;get value of first parameter
           MOV SI,[BP+8]       ;SI points to second
           MUL [SI]            ;multiply second by first
           MOV SI,[BP+6]       ;SI points to third
           MOV [SI],AX         ;leave answer in third
           POP BP              ;restore BP
           RET 6               ;far RETurn to BASIC
                               ;

ADDER      ENDP
CSEG       ENDS
           END
```

This program might be called from BASIC with this:

```
100 DEF SEG = &H1C00      'seg. addr. for 128K PCjr
110 BLOAD "ADDER.BSV",0   'program named "ADDER.ASM"
120 ADDER=0: A%=3: B%=5   'specify address and parameters
130 CALL ADDER (A%,B%,C%) 'CALL the machine language
140 PRINT C%              'print the result
```

All parameters must be integers. In this example, if A% holds 3 and B% holds 5, C% should hold 15 when the subroutine returns to BASIC. If your program returns a value (or more than one), it's probably easiest to place the value in a BASIC variable (like C% above). It is possible to write a program that returns a value directly, with the USR command. See the BASIC manual for details.

If you like, you can assemble and link ADDER.EXE, enter DEBUG with EXELOAD, use the N and E commands, execute EXELOAD, quit DEBUG and enter BASIC, BSAVE the program, and test it. The program serves as a good example of the EXELOAD technique, since it would be hard to put a bug in an 18-line program.

Accessing Parameters from the Stack

You may have been a little puzzled by the displacements used with BP to access the addresses of the variables. A closer look will help you see the reasoning. Remember, a BASIC CALL with parameters pushes a two-byte *address* for each parameter, not a one-byte value. BASIC first pushes the three word-length addresses onto the stack, and then executes a far CALL, leaving two words of the return address (four bytes) on the stack. Then, to save BP, we PUSH it onto the stack, depositing another two bytes, or six in all. So, to back up to the actual parameters, we start with [BP+6]. This skips over the intervening six bytes, pointing us to the last parameter pushed by the CALL statement. We then work our way backwards by twos as we load in the parameters nearer to the beginning of the CALL parameters. Thus, the sum is put in [BP+6], which holds a pointer to the last variable specified. In our example, that was C%. [BP+8] holds the pointer to B%, and [BP+10] holds the pointer to A%.

As a general rule, if you have a total of n arguments, the displacement from BP of variable M (1, 2, 3 . . . n) is $2*(n-M)+6$.

Removing Parameters

One other peculiarity about this program is that it ends, not with a normal RET, but with a RET pop-value instruction. This form of the RET instruction, as we discussed in Chapter 6, is used to dispose of PUSHed parameters for a subroutine. With BASIC, it's the programmer's responsibility to remove the appropriate number of bytes from the stack on exit from the program. Assuming, as above, that n arguments were specified in the CALL statement, your program should end with

RET 2 * n

Types of Parameters

BASIC has four variable types, but you'll only need to concern yourself with two. BASIC saves real numbers, both single- and double-precision, in a format difficult to use with 8088 machine language. However, BASIC's integer types (declared with a % suffix) and string types (with the $ suffix) are easier to handle. Integers, as you may have deduced from the sample program above, are stored by BASIC as normal, word-sized signed values, just like machine language. To access one of these variables, you must first get its address from the stack, and then get the actual value contained in that address. Here we're moving the value of the last parameter of the CALL statement into DX:

MOV BX,[BP+6]
MOV DX,[BX]

Strings are handled differently. The address on the stack doesn't point to the string itself. Instead, it points to a string descriptor, three bytes long, with the following format:

byte 0   length of the string
bytes 1,2 address of the string in memory (a word value)

To look at a string in memory, you first load the address of the string descriptor off the stack, then load the address of the string itself from the string descriptor. BASIC allows you to modify the actual string as you please, but you can't change its length or its address. The string descriptor should be kept intact.

Entering and Exiting

When BASIC gives your subroutine control, the only registers that are explicitly set are the segment registers. CS holds the current DEF SEG value, and DS, ES, and SS hold the default DEF SEG value of BASIC's work area.

Most .EXE programs immediately begin by setting the DS and ES registers to point to their own data segments. This may be a mistake if your subroutine takes parameters from BASIC, since you must keep at least one segment register pointing into BASIC's work area in order to read the values of the parameters which were passed. Often the best approach for a long program is to begin by setting DS to point to your data segment, and use ES as a segment override to read the variable parameters. Of course, you could do it the other way around, or even use the SS register as a segment override.

The SS register, however, often has to be changed as well. All DOS .EXE files define their own stack, and DOS automatically sets SS and SP to point to the correct part of memory when such files begin to execute. However, with BASIC, the burden of managing the stack is on the programmer. When BASIC gives control to your program, the stack has only room for eight word-sized values. If you need more stack space, you will have to set SS and SP to point to your own stack. Remember, however, to save the initial values, so they can be recovered just before returning to BASIC. Unfortunately, most DOS and BIOS interrupt routines use more than 16 bytes of stack space, so if you use any interrupt routines you will almost certainly need to switch the stack registers to point to your program's own stack. Of course, if you don't use more than 16 bytes of stack space, you don't need to move the stack; nor, in fact, do you need to define a stack in your source file at all, and you can ignore the Linker's no stack message.

The only requirement when you leave the program is that the segment registers (CS, DS, ES, and SS) have the value they had when your subroutine took over. SP and apparently BP also need to be reset to their initial values.

Here's a program framework that you can use for long BASIC/machine language programs:

```
SSEG        SEGMENT STACK 'STACK'
STK         DW 64 DUP(?)            ;define a stack area
SSEG        ENDS
                                    ;
DSEG        SEGMENT 'DATA'
SP_STORE    DW ?                    ;store SP here
SS_STORE    DW ?                    ;store DS, ES, SS here
... your data here...
DSEG        ENDS
                                    ;
CSEG        SEGMENT
            ASSUME CS:CSEG,DS:DSEG
PROGRAM     PROC FAR
            MOV AX,DSEG             ;initialize DS
            MOV DS,AX
            PUSH BP                 ;save BP on BASIC
                                    ;stack
            MOV BP,SP               ;BP points at BASIC
                                    ;stack
            MOV SI,[BP+6]           ;read parameters from
                                    ;BASIC stack
            MOV AX,ES:[SI]          ;get a value...
... read all the parameters in here...
            MOV SS_STORE,SS         ;save DS, ES, SS
            MOV SP_STORE,SP         ;save stack pointer
            MOV AX,SSEG             ;initialize our stack
            MOV SS,AX
            MOV SP,SIZE STK         ;use SIZE operator
... your program goes here...
            MOV SS,SS_STORE         ;reload SS with
                                    ;BASIC's segment
            MOV SP,SP_STORE         ;reset BASIC's stack
            MOV DS,SS_STORE         ;do the same with DS
            POP BP                  ;recover BP from
                                    ;BASIC's stack
            RET n                   ;RET with pop-value
PROGRAM     ENDP
CSEG        ENDS
            END
```

This program template assumes that you need to set up your own stack (whether you use interrupt routines or for some other reason), and assumes that you leave ES pointing to the BASIC data segment. Just remember, DS, ES, and SS must point to the BASIC work area when your machine language routine ends.

The sample program for this chapter is "SCROLL.ASM." Enter it, assemble and link it, then load it into memory with EXELOAD. When you enter BASIC, save it (with DEF SEG and BSAVE). Then, you can enter and run two short BASIC programs written to show off the scroll routine. SCROLL-1 must be used with the color board for the proper effect; SCROLL-2 can be used with color, monochrome, 40- or 80-columns. Don't forget to change the DEF SEG at the start of the two BASIC programs.

As you have seen, interfacing machine language routines with BASIC is substantially unlike DOS programming. You don't push a return address onto the stack, because BASIC has already done that. You do have to initialize your own stack, since BASIC doesn't do that. You have to reset DS, ES, and SS for BASIC; DOS doesn't care. However, the programming is not that much different from DOS, and the rewards of using machine language in conjunction with BASIC are certainly substantial enough to justify any added complexity.

Program 10-1. Work Area

```
100 CLOSE:WORKSEG=VARPTR(#3)+51
110 FOR I=WORKSEG TO WORKSEG+11
120 READ BYTE:POKE I,BYTE
130 NEXT: CALL WORKSEG(A%)
140 PRINT "Lowest segment for external machine
    -language: ";
150 A%=A%+4096:PRINT HEX$(A%);" hex (";INT(A%/
    64);"K )"
160 DATA &h55,&h8b,&hec,&h8b,&h76,&h06,&h8c,&h
    1c,&h5d,&hca,&h02,&h00
```

Program 10-2. EXELOAD.ASM

```
        page ,96
        title Load an .EXE file for BASIC

; EXELOAD.ASM
;
; Invoke EXELOAD with DEBUG EXELOAD.EXE
;   specify the load file's name with the N command
;   specify the segment load address with E CS:12
;
bdos    equ 21h                 ;DOS function interrupt
setblok equ 4ah                 ; function to modify mem blocks
```

```
exec      equ 4bh                         ; function to load/execute
overlay   equ 3                           ; subfunction to load
;
upa       equ byte ptr ds:[80h]           ; PSP's unformatted parms area
;
eseg      segment 'PARMS'                 ; this segment holds parameters
p_block   dw ?,?                          ; used by DOS, pointed to by ES
eseg      ends
;
sseg      segment stack 'STACK'           ; define stack segment
          dw 128 dup(?)                   ; ... as 256 bytes
sseg      ends
;
cseg      segment 'CODE'
          assume cs:cseg,es:eseg,ss:sseg
exeload   proc far
          push ds                         ; set up far RETurn on stack
          mov ax,0
          push ax

          mov bx,28h                      ; set current block size
          mov ah,setblok                  ; to 280H bytes
          int bdos                        ; via DOS

          mov ax,eseg                     ; make ES point to ESEG
          mov es,ax
          mov ax,1700h                    ; segment address to load at
```

```
        mov  p_block,ax           ;store in parameter block
        mov  p_block+2,ax         ; for DOS's EXEC function
        mov  dx,81h               ;start of string (DS:DX)
        cmp  byte ptr ds:[81h],' '   ;check for leading space
        jne  skip                 ; no space, DX = 81h
        inc  dx                   ; space, so DX = 82h
        mov  bl,upa               ;let BX = [80h]
skip:   mov  bl,upa
        mov  bh,0
        mov  upa+1 [bx],0         ;convert to ASCIIZ

        mov  bx,offset p_block    ;ES:BX = parameter block
        mov  al,overlay           ;specify load-don't-exec option
        mov  ah,exec              ;load program function of DOS
        int  bdos

        ret                       ;far RETurn to DEBUG
exeload endp                      ;end of procedure
cseg    ends                      ;end of segment
        end  exeload              ;end of source code
```

Program 10-3. SCROLL.ASM

```
        page ,96
        title Scroll text screen right or left.

; SCROLL.ASM
;
; call this routine with two integer parameters:
;
;   CALL SCROLL (SHIFT%,ATTRIBUTE%)
;
; SHIFT% gives the distance to shift the screen (pos. or neg.)
; ATTRIBUTE% is the new attribute to use on the blanked area
;
video     equ 10h                 ;video I/O interrupt
get_vid   equ 15                  ; get video status
;
dseg      segment 'DATA'
;
ss_store      dw ?                ;store BASIC's SS here
sp_store      dw ?                ;store BASIC's SP here
;
screen_size   dw ?                ;size of current screen (chars)
row_width     dw ?                ;length of one row (bytes)
shift         dw ?                ;-1 or 1 for direction
attribute     db ?                ;attribute for blank line
;
sizes         dw 1024,2048        ;size of WIDTH 40, WIDTH 80
```

179

```
widths          dw 80,160          ;byte row width (as SIZES)
;
dseg    ends
;
sseg    segment stack 'STACK'      ;stack area used only during
stk     dw 64 dup(?)               ; program execution
sseg    ends
;
cseg    segment 'CODE'
        assume cs:cseg,ss:sseg,ds:dseg
scroll  proc far
;
        mov ax,dseg                ;initialize DS
        mov ds,ax
        push bp
        mov bp,sp                  ;initialize BP for stack
        mov si,[bp+6]              ;get second parameter
        mov ax,es:[si]
        mov attribute,al           ;store attr in our data area
        mov si,[bp+8]              ;get first parameter
        mov di,es:[si]            ;get shift request into DI
        cmp di,0                   ;check for no movement
        jnz re_stack               ;not zero, skip abort
        push es                    ;set DS to ES via the stack
        pop ds                     ;(BASIC's DS = ES)
        pop bp                     ;recover BP
        ret 4                      ;abort back to BASIC
```

```
; adjust stack segment
;
re_stack:
        mov ss_store,ss        ;re-make stack
        mov sp_store,sp        ;store SS in DSEG
        mov ax,sseg            ; and SP
        mov ss,ax              ;reset SS to our SSEG
        mov sp,size stk        ;and SP to the top of STK
;
; using BIOS, set up some registers:
; ES points to start of video area
; initialize ROW_WIDTH and SCREEN_SIZE
;
process:
        mov dx,0b800h          ;default start of video
        mov ah,get_vid         ;get video mode into AL
        int video
        cmp al,7               ;test for monochrome mode
        jne p1                 ; no
        mov dx,0b000h          ; yes, set video to B0000
        mov al,2               ; now pretend it's mode 2
p1:     cmp al,4               ;test for a graphics mode
        jb p2                  ; no, so begin execution
        jmp done               ; yes, so skip to end
p2:     and ax,2               ;AX = 0,2 for 40-,80-columns
        mov si,ax              ;move into an index register
```

```
        mov ax,widths [si]      ;get width of a row on screen
        mov row_width,ax        ; store it
        mov ax,sizes [si]       ;get size of total screen
        mov screen_size,ax      ; store it (as a word quantity)
        mov cl,4                ;convert from words ...
        shr ax,cl               ; to segment paragraphs / 2
        mul bh                  ;multiply by page number
        shl ax,1                ;restore to paragraphs
        add dx,ax               ;add to base of video memory
        mov es,dx               ;point our extra segment at it

p3:
        mov shift,1             ;default sign of shift-count
        cmp di,0                ;test DI (shift-count) for +,-
        jns p3                  ;it is positive; go shift
        neg shift               ;reset to negative (-1)
        neg di                  ;make DI positive ( ABS(DI) )
        mov bx,di               ;BX is our count-down register

;
; here we prepare to handle the actual scrolling each time
; initialize DX (line counter) and DI/SI/DF (for MOVS)
;
shift_loop:
        mov dx,25               ;clear 25 rows
        mov di,0                ;shift left (default)
        mov si,2                ;and go up for string ops
        cld                     ;test for right or left
        cmp shift,0
```

```
        js line_loop            ;left is correct
        mov ax,row_width        ;length of one line
        mov cl,25               ;number of lines
        mul cl                  ;size of screen
        sub ax,2                ;last location on screen
        mov di,ax               ;put in index register
        lea si,[di-2]           ;end of screen minus 1 char
        std                     ;and go down for string ops
;
; Now we run through 25 lines with MOVS and STOS
;
line_loop:
        mov cx,row_width        ;get length of line
        shr cx,1                ;convert to words
        dec cx                  ;don't move all of it
rep_1:  cli                     ;disable interrupts briefly
        rep movs word ptr [di], word ptr es:[si]
        jcxz rep_2              ;all REPs done
        dec cx                  ;auto-decrement CX
        jmp rep_1               ;and resume
rep_2:  sti                     ;turn interrupts back on
        mov al,' '              ;clear to a space value
        mov ah,attribute        ; with specified attribute
        stosw                   ;put at end of line (move DI)
        lodsw                   ;move SI as well as DI
        dec dx                  ;check for more lines
        jnz line_loop           ;yes, so loop back
```

```
        dec bx              ;check for more shifts
        jnz shift_loop      ;yes, so loop back
;
; POP the segments, restore BASIC's stack, POP BP, and RETurn
;
done:   mov ss,ss_store     ;get values from DSEG
        mov sp,sp_store     ;(BASIC's SP:SS)
        mov es,ss_store     ;(and ES = SS)
        mov ds,ss_store     ;(note BASIC's DS = SS)
        pop bp              ;restore BP
        ret 4               ; and return to BASIC
;
scroll  endp
cseg    ends
        end
```

Program 10-4. SCROLL-1.BAS

```
100 DEF SEG = &H1700
110 BLOAD "SCROLL.BSV",0
120 SCROLL=0: SHIFT=1: AT%=0: FACTOR=1.12: LIM
    IT=30
130 AT%=(AT%+16) MOD 256: SHIFT%=SHIFT
140 CALL SCROLL (SHIFT%,AT%)
150 SHIFT=SHIFT*FACTOR: SHIFT%=SHIFT
```

```
160 IF SHIFT>LIMIT OR SHIFT<.5 THEN FACTOR=1/F
    ACTOR
170 GOTO 130
```

Program 10-5. SCROLL-2.BAS

```
100 DEF SEG=&H1700: BLOAD "SCROLL.BSV",0
110 SCREEN 0,0,0: CLS: KEY OFF: DEFINT A-Z: RA
    NDOMIZE TIMER
120 SCROLL=0: SHIFT=1: ATTRIBUTE=7: HEIGHT=10:
    DIR=1
130 LOCATE HEIGHT,1: IF DIR=1 THEN PRINT "/";
    ELSE PRINT "\";
140 CALL SCROLL (SHIFT,ATTRIBUTE)
150 IF RND(1)<.15 THEN DIR=-DIR: GOTO 130
160 IF HEIGHT+DIR>25 OR HEIGHT+DIR<10 THEN DIR
    =-DIR: GOTO 130
170 HEIGHT=HEIGHT+DIR: GOTO 130
```

3
Interrupts

11
Overview of Interrupts

In this chapter we'll examine the use of interrupts on the 8088 microprocessor. You have used interrupts in earlier chapters in a cookbook fashion: the DOS function call, INT 21H, for example. Here we'll discuss how interrupts work and how the 8088 and MS-DOS make use of them. (There is an excellent, if technical, discussion of interrupt structure on pages 8-30 through 8-42 of Rector's and Alexy's *The 8086 Book*, published by Osborne/McGraw-Hill.) In the next two chapters, we'll continue with the subject of interrupts, focusing on the PC.

Why Interrupts?

First of all, let's discuss what an interrupt is. We all are well-acquainted with many types of interruptions: the telephone ringing, the smoke alarm going off, a young child wanting our attention. However, in a computer system, interrupts are positively advantageous.

The computer is always connected to a variety of other devices. Some of them are clearly separate—disk drives, modems, other microprocessors—and some less so—internal clocks and timers, for example. For a computer to handle input and output properly, it has to be prepared for information from all of these devices at any time. There are only two ways for the 8088 to find out what's happening with these external devices.

1. The computer can routinely take time off from its various tasks to poll all the attached devices. In other words, the 8088 checks the appropriate input/output ports to see if anything is happening.
2. The devices let the computer know when something happens.

As you can imagine, this second alternative makes more sense. That way, the computer is spared having to spend a substantial amount of time checking all the attached peripherals. This second method is the interrupt technique. In

189

short, whenever some external device has something to tell the microprocessor, it interrupts it. The keyboard, for example, interrupts the microprocessor whenever a key is struck.

The 8088 has a much more powerful system of interrupts than most eight-bit microprocessors. Each interrupt on the 8088 has a priority level, from interrupt 0 (the highest) to 255 (the lowest). Whenever the 8088 gets two interrupts at the same time, the lower-numbered interrupt is handled first.

Software Interrupts

In general, external interrupts (interrupts from peripherals) won't concern you. Software interrupts (interrupts requested by your own program as part of the normal program flow) are of more concern to the programmer. The interrupt number then becomes not a measure of an interrupt's priority, since you can call only one interrupt at a time, but rather a convenient index with which to access specific interrupt routines. These software interrupts are designed to give the programmer access to all the power of DOS and BIOS.

Basically, using software interrupts is similar to CALLing the system routines. However, using the INT command lets you call a routine without knowing where it is. You simply use the INT command in your program and let the computer figure out where the requested routine is located.

The idea of something interrupting itself is most peculiar. In fact, as you can imagine, the rationale behind these software interrupts is entirely different from the reason for the hardware interrupts discussed above. Why not simply have your program CALL any DOS or BIOS routines it needs to use? There are a few convincing reasons for using interrupts:

1. Simplicity. Putting **INT 10H** in your program is obviously preferable to, for example, **CALL F000:0D0B:** It takes fewer bytes of program memory (two versus five), and it is considerably easier to remember.
2. Portability. A portable program is one that will run without modification on a variety of different machines. For example, most machine language programs written on the IBM PC will run on the PCjr, even though the crucial routines in DOS and BIOS are in different places. A **CALL F000:0D0B** on one machine, for example, is a **CALL F000:F065** on another. Portable programs thus always use

the system INTerrupts and let the computer figure out where the appropriate routines are located.

How Interrupts Work

No matter whether an interrupt is a software interrupt or a hardware interrupt, the basic mechanism used to handle them is the same. There are three ways for the computer to know which interrupt you want. The number can be specified by an external device requesting an interrupt, by the program itself (as in INT 21H), or the number can be implicit in the software command.

Once the computer knows which interrupt number is being requested, it locates the interrupt-handling routine (also know as the interrupt service routine). The first 1024 bytes of memory (00000H to 003FFH) are given over to storing the starting addresses of each interrupt routine in *segment:offset* form. (Thus, 256 interrupt vectors, each four bytes long, add up to 1024 or one K.) It is possible to modify these vectors so that they point to your routines rather than the computer's, but doing so is a rather advanced technique.

Now the computer knows where the subroutine is located. It pushes three words onto the stack: the 16-bit flags register, the current code segment (CS), and the current instruction pointer (IP). Next it loads the appropriate segment:offset value from the interrupt vector area. At this point the interrupt routine is given control. As you can see, this is much like a far CALL (such as the CALL F000:0D0B mentioned above). The only difference is that the flags register is also saved on the stack. We'll discuss why in a moment.

At this point, CS:IP holds the start address of the interrupt routine; the routine begins to execute. When the interrupt routine is finished, it executes an IRET instruction (Interrupt RETurn). This instruction is like the standard far RETurn, but it also pops the flags register off the stack. Now, CS:IP points back into the main program at the point where the interrupt was called, and the main program continues from where it left off.

Why save the flags register? Saving and then restoring the flags register allows a program to be stopped in the middle of execution by an external interrupt and then to resume exactly where it left off. For example, the clock-updating routine, which is called 18.2 times each second by one of the PC's timers, saves and then restores all the registers that it modifies. (Imagine the registers in your program changing 18.2 times a second!)

For those interrupt routines that are called only with software interrupts (and that covers most routines), certain registers are not saved. These are the registers that are used to pass parameters. For example, the AX register is very rarely saved by any of the common interrupts; some interrupts, like the absolute disk read and write routines (INT 25H and 26H), alter all but the segment registers. Since these routines are always called predictably from within program code, you don't have to worry about registers changing randomly. If you need to save registers, simply place PUSH instructions before the interrupt call, and POP instructions after it.

Interrupt Control Opcodes

We've already discussed the primary interrupt commands, INT and IRET. INT allows you to call any of the 256 interrupt routines simply by specifying

INT *number*

where *number* ranges from 0 to 255. IRET (Interrupt RETurn) is the instruction used to return from an interrupt. You'll have no need to use IRET yourself until you're an advanced programmer, but you'll need to be able to recognize it to understand interrupt routine program listings, such as those in BIOS.

There are, as we've briefly mentioned, two other interrupt generating opcodes. The first of these is INT 3. In appearance this is the same as the INT number form above, but in fact the INT 3 command is only one byte, as opposed to the standard two-byte INT instruction. INT 3 is used by DEBUG to set breakpoints, and will be discussed in more detail below.

The second specialized interrupt command is INTO. This command (INTerrupt on Overflow) is a *conditional interrupt*. Normally, a program that deals with signed math needs to have a way to handle overflow. If INTO is placed after a math operation, it will execute an INT 4 if the overflow flag is set. This interrupt opcode, like INT 3, is only one byte. As a rule, you won't be needing to use this interrupt. Generating an interrupt on overflow is a slight case of overkill for the beginning to intermediate programmer. Normally, a JO (Jump on Overflow) will serve your purpose just as well.

There are two other interrupt control commands, CLI and STI. The CLI command (CLear Interrupt flag) disables (prevents) the microprocessor from responding to external interrupts (such as the clock interrupt mentioned above). Conversely, the STI command (SeT Interrupt flag) enables interrupts. (6502 programmers, beware! The SEI and CLI commands on the 6502 are exactly the reverse of the seemingly equivalent 8088 commands, STI and CLI. SEI, on the 6502, SEts the Interrupt *disable* flag; STI, on the 8088, SeTs the Interrupt *enable* flag.) Bear in mind, though, that when an interrupt is actually executed, the computer executes an automatic CLI and also clears the trap flag (discussed below). This insures that the interrupt itself will not be interrupted. However, the interrupt (and trap) flags are reset when the IRET is executed, since the flags register, including these two flags, is popped from the stack.

Software interrupts and non-maskable interrupts are both exempt from the setting of the interrupt flag. Non-maskable interrupts are external interrupts, generally of some urgency, and can't wait for the interrupt flag to be cleared. We'll discuss the 8088's non-maskable interrupt, INT 2, below.

The Fixed 8088 Interrupts

A certain number of 8088 interrupts are preset for all 8088 systems, regardless of whether they run PC-DOS, MS-DOS, or scientific or business systems. These are the first five interrupts, numbers 0 through 4. Each of these interrupts is non-maskable and therefore will ignore any CLI or STI commands.

Interrupt 0, Divide Overflow. When specifying a DIV or IDIV instruction, it's possible to create a result that is too large. For example, requesting

```
MOV AX,1234H    ;dividend in AX (a word)
MOV BL,2        ;divisor in BL (a byte)
DIV BL          ;quotient to be in AL (a byte)
```

will cause a Divide Overflow interrupt. As you can see, the result (91AH) is too large to fit into AL. An even more extreme case occurs when you put 0 into BL, then execute a DIV BL. When a Divide Overflow condition occurs, the divide logic automatically calls interrupt 0. In PC-DOS, this interrupt calls a routine which prints:

Divide Overflow

and drops out of your program back to the command level of
DOS (the A> prompt). (DOS 2.00 users should note that the
DOS routine responsible for this will cause the computer to
crash. DOS 1.10 and 2.10 divide overflow routines work correctly.) You can, if you wish, revector this interrupt to point to
your own divide overflow routine (an advanced technique).
This interrupt is the only runtime error message you can get in
machine language.

Interrupt 1, Single Step. This interrupt is used only by
DEBUG. It is triggered after every instruction when the trap
flag (mentioned above) is set. When the trap flag is set, the
computer calls interrupt 1 after every program instruction.
Normally, the trap flag is clear, so the INT 1's are not generated. Furthermore, the INT 1 vector normally points directly
to an IRET in DOS. This effectively cancels any INT 1's, since
nothing happens and the flags, CS, and IP are immediately restored.

The trap flag can't be set by a single program instruction.
Instead, you must follow this procedure:

```
PUSHF        ;AX holds the flags as follows (bit 15 first)
POP AX       ; 0,0,0,0,OF,DF,IF,TF,SF,ZF,0,AF,0,PF,0,CF
OR AX,100H   ;now we set bit 8 (TF) to 1
PUSH AX      ;finally, we return the changed flags register
POPF         ; via the stack
```

The interrupts will become enabled after the next instruction.
The entire 16-bit flags register is moved into the AX register,
then the appropriate bit (bit 8) is set with the OR instruction.
Then the modified flags word is transferred back to the flags
register, again via the stack. Starting with the instruction after
the POPF instruction, each instruction will be followed by an
interrupt 1. To turn off single-stepping, you must transfer the
flags to AX (via the stack), AND AX,0FEFFH, then return the
flags to the flags register.

DEBUG uses the Single Step interrupt to handle its Trace
function. Though you will rarely find a use for this interrupt
within your programs, you will no doubt be using the DEBUG
Trace function. A warning about the Trace function: It occasionally appears to drop opcodes during the trace.

Interrupts are automatically disabled whenever a segment
register is loaded (with MOV or POP). This exception to the

normal rules of interrupt execution was designed explicitly to protect a sequence such as the following:

MOV SS,AX   ;assuming AX has the new stack segment
MOV SP,100H   ;100H or whatever SP value you wish

Without this exception, an external interrupt could be triggered between the two stack-setting commands, creating havoc by storing information in some area not meant to be a stack at all (remember, INT pushes the flags, CS, and IP at the current SS:SP). We can see the interrupts being disabled when DE-BUG occasionally drops opcodes from its trace list. These opcodes have been executed; they're just not displayed, since loading a segment register turns off all interrupts, including Single Step.

Interrupt 2, NMI (Non-Maskable Interrupt). This is the highest priority hardware interrupt (the previous two are invariably software interrupts). Furthermore, this is the only external interrupt that can override the CLI command. For most non-MS-DOS systems, the NMI is used to signal some traumatic event within the system: an imminent power failure, for example. However, the IBM PC uses the NMI solely to handle keyboard input. It's usually a good thing for the user, too, since the keyboard Ctrl-Alt-Del sequence must be non-maskable if it's to work when interrupts have been disabled by CLI.

As a programmer, you will have little need to involve yourself with INT 2 directly. The interrupt handler for interrupt 2 is responsible solely for converting the keyboard data into scan codes. We'll discuss the most useful keyboard interrupt, INT 16H, in the next chapter.

Interrupt 3, Breakpoint. This interrupt, like the Single Step interrupt above, is used almost exclusively by and with DEBUG. Whenever you specify the Go command with extra parameters, like

G 37,4B

DEBUG puts the one-byte INT 3 instruction at the specified breakpoints (37 and 4B here) and saves their previous contents. Since INT 3 is a one-byte instruction, it can replace any one 8088 opcode without interfering with the next. When the program hits the breakpoint, DEBUG stops the program's execution and restores the old contents of the breakpoint byte(s).

195

INT 3 can also be used, with DEBUG, to replace the initial PUSH/PUSH sequence and final RETF. INT 3, if used explicitly to end your program, will simply return you to the DEBUG command level without restoring DS and the other registers to their initial values (as happens when you use RETF).

When you're not using DEBUG, the interrupt number 3 points directly to an IRET instruction, like INT 1 above.

Interrupt 4, Overflow. This interrupt has been described above in connection with the INTO command. In short, this interrupt will execute if INTO is specified and the overflow flag is set. INT 4 normally doesn't handle overflow; it defaults to an IRET just like INT 1 and INT 3.

We suggest that you not write any of your own interrupt handlers until you are quite advanced. Now that we've examined the technical details of interrupts and have begun to understand their structure and general use, we can proceed to discuss the details of the most useful BIOS and DOS interrupts in the next two chapters.

12
BIOS Interrupts

Now that we've discussed the technical side of the interrupts—the interrupt mechanism and structure, the inferrupt commands, and the predefined 8088 interrupts—we can discuss the PC-DOS interrupts in more detail. In the next two chapters, we'll turn from the technical aspects of interrupts to a discussion of the interrupt routines that make up the Disk Operating System (DOS) and the Basic Input/Output System (BIOS).

As we discussed in earlier chapters (when you used DOS interrupt 21H), one interrupt can often perform more than one particular function. For several of the BIOS interrupts, a variety of functions are available with one interrupt call: interrupt 10H, for example, has 17 functions. For all the BIOS routines, you select a function by placing the number of the function in AH prior to calling the routine. So, to call function 8 of interrupt 10H, you would write

MOV AH,8   ;select function number 8
INT 10H   ;call interrupt 10 hex

Other parameters also must be specified for many of these functions. For example, to output a character with INT 10H, you have to put the character in AL as well as the function number in AH. Conversely, many functions return values; the read keyboard function, for example, returns in AX the value of the last key pressed. Registers that are not used for returning values are always preserved by BIOS routines. (AX, however, is never preserved, and can be any value when the routine returns to your program.)

The Video Handler Interrupt, INT 10H
This interrupt is very powerful. You will probably be using this routine more frequently as your programs begin to use the power of the screen for advanced text handling and machine language high-resolution graphics.

Luckily, the functions provided with this interrupt are grouped together fairly logically, but there are some exceptions. The table at the end of this section outlines the INT 10H functions (in terms of their input and output).

PC users must make special note of the color/graphics functions. Much of the video handler is devoted to the color/graphics board, and so the monochrome board can make only limited use of this function. When you're using the monochrome board, functions 5, 11, 12, and 13 shouldn't be used. However, if your PC has both monochrome and color/graphics boards, you can switch from one to the other with the DOS 2.00 MODE command (MODE COL for color/graphics and MODE MONO for monochrome). PCjr owners can use all of these functions as they wish. Note also that the PCjr BIOS has increased the power of functions 5 and 11, as well as added an entirely new function, number 16.

Display Handling Functions (AH = 0, 5, 14 Decimal)

Set Video Mode (AH = 0). The first function available with INT 10H is very similar to the BASIC SCREEN command. However, the video modes are numbered differently, which can be confusing if you're not careful. To use this function place the function number, 0, in AH, and the desired mode number in AL. Table 12-1 is a list of mode numbers, along with the BASIC commands that create the same effect. Bear in mind that the set video mode function always clears the screen and homes the cursor when called, whereas the BASIC SCREEN command won't if the requested mode is the same as the current mode. (The set video function also sets the active page to 0.)

The extended graphics modes are available only on the PCjr. Also note that the PCjr BASIC command SCREEN for SCREENs 3 through 6 is available only with Cartridge BASIC. For more detailed information on the graphics modes, see the *IBM Technical Reference Manual*.

Here's a brief example of how to use this function, setting the computer to graphics mode 4 (320 × 200, 4 colors).

```
MOV AH,0    ;function 0, set mode
MOV AL,4    ;mode 4, 320 × 200, 4 colors
INT 10H     ;call the video I/O routine
```

This is the equivalent of the BASIC command SCREEN 1,1,0.

Table 12-1. Video Interrupt Function 0 Mode Settings

Mode # Name of Mode	BASIC Equivalent
Text Modes	
0 40 × 25, black/white	SCREEN 0,0,0: WIDTH 40
1 40 × 25, color	SCREEN 0,1,0: WIDTH 40
2 80 × 25, b/w	SCREEN 0,0,0: WIDTH 80
3 80 × 25, color	SCREEN 0,1,0: WIDTH 80
Graphics Modes	
4 320 × 200, 4 colors	SCREEN 1,1,0
5 320 × 200, b/w, 4 shades	SCREEN 1,0,0
6 640 × 200, black & white	SCREEN 2,0,0
7 can't set mode 7 (refers to PC's monochrome board)	
Extended Graphics Modes	
8 160 × 200, 16 colors	SCREEN 3,1,0
9 320 × 200, 16 colors	SCREEN 5,1,0
10 640 × 200, 4 colors	SCREEN 6,1,0

Select Active Display Page (AH = 5). This function allows you to choose which of the text pages to display on the screen. If you're a fairly advanced BASIC user, you may be familiar with this concept. For text modes, the PC family has the ability to make more than one screen (or page) available to the programmer at one time. Obviously, only one page of information can be displayed on the screen. However, you can be working on another page at the same time, which you display only when it's complete. Using multiple pages and page flipping eliminates the annoying flicker of putting new information directly onto the screen.

To use this function, AH holds 5, and AL holds the page requested. The range for AL is 0 to 7 for 40 columns, and 0 to 3 for 80 columns. (The video memory area is 16K long, and each 40-column screen takes 2K while an 80-column screen takes 4K.) The monochrome board does not support this function.

An additional use for this function has been added on the PCjr, one which allows you to select which 16K block of memory of system RAM to use for display. On the PC, the memory used for the color/graphics screen is invariably stored at B8000H.

On the PCjr, however, the video memory is simply a piece of the main system RAM. Normally the 16K at the top

199

end of memory is allocated for screen memory. But, with this video function, a 128K PCjr can support eight different 16K screen-memory blocks. This becomes useful when you need to use one of the computer's extended graphics modes, modes 9 and 10. Since these modes require 32K, you clearly can't get by with just the 16K at the top end of memory. So the PCjr's block of screen memory must be moved down one unit (16K), to leave a total of 32K available at the top of memory. You will also need to move the 16K screen-memory area around for graphics page flipping, since the standard graphics modes use 16K for one page.

BASIC also makes use of this function to access the two extended 32K modes. Normally, BASIC leaves the screen-memory area at the top of memory. However, since the two 32K modes need more than the default 16K, you have to allocate more memory to the screen area with the BASIC command CLEAR ,,,32768. To use these modes from machine language, you have to do exactly the same thing: make 32K available for the screen. Furthermore, BASIC can do page flipping when in graphics mode, if enough memory is allocated to it. BASIC moves the 16K screen memory area around to do this just as machine language does.

There are two separate registers controlling this 16K area. You can select which 16K block contains the screen you're displaying, as well as which 16K block will mirror the B8000 area of memory. As we mentioned above, the PC's graphics screen is at B8000H, while the PCjr's screen can move around. For compatibility, the PCjr has a provision to send any MOVes in the B8000 area (which is empty memory in the PCjr) to the real 16K of screen memory in the system RAM. The register controlling which block to display is called CRTREG. The register controlling which block to vector B8000 requests to is called CPUREG. Normally, both of these registers are changed at the same time. To set and read these registers separately or in conjunction, pass the following values in AL:

80H to read CRTREG into BH and CPUREG into BL
81H to set CPUREG to the value in BL
82H to set CRTREG to the value in BH
83H to set CPUREG to BL and CRTREG to BH

You will almost always be setting CRTREG and CPUREG together (option 83H). For example, to set both CRTREG and

CPUREG down one block, to allow for one of the 32K graphics modes, do the following:

```
MOV AH,5      ;function 5, select active page
MOV AL,80H    ;read CRTREG/CPUREG to BH/BL
INT 10H
DEC BH        ;set CRTREG and CPUREG to...
DEC BL        ;... one block lower in memory
MOV AH,5      ;function 5 again
MOV AL,83H    ;set CRTREG/CPUREG to BH/BL
INT 10H
```

And don't forget to repeat this process in reverse (replacing DEC with INC) before you exit. The results otherwise are interesting, but not desirable.

Read Video State (AH = 15). This routine returns the information set by functions 0 and 5. You don't need to set any parameters except AH = 15. To call this function, use

```
MOV AH,15   ;function 15, current video state
INT 10H     ;call video I/O routine
```

This routine returns the following information:

- AL holds the mode currently set. This is the same number that you specify when using function 0 (see Table 12-1).
- AH holds the number of character columns on the screen. This value is returned according to the mode:

```
decimal 80   for modes 2, 3, 6, and A
40           for modes 0, 1, 4, 5, and 9
20           for mode 8
```

- BH holds the number of the current active display page (which page is being displayed on the screen). BH ranges from 0 to 7 in 40-column text modes, 0 to 3 for 80-column text, and is always 0 for all graphics modes.

  Some of the video functions require you to specify which page you want to work with; calling function 15 beforehand tells you what page is being displayed. Thus, for simple applications, you'll usually continue to use the page you started on; function 15 tells you the number of that page.

Cursor-Handling Routines (AH = 1, 2, 3)

The video handler interrupt, INT 10H, can also be used to control the cursor. This is done by placing the proper value in

AH for the function you want. (See Table 12-3 for a complete list of the INT 10H functions.)

Set Cursor Type (AH = 1). This rarely used routine allows you to set the size of the cursor. The line to start the block shape is placed in CH, and the line it should end is in CL. The color/graphics cursor, for example, starts on line 6 and ends on line 7 (the first line is line 0). To turn off the cursor altogether, call this routine with 20H in CH. Note that the LOCATE command, in BASIC, can be used to change the size of the cursor (see the BASIC manual). To return the cursor to its normal shape, call function 0 (set mode). You can, of course, also use this function to return the cursor to its original shape.

Set Cursor Position (AH = 2). This routine can place the cursor anywhere on a specified display page. DH holds the new row for the cursor (from 0 to 24), and DL the column. The column can be 0 to 79 in 80-column mode, 0 to 39 in 40 columns, or 0 to 19 in 20 columns (video mode 8). Since the PC keeps separate cursor positions for each of the possible display pages (up to eight pages in 40-column mode), you also have to specify, in BH, the page number of the cursor that you're moving.

For simpler applications, a call to the set cursor routine is often preceded by a call to the read video state routine, number 15. Thus, for example, to set the cursor on the current page to the center of the screen:

```
MOV AH,15    ;read the current video state
INT 10H      ;video I/O call
             ;now AL holds mode, AH holds columns, and BH
             ;holds display page
SHR AH,1     ;divide width (columns) by 2
MOV DL,AH    ;and place in columns register
MOV DH,12    ;put half of 25 in rows register
             ;DL holds half width, DH holds half height, BH
             ;holds page
MOV AH,2     ;function 2, set cursor position
INT 10H      ;video I/O call
```

Read Cursor Position (AH = 3). This routine returns the current settings of the last two routines, 1 and 2. To read the cursor position, AH holds 3 and BH holds the page number (BH must be 0 for graphics modes). On return from the interrupt call, DH, DL will hold the row and column of the cursor on the specified page. Additionally, CH, CL will hold the cursor type (from function 1 above). This routine can, for example, be used to move the cursor to a specific position on the current line (equivalent to the BASIC's TAB). If you are unsure what screen line the cursor is on, but want to set the column to 60, you can use the following code fragment to change only the column, on the current page:

```
MOV AH,15   ;get current video state
INT 10H     ;... we need the page number in BH
MOV AH,3    ;read cursor position (page in BH)
INT 10H
MOV DL,60   ;set DL to 60, leave DH (row) alone
MOV AH,2    ;set cursor position (page in BH)
INT 10H
```

This would be equivalent to the BASIC statement

PRINT TAB(60);

Read Light Pen Position (AH = 4)

This one is very rarely used, so we'll summarize. Call INT 10H with AH = 4, and AH will return 1 if the light pen was triggered; otherwise, it will return 0. If AH = 1, DH, DL will also hold the row, column being pointed at, and BX, CH will hold the graphics mode pixel x,y coordinates.

Scroll Active Page Up or Down (AH = 6, 7)

INT 10H can also be used to scroll the active page. These two functions can be quite useful. The two have almost the same format, so we'll treat them as one command. They allow any part of the current active page (a window) to be scrolled up or down any number of lines. In addition, you set the attribute to be used on the blank line (see the "Flash" program in Chapter 5 for a description of the attribute byte). Here are the input parameters for the two routines:

(CH,CL) = row, column of the upper left corner of the window

(DH,DL) = row, column of the lower right corner of the window

(AL)   = number of lines to scroll the window up or down

(BH)   = attribute to be used on blank line(s)

One convenient feature of this routine is that you can use it to blank any area of the screen simply by specifying 0 for AL. If you use 0 for AL, functions 6 and 7 produce identical results, and the entire window is set to the attribute in BH. Otherwise, function 6 (scroll up) will give you (AL) blank lines of attribute (BH) at the bottom of the window, while function 7 (scroll down) produces blank lines at the top of the window.

The most common use of the scroll routines is simply to blank the entire screen. Here's how to blank the screen:

```
MOV CX,0    ;CH=0, CL=0 for top left of screen
MOV DL,79   ;for 80 columns; use 39 for 40 columns
MOV DH,24   ;bottom line of screen
MOV AL,0    ;select clear whole screen option
MOV BH,7    ;set to standard white-on-black
MOV AH,6    ;(scroll up)
INT 10H
```

Character Handling Routines (AH = 8, 9, 10, 14 Decimal)

There are four useful character handling routines that can be accessed using INT 10H. Three of the routines allow you to write to any page display.

Multi-Page Character Handling Routines (AH = 8, 9, 10). Each of these routines will allow you to write characters to any display page depending on which page is specified in BH. (However, if you're reading or writing characters in a graphics mode, you don't have to specify BH, since there's only one graphics page.) These are the only routines that allow placing text on a screen other than the current active page, so you will no doubt grow quite familiar with them when you start using multiple screens in machine language. The thing to remember with these routines is that the cursor (on whichever page) is not automatically moved when the character is written. If you use the character-output routine in this group (AH = 10), and try to print a string of characters, they'll all be written to the same position, each on top of the last.

The first of these routines, AH = 8, is the routine to read the attribute and character at the current cursor position (remember, each text screen has its own cursor position). To use this routine, AH holds 8 and BH holds the display page before calling INT 10H. On return, AL holds the character and AH holds the attribute. Note that characters on graphics screens don't have attributes.

The other two routines control the writing of characters to any page, with the option to write the attribute as well (AH = 10 for character only, AH = 9 for attribute and character). To use these routines, AH holds 9 or 10, BH has the page number, and the character to write must be in AL. For function 9 (write attribute/character) in text modes, BL must hold the new attribute byte. For function 10 in text modes, BL doesn't have to be specified. For either function in graphics modes, BL holds the color of the character to be written. (For a discussion of the color, as opposed to the attribute, of a character, see the write dot function, number 12. Note that setting the high bit in BL for graphics causes the character to be XORed onto the screen, as in function 12.) The use of BL and BH is outlined in Table 12-2.

Table 12-2. Use of BL and BH with Functions 9 and 10

	Text Modes	Graphics Modes
function 9	BL attribute	BL color
	BH display page	BH —
function 10	BL —	BL color
	BH display page	BH —

One other register, CX, must be set to use these two routines—it holds the number of characters to write. This lets you repeat the character in AL along the same row several times. However, you can't wrap around to a new line. Here's an example of a routine that puts a string of 80 horizontal double-line characters, in light blue on dark blue, at the bottom of 80-column page 2. (This applies, of course, only to the color/graphics board; for monochrome, you would use some other value in BL, and make sure BH was 0, since only one page is provided for monochrome.)

```
MOV BH,2          ;page 2
MOV DH,24         ;bottom row
MOV DL,0          ;first column
MOV AH,2          ;function 2, set cursor
INT 10H
MOV AL,205        ;double horizontal line character
MOV BL,1*16+9     ;light blue (9) on dark blue (1)
MOV BH,2          ;page 2
MOV CX,80         ;repeat 80 times (a full row)
MOV AH,9          ;function 9, write attribute/character
INT 10H
```

205

The Write Teletype Routine (AH = 14). This is a some-what more useful routine for most single-page applications—it handles moving the cursor as well as writing the characters. (Don't worry about IBM's peculiar name for this function.) However, it allows writing only to the current active page.

This routine is similar to the DOS function character output routine you've seen used in other programs ("Primes," for example). However, there are differences between this routine and the equivalent DOS function routine (the display output function, AH = 2). This function is significantly faster than the equivalent DOS functions, in part because it does not echo to the printer when Shift-PrtSc (Fn-Echo on the PCjr) is pressed, nor does it support the DOS 2.00 "piping" feature (see Chapter 13 for a discussion of DOS 2.00 piping). Note that this routine is an exception to the usual rule that the contents of AX are destroyed. The teletype function preserves AL.

The routine itself is simple. It outputs the character in AL directly to the active page. For graphics modes, BL must hold the color to plot the character in. So, to output an exclamation point to the current (text) screen, simply code:

```
MOV AL,'!'
MOV AH,14
INT 10H
```

Several characters are handled specially by this BIOS routine:

```
 7  ring the bell (beep!)
 8  backspace (go back one space, but don't delete)
10  linefeed (go down to the next line, same column)
13  carriage return (go back to the beginning of this line)
```

You'll notice that there are some differences from the way BASIC handles its special characters: Both the backspace and the carriage return are handled differently. BASIC doesn't use CHR$(8) for backspace (it prints a graphics character), but BIOS does. More significantly, the carriage return character, CHR$(13), tells BASIC to go to the beginning of the next line, whereas the carriage return makes BIOS go to the beginning of the current line. To go to the start of the next line in BIOS, you must first print an ASCII 13, and then an ASCII 10 (linefeed) to go down to the start of the next line. The 13–10 sequence is often seen in machine language programs.

Graphics Interface Functions (AH = 12, 13 Decimal)

These routines are both exceedingly simple, yet quite powerful. To use the write dot routine, AH = 12, CX, DX must hold the x,y coordinates of the pixel to be plotted and AL must hold the color to use. The color (technically, the palette register) can be any of the legal colors for the graphics mode you're in:

0 or 1   mode number 6
0 to 3   mode numbers 4, 5, and A
0 to 15   mode numbers 8 and 9

One useful capability of the write dot routine is that you can XOR the dot onto the graphics screen by setting the high bit (bit 7) in AL. This is equivalent to adding 80H to the color value you've selected. Usually, this XORing mode is used for moving shapes around. Advanced BASIC users may be familiar with this idea from the XOR option of the graphics PUT command. In brief, the XOR feature of the write dot function allows you to plot a shape directly over the background. Then, to erase it, simply XOR the shape again. Since two successive XORs return a dot to its original state, the XORed shape has now disappeared, and you can plot it at some other location. See Chapter 8 for more details on XOR. Here's an example of plotting a dot of color 2 at 67,31, with XOR mode:

```
MOV CX,67      ;x coordinate is 67
MOV DX,31      ;y coordinate is 31
MOV BL,2+80H   ;color (palette register) is 2, with XOR bit set
MOV AH,12      ;function 12, write dot
INT 10H
```

A line-drawing procedure using this function is included at the end of the chapter.

The counterpart of this routine is the read dot function, AH = 13. For this, too, you specify CX, DX as the x,y coordinates. The INT 10H call returns with the dot color in AL (recall that an off dot will always return with AL = 0).

Palette Interface Routines (AH = 11, 16 Decimal)

These INT 10H functions are used to change the screen display colors. There are differences here between the various IBM machines.

Set Color Palette (AH = 11). This call allows you to select the colors to be used on the screen. First we'll discuss how this function is used on the PC. PC and PC/XT owners have distinctly less powerful graphics, as we have seen when discussing the set video mode function, and this is reflected in this function as well.

To choose one of the two different subfunctions available with the set palette function, set BH to 0 or 1. When BH is 0, function 11 will set the border/background color to the value in BL. BL should be a number from 0 to 15. In graphics modes 4 and 5 (320 × 200 four-color) this function sets the border and background colors (the background color is equivalent to color 0). In BASIC, the COLOR command can be used to the same effect. In the text modes (0 through 3), this call sets the border color. The background color in text mode, by contrast, is set by the attribute byte of each character.

The other subfunction, for which BH = 1, allows you to choose one of two palettes to use with the 320 × 200 four-color mode (modes 4 and 5). Two palettes of colors are available. The palette determines the colors of the pixels on the screen. One palette consists of the colors white, magenta, and cyan. This palette, number 1, is selected by BIOS when you enter mode 4 or 5 with BIOS. The other palette, number 0, contains the colors brown, red, and green. To select a palette, BH must hold 1, and AL must hold the palette number. The available palette colors are summarized below:

palette 0: green, red, brown for colors 1, 2, 3
palette 1: cyan, magenta, white for colors 1, 2, 3

This switchable palette allows you to have either the colors green, red, and brown or the colors cyan, magenta, and white, on the screen at one time, as well as the background color (set by the BH = 0 subfunction). Switching between the palettes immediately changes the colors of all the pixels on the screen.

The PCjr has extended the power of these two functions considerably. On the PC, the first function, BH = 0, is able to set the graphics background color only for 320 × 200 four-color mode. On the PCjr, we can set the background color for any graphics mode (all seven). If you call the set color palette function with BH = 0 in a graphics mode, the color specified in AL becomes the new background color, color 0, as well as the border color.

The second function, BH = 1, is limited on the PC to choosing palette 0 or 1 for graphics modes 4 and 5. The PCjr can use the BH = 1 function to set palette 0 or palette 1 in extended graphics mode 10. In addition, the PCjr can set a palette for the 640 × 200 two-color mode. Normally, on the PCjr, mode 6 has white characters on whatever background color you select. However, you can select black characters on the background also. The white foreground is palette 0 (the default), while the black foreground is palette 1. But you probably won't need to concern yourself with palettes if you have a PCjr, since the next function allows you to set each palette register independently to whatever color you wish.

Set Palette Registers (AH = 16). This palette control function is only for the PCjr. It allows you to select which colors are to be used with which palette registers, for both text and graphics modes. When you enter one of the two 16-color modes (numbers 8 and 9), or one of the alphanumeric modes (numbers 0 through 3), the PCjr makes a one-to-one match between the 16 palette registers and the 16 colors. Palette register 0 corresponds to color 0 (black), 1 corresponds to 1 (blue), 2 to 2 (green), and so forth. The four-color modes default to black, cyan, magenta, white (palette 1) and the two-color mode to white-on-black (palette 0).

However, it is possible to select any combination of colors to be used with any of the palette registers. They could all be set to black (thus making a picture invisible while, perhaps, it's being drawn or loaded), or they could be set to change appropriately during a game to show the passage of time, strength, points, or whatever. To change one palette register independently of the others, you call INT 10H with AH = 16 and AL = 0. Then palette number (BL) is set to color (BH), which you have specified. These commands are similar to the BASIC command PALETTE. For example, to duplicate the BASIC command PALETTE 4,15, which sets palette register 4 to bright white, code:

```
MOV AL,0    ;select subfunction to set palette register
MOV BL,4    ;set palette register 4...
MOV BH,15   ;... to color 15 (bright white)
MOV AH,16   ;select function 16, set palette registers
INT 10H
```

There is a similar function to change the border color. Call the set palette register function with AL = 1, and put the border color in BH.

There is one other, more specialized option with this function. This option allows you to set all 16 of the palette registers, as well as the background, just as PALETTE USING does in BASIC. To use this option, set AL to 2 (and AH to 16); DS:DX should point to a list of colors. The first 16 bytes (numbers 0 through 15) are the colors to be assigned to palette registers 0 through 15. The seventeenth byte, at offset 16 within the table, sets the color of the border.

Table 12-3. Functions Available with INT 10H

(AH) function name

0 set mode
input	(AL)	= new mode number

1 set cursor type
input	(CH)	= start line for cursor, (CL) = end line

2 set cursor position
input	(BH)	= display page, (DH,DL) = new row, column

3 read cursor position
input	(BH)	= display page
output	(DH,DL)	= row, column, (CH,CL) = cursor mode

4 read light pen position
output	(AH)	= 0 if light pen switch not down/not triggered
	(AH)	= 1 if valid light pen values in registers
	(DH,DL)	= row, column, (BX,CH) = pixel x,y

5 select active page
input	(AL)	= page value (valid 0–3 or 0–7)
or (for PCjr):		
	(AL)	= 80H, read CRT/CPU registers (see output)
	(AL)	= 81H, (BL) = new CPU page register
	(AL)	= 82H, (BH) = new CRT page register
	(AL)	= 83H, (BL) = CPU register, (BH) = CRT register
if bit 7 (80H) of AL is set, then		
output	(BL)	= CPU register, (BH) = CRT register

6 scroll active page up, lines blanked at bottom
        input   (AL)   = number of lines, or (AL) = 0
                              to blank window
                 (CH,CL) = upper left corner of window
                              (row,column)
                 (DH,DL) = lower right corner of window
                              (row,column)
                 (BH)   = attribute to use on blank line(s)
7 scroll active page down, lines blanked at top
        input as above for function 6
8 read attribute/character at current cursor position
        input   (BH)   = display page (for text modes)
        output (AL)   = character read, (AH) =
                              attribute (text only)
9 write attribute/character at cursor position
        input   (BH)   = display page (for text modes)
                 (AL)   = character, (BL) = attribute or
                              color
                 (CX)   = count of characters to write
10 write character only at cursor position
        input as above, but (BL) used only in graphics modes
11 set color palette
        input   (BH)   = 0 for background, (BL) =
                              background color
                 (BH)   = 1 to select palette, (BL) =
                              palette number
12 write dot
        input   (CX,DX) = pixel x,y, (AL) = palette
                              register
13 read dot
        input   (CX,DX) = pixel x,y
        output (AL)   = dot read
14 write teletype to active page
        input   (AL)   = character, (BL) = color (graph-
                              ics modes only)
15 return current video state
        output (AL)   = display mode, (AH) =
                              columns, (BH) = page
16 set palette registers (PCjr only)
        input   (AL)   = 0, (BL) = palette register, (BH)
                              = color
                 (AL)   = 1, (BH) = border color
                 (AL)   = 2, (DS:DX) points to a 17-byte
                              color buffer holding 16 register
                              colors + border color

Keyboard I/O, INT 16H

This interrupt allows communications with the keyboard with a minimum of difficulty and a maximum of control. However, before we get into the details of how to use this interrupt, it is necessary to discuss how the PC reads the keyboard.

Scan Codes and ASCII Codes

Many computers have a separate chip that controls the keyboard. This chip converts keypresses to standard ASCII codes, taking into account the status of other keys, such as the Caps Lock or Ctrl keys. For example, if the keyboard chip sensed key number 25 being pushed (scan code 25) while the Shift key was down, it might send ASCII code 80 (an uppercase P) to the system microprocessor.

The PC, on the other hand, does all the translating from scan codes to ASCII under software control. This allows a program to get much more information from the keyboard than would be possible if the system had access only to the ASCII codes. Using INT 16H, the program can sense when the Ins, Caps Lock, Num Lock, or Scroll Lock key is pushed, as well as the toggled (on or off) state of each one. Additionally, it can sense whether the Right Shift, Left Shift, Ctrl, or Alt key is being depressed.

The keyboard function that reads a key always returns two values. One of these values is the ASCII code for the key pressed, taking into account the Shift, Ctrl, or Alt key concurrently pressed. This value is usually most useful. The other value is the scan code. This code reflects, in most cases, the key that was pressed, and not the Shift, Ctrl, or Alt key simultaneously pressed. Sometimes, the ASCII code is returned as 0, and you have to use the scan code to identify the actual key. IBM refers to these ASCII zero codes as extended codes. BASIC users may be familiar with extended codes. When the INKEY$ statement returns an ASCII zero as the first byte, the zero marks an extended code, and the second byte, the scan code, is used to identify the key.

Table 12-4 shows the scan code for each key on the keyboard, as well as the ASCII code and character associated with it. In the three columns following are listed the ASCII codes you get by pressing Shift, Ctrl, or Alt with the listed key; the scan code usually stays the same no matter what Shift key you press. For most keys, we've given the character in quotes, and the ASCII code in parentheses. Some keys (like Enter) don't produce a printable character; therefore, just the ASCII code is given. You may also notice that some combinations of keys (like Alt-Esc) are listed with a long dash (—). This means that this combination doesn't return anything with INT 16H.

There is one exception. Normally, as we mentioned above, the scan code stays the same no matter what Shift keys you press. However, the PC keyboard identifies certain combinations of keys as representing "new keys." These are always extended codes, as mentioned above. For example, the 5 key on the top row of the keyboard is normally scan code 6. But when you press Alt-5, the keyboard creates a new scan code for the key, 124, and gives it an ASCII code of zero. When an extended code with a new scan code is generated, the notation <0,n> is used to identify the new scan code: n is the value of the new scan code, and the 0 refers to the ASCII code of zero.

Some keys and combinations of keys normally return an ASCII code of zero (and are thus extended codes), but the scan code remains the standard scan code given in the leftmost column. These are indicated simply by placing a 0 in the appropriate column. The standard A to Z keys, for example, normally return an ASCII code. But when you use the Alt key with one of these keys, they return an ASCII code of zero, although the scan code stays the same.

All key names given are those for the PC's 83-key keyboard; PCjr owners see the PCjr Conversions Table (Table 12-5) following. Keys not directly available on the PCjr keyboard are marked with a star.

Certain keys change the values listed in Table 12-4. The Caps Lock key reverses the base and uppercase values listed for the A to Z keys each time it is pressed. The Num Lock key reverses the base and uppercase values for the numeric pad keys (scan codes 71 through 83) each time it is pressed. On the PCjr, Num Lock mode also makes the top row of numeric keys look like the PC's numeric pad.

One other feature is available through the keyboard routine. If you hold down the Alt key and enter a decimal number, you can enter any character code from 0 to 255. To enter character 234, you would hold down the Alt key, enter 234, then release the Alt key. The keyboard routine treats this as ASCII 234 but scan code 0. On the PC, you use the numeric keypad; on the PCjr, you use Alt-Fn-N and the top row of numeric keys.

Table 12-4. Key Codes on the 83-key Keyboard

All codes given in decimal   ⟍ASCII

Scan Code	Base Case		Uppercase		Ctrl-	Alt-
1 Esc	27		27		27	—
2 top row 1	"1"	(49)	"!"	(33)	—	<0,120>
3 top row 2	"2"	(50)	"@"	(64)	<0,3>	<0,121>
4 top row 3	"3"	(51)	"#"	(35)	—	<0,122>
5 top row 4	"4"	(52)	"$"	(36)	—	<0,123>
6 top row 5	"5"	(53)	"%"	(37)	—	<0,124>
7 top row 6	"6"	(54)	"^"	(94)	30	<0,125>
8 top row 7	"7"	(55)	"&"	(38)	—	<0,126>
9 top row 8	"8"	(56)	"*"	(42)	—	<0,127>
10 top row 9	"9"	(57)	"("	(40)	—	<0,128>
11 top row 0	"0"	(48)	")"	(41)	—	<0,129>
12 top row –	"-"	(45)	"_"	(95)	31	<0,130>
13 =	"="	(61)	"+"	(43)	—	<0,131>
14 Backspace	8		8		127	—
15 Tab	9		<0,15>		—	—
16 Q	"q"	(113)	"Q"	(81)	17	0
17 W	"w"	(119)	"W"	(87)	23	0
18 E	"e"	(101)	"E"	(69)	5	0
19 R	"r"	(114)	"R"	(82)	18	0
20 T	"t"	(116)	"T"	(84)	20	0
21 Y	"y"	(121)	"Y"	(89)	25	0
22 U	"u"	(117)	"U"	(85)	21	0
23 I	"i"	(105)	"I"	(73)	9	0
24 O	"o"	(111)	"O"	(79)	15	0
25 P	"p"	(112)	"P"	(80)	16	0
26 [	"["	(91)	"{"	(123)	27	—
27]	"]"	(93)	"}"	(125)	29	—
28 Enter	13		13		10	—
30 A	"a"	(97)	"A"	(65)	1	0
31 S	"s"	(115)	"S"	(83)	19	0
32 D	"d"	(100)	"D"	(68)	4	0
33 F	"f"	(102)	"F"	(70)	6	0
34 G	"g"	(103)	"G"	(71)	7	0
35 H	"h"	(104)	"H"	(72)	8	0
36 J	"j"	(106)	"J"	(74)	10	0
37 K	"k"	(107)	"K"	(75)	11	0
38 L	"l"	(108)	"L"	(76)	12	0
39 ;	";"	(59)	":"	(58)	—	—
40 '	"'"	(39)	" ' "	(34)	—	—
41 ' *	" ' "	(96)	" "	(126)	—	—
43 *	" "	(92)	"|"	(124)	28	—
44 Z	"z"	(122)	"Z"	(90)	26	0

ASCII.

Scan Code	Base Case	Uppercase	Ctrl-	Alt-
45 X	"x" (120)	"X" (88)	24	0
46 C	"c" (99)	"C" (67)	3	0
47 V	"v" (118)	"V" (86)	22	0
48 B	"b" (98)	"B" (66)	2	0
49 N	"n" (110)	"N" (78)	14	0
50 M	"m" (109)	"M" (77)	13	0
51 ,	"," (44)	"<" (60)	—	—
52 .	"." (46)	">" (62)	—	—
53 /	"/" (47)	"?" (63)	—	—
55 PrtSc *	"*" (42)	—	<0,114>	—
57 (space bar)	" " (32)	" " (32)	" " (32)	" " (32)
59 F1*	0	<0,84>	<0,94>	<0,104>
60 F2*	0	<0,85>	<0,95>	<0,105>
61 F3*	0	<0,86>	<0,96>	<0,106>
62 F4*	0	<0,87>	<0,97>	<0,107>
63 F5*	0	<0,88>	<0,98>	<0,108>
64 F6*	0	<0,89>	<0,99>	<0,109>
65 F7*	0	<0,90>	<0,100>	<0,110>
66 F8*	0	<0,91>	<0,101>	<0,111>
67 F9*	0	<0,92>	<0,102>	<0,112>
68 F10*	0	<0,93>	<0,103>	<0,113>
71 Home*	0	"7" (55)	<0,119>	see text
72 (cursor up)	0 *(24)*	"8" (56)	—	see text
73 Pg Up*	0	"9" (57)	<0,132>	see text
74 numeric pad –*	"–" (45)	"-" (45)	—	—
75 (cursor left)	0 *(27)*	"4" (52)	<0,115>	see text
76 numeric pad 5*	—	"5" (53)	—	see text
77 (cursor right)	0 *(26)*	"6" (54)	<0,116>	see text
78 numeric pad + *	"+" (43)	"+" (43)	—	—
79 End*	0	"1" (49)	<0,117>	see text
80 (cursor down)	0 *(25)*	"2" (50)	—	see text
81 Pg Dn*	0	"3" (51)	<0,118>	see text
82 Ins	0	"0" (48)	—	see text
83 Del	0	"." (46)	—	—

Table 12-5 lists all of the conversions for the PCjr's 62-key cordless keyboard. The cordless keyboard can access every key on the 83-key PC keyboard, although some of the conversions are rather odd.

Table 12-5. PCjr Conversions

F1 through F10	Fn-1, 2, 3, 4, 5, 6, 7, 8, 9, 0
Ctrl-Break	Fn-B (Break), or, Ctrl-Fn-S
Ctrl-PrtSc	Fn-E (Echo), or, Ctrl-Fn-P
Shift-PrtSc	Fn-P (PrtSc)
Ctrl-Num Lock	Fn-Q (Pause)
Scroll Lock	Fn-S (Sc Lock)
Num Lock	Alt-Fn-N
Pg Up	Fn-cursor left (Pg Up)
Pg Dn	Fn-cursor right (Pg Dn)
Home	Fn-cursor up (Home)
End	Fn-cursor down (End)
numeric keypad −	Fn-minus
numeric keypad +	Fn-equals ("=/+" key)
numeric keypad .	Shift-Del
numeric keypad numbers	top row numbers in Num Lock mode
backslash (\ )	Alt-slash (/)
open quote (')	Alt-single quote (')
vertical bar (¦)	Alt-open bracket ([)
tilde (~)	Alt-close bracket (])
asterisk (*) from PrtSc	Alt-period

The Keyboard Interrupt Functions (INT 16H)

Now that we have run through the scan codes available on the PC and PCjr, let us turn our attention to the interrupt itself. To use this interrupt, as always, place the function number in AH, then issue INT 16H.

Read Keyboard (AH = 0)

This is the workhorse of the keyboard interrupt routine. When you call this routine, the computer checks to see if a key has been pressed; if not, it waits for one. Then, the computer returns the scan code in AH and the standard ASCII code in AL. However, if the ASCII code (AL) holds 0, AH will hold the extended code for the key that was pressed. For example, if we want to write a routine that waits until Alt-Q is pressed, we write it as follows:

```
NO_ALT_Q:  MOV AH,0        ;read keyboard function
           INT 16H         ;keyboard I/O
           CMP AL,0        ;test for an extended code
           JNE NO_ALT_Q    ;not Alt-Q
           CMP AH,10       ;test for Q's scan code
           JNE NO_ALT_Q
```

Get Keyboard Status (AH = 1)

This function sets the zero flag depending on whether the keyboard buffer is empty or not. If the keyboard buffer is empty, the zero flag indicates 0; if the flag is not 0, then a code is waiting to be read. The key waiting to be read is echoed into the AX register (ASCII in AL, scan code in AH). However, the key still has to be read to clear the buffer. This fragment of code calls a keyboard-handling routine whenever a key is pressed:

```
            MOV AH,1          ;get status function
            INT 16H           ;keyboard I/O
            JZ NO_CODE        ;ZF is set, so buffer empty
            CALL READ_KBD     ;character ready: go process
NO_CODE:                      ;continue with program
```

Get Current Shift Status (AH = 2)

This function allows you to check the status of the keyboard. The status byte is returned in AL. Each bit relates the status of a "shift key." Some of the bits are set only when the key is actually being held down. Some are set to 0 or 1 depending on whether the function selected by that key is on or off (for example, normally the bit that tests for Caps Lock on is 0; when you push Caps Lock once the bit becomes 1, then 0 when you push it again).

Here is the status byte returned in AL:

bit 0 Right Shift key depressed
bit 1 Left Shift key depressed
bit 2 Ctrl key depressed
bit 3 Alt key depressed
bit 4 Scroll Lock is on
bit 5 Num Lock is on
bit 6 Caps Lock is on
bit 7 Insert mode is on

An additional byte contains more status flags. This byte, called KB_FLAG_1, is at the same location on the PC, PC/XT, and PCjr. One can hope that it will not be moved in later members of the PC family. Regardless, it is inadvisable to use this byte in a program meant for public use, since IBM gives us no guarantee that it will remain in the same place in later PC generations. In any event, the byte is at location 0040:0018 (or 00418 absolute). You can read it with the following sequence:

MOV AX,40H   ;set segment DS to 0040
MOV DS,AX
MOV AL,BYTE PTR DS:[18H]   ;get byte from offset 0018

This byte returns the following:

bit 0 (unused)
bit 1 Ctrl-Alt-Caps Lock is depressed (PCjr only)
bit 2 audio feedback (click) is on (PCjr only)
bit 3 (used internally by BIOS, always 0)
bit 4 Scroll Lock key is depressed
bit 5 Num Lock key is depressed
bit 6 Caps Lock key is depressed
bit 7 Insert key is depressed

A third keyboard byte exists on the PCjr, holding the status of the Fn key and keypress repeat rate, at 0040:0088. This byte is of little use.

The data obtained through BIOS, as well as from KB_FLAG_1 (if necessary), may be used to give you a greater degree of control over the keyboard, should one of your programs need it.

Set Key Repeat Rate (AH = 3)

This function is valid only for the PCjr. The key repeat rate is the rate at which the keys repeat when you hold them down, as well as the initial delay before they begin to repeat. The INT 16H interrupt function can set them as follows:

AL = 0 restore rate to normal
AL = 1 increase initial delay
AL = 2 slow repeat speed by one-half
AL = 3 combine effects of AL = 1 and AL = 2
AL = 4 turn off repeat

Set Keyboard Click (AH=4)

This function is also new to the PCjr. The keyboard click can be controlled with Alt-Ctrl-Caps Lock, or it can be controlled from software as follows:

AL = 0 turn off keyboard click
AL = 1 turn on keyboard click

DOS provides a variety of keyboard input routines which are good for some purposes, as we shall discuss in the next chapter. INT 16H, however, gives you finer control over keyboard input, and for that reason is often used in preference to the DOS functions.

Table 12-6. Functions Available with INT 16H

(AH)   Function name

0   read character from keyboard
           output (AL) = ASCII, (AH) = scan code
1   get keyboard status
           output (ZF) = 0 if buffer empty, = 1 if key ready
               if key ready, a copy is placed in (AX)
2   get shift status
           output (AL) = shift status
                       bit 0 Right Shift key depressed
                       bit 1 Left Shift key depressed
                       bit 2 Ctrl key depressed
                       bit 3 Alt key depressed
                       bit 4 Scroll Lock is on
                       bit 5 Num Lock is on
                       bit 6 Caps Lock is on
                       bit 7 Insert Mode is on
3   set key repeat rates
           input (AL) = new setting for repeat
                       0 restore default rate
                       1 increase initial delay
                       2 slow repeat speed by one-half
                       3 combine effects of AL = 1 and AL = 2
                       4 turn off repeat
4   set keyboard click
           input (AL) = 0 for off, (AL) = 1 for on

Other BIOS Interrupts

We'll take up where we left off in the last chapter, and briefly run through the interrupts from 5 to FH.

Low-Level Interrupts

Interrupt 5—Print Screen is called whenever you push Ctrl-PrtSc (Fn-PrtSc on the junior). As you no doubt know, this routine dumps the contents of the screen to the printer. If you need to dump the screen from within a program, you can call this routine by simply inserting

INT 5

in your program. No registers are affected, but the routine returns its status in a byte at segment 50, offset 0 (50:0, absolute 00500):

50:0 = **0**   successful print screen
     = **1**   print screen in progress (during operation)
     = **0FFH**   error encountered during printing

Interrupts 6 and 7 are unused in the PC, PCjr, and PC/XT.

The 8259A Interrupts, 8 through 0FH, are all handled by the 8259A chip. Interrupt 8 is the clock tick interrupt that triggers about 18.2 times per second. This interrupt updates the clock and then calls INT 1CH, which normally points to an IRET (see the discussion of INT 1CH in this chapter).

There are two other interrupts in this group, INT 9 and INT 0EH. The first is one of the low-level keyboard decoding routines, the second, a routine which is triggered by disk errors. The rest of the routines in this group (A through D, and F) are unused and reserved in the PC, PC/XT, and PCjr.

The Equipment Determination Routines (INT 11H and 12H)

These two routines are useful for writing programs meant to run on a variety of PC models. The first interrupt, INT 11H, returns a word in AX which describes attached equipment bit by bit. Note that where two bits select an option, the bit pairs are given as binary numbers (that is, 00_2, 01_2, 10_2, and 11_2).

bits   description
0   1 = disk drive(s) are attached (see bits 6, 7)
1   (unused)
2, 3   system board RAM size (not including added memory):
          00_2 = 16K, 01_2 = 32K, 10_2 = 48K, 11_2 = 64K
4, 5   initial video mode:
          00_2 (unused)
          01_2 = 40 × 25 b/w, color/graphics (PCjr default)
          10_2 = 80 × 25 b/w, color/graphics
          11_2 = 80 × 25 b/w, using b/w card (PC default)
6, 7   number of disk drives, if bit 0 = 1:
          00_2=1, 01_2=2, 10_2=3, 11_2=4
8   0 = the system allows direct memory access (DMA)
9–11   number of RS-232 cards (0–7)
12   1 = game I/O (joysticks, etc.) is attached
13   1 = a serial printer is attached (PCjr only)
14, 15   number of printers attached (0–3)

The other interrupt, INT 12H, returns the amount of memory

available on the system board. The value is returned in increments of one K byte in AX. However, this value only represents the amount of memory on the system board, and doesn't take into account any add-on memory. So, for most purposes, this interrupt is useless. The word at segment 40H, offset 15H (absolute address 00415H), holds the actual size of memory in K bytes on the PC, XT, and PCjr.

Disk I/O (INT 13H)

This interrupt is the lowest level of disk access available through the operating system. Rather than dealing with files, or with relative sectors, this routine deals directly with the track, sector, and head of the sector you want to load or save. It's unlikely that you'd want to use this interrupt, unless you were writing your own personal DOS, or writing a disk-repair utility. However, the available functions are summarized in Table 12-7.

Table 12-7. Functions Available with INT 13H

(AH) Name of function and input/output parameters

0   reset disk system (do this for errors, then try again)
1   read the status of the disk system into AL (see below)
        00H = operation successful
        01H = bad command given to disk I/O
        02H = address mark not found
        03H = write attempted on write-protected disk
        04H = requested sector not found
        08H = DMA overrun on operation
        09H = attempt to DMA across 64K boundary
        10H = bad CRC (checksum) on disk read
        20H = controller has failed
        40H = seek operation failed
        80H = attachment failed to respond (time-out error)
2   read the desired sectors into memory
      input   (DL)   = drive number (0 to 3)
                  (DH)   = head number (0 or 1)
                  (CH)   = track number (0 to 39)
                  (CL)   = sector number (1 to 8, or 1 to 9)
                  (AL)   = number of sectors (1 to 8, or 1 to 9)
                (ES:BX) = address of buffer for data
      output (AH)   = error number (as above)
                        carry flag set if (AH) does not equal zero
                (AL)   = number of sectors read (PCjr only)

3   write the desired sectors from memory
      input and output parameters identical to function 2
4   verify the desired sectors (check CRC and so forth)
      parameters identical, but ES:BX is not required
5   format the desired track
      input the same, but (CL) and (AL) are not needed
      ES:BX must point to a format-information buffer.

    This format-information buffer holds a series of fields of data, one for each sector on the track. Each field is four bytes long, holding track number, head number, and sector number, followed by a byte indicating how long the sector is (0 = 128 bytes, 1 = 256 bytes, 2 = 512 bytes, 3 = 1024 bytes). There must be one field for each sector on the track.

RS-232 I/O, INT 14H

Should you need to use this interrupt (to write a modem-handling program, for example), we recommend that you refer to the *Technical Reference Manual*.

Cassette I/O, INT 15H

Since cassette drives are becoming less popular (and since you must have a disk drive for your assembler disk if you're reading this), we'll skim briefly through this topic. For the interested, however, Table 12-8 contains a brief summary of the cassette I/O functions.

Table 12-8. Cassette I/O Functions

(AH)   Function name and input/output

0   turn cassette motor on
1   turn cassette motor off
2   read data from the cassette
      input   (CX)   = number of bytes to read
               (ES:BX) = pointer to data buffer
      output   (DX)   = number of bytes actually read
               (AH)   = error condition if carry is set:
               01   = CRC (checksum) error detected
               02   = data transitions are lost
               04   = no data was found
3   write data to cassette
      input as above; on output, no error returns

Printer I/O—INT 17H

This function is useful for controlling any printers attached to your system. The available options, summarized in Table 12-9, are largely self-explanatory.

Table 12-9. Printer I/O Functions

(AH) Function name and input/output

0   print character
    input   (AL) = character to be printed
            (DX) = number of printer to be used (0, 1, or 2)
    output (AH) = status byte (below)
      (bit 0 set indicates character not printed)

1   initialize the printer port
    input   (DX) = printer to be initialized (0–2)
    output (AH) = status byte

2   read the printer status byte into AH
    input   (DX) = printer number (0–2)
    output (AH) = status byte:
               bit 0 time-out
               bits 1, 2 (unused)
               bit 3 I/O error
               bit 4 printer selected (on-line)
               bit 5 out of paper
               bit 6 acknowledge
               bit 7 not busy

BASIC Start, System Warm Boot, and Time-of-Day Routines (INT 18H, 19H, 1AH)

INT 18H will start up BASIC; INT 19H will reboot from disk. It's unlikely that you'll ever need either of these.

INT 1AH, on the other hand, is convenient for timing applications. The time-of-day clock in the PC family is incremented 18.2 times per second by the 8253 timer. This interrupt provides a way to read and set this counter. The counter is in two words, and all the time-of-day functions use DX as the low word, and CX as the high word. The functions available are listed in Table 12-10.

Table 12-10. Functions for the Time-of-Day Routine

(AH) Function name and input/output

0   read the current clock setting
       output (DX,CX) = low word, high word of counter
              (AL)   = 0 if less than 24 hours since timer read
1   set the clock
       input   (DX,CX) = low word, high word of new setting
80H set the sound source on the PCjr (beeper, sound chip, etc.)
       input   (AL)   = 00 to 03

To insert a specific delay into your program, you might write a procedure like the following:

```
;
; pass in BX the number of 18.2's you wish to wait
; AX, BX, CX, and DX are destroyed by this routine
;
WAIT        PROC NEAR
            MOV AH,0        ;read the clock setting
            INT 1AH         ;time-of-day interrupt
            ADD BX,DX       ;find out when time is up
W_LOOP:     MOV AH,0        ;read the clock again
            INT 1AH
            CMP DX,BX       ;is time up yet?
            JNE W_LOOP      ; no, so loop back
            RET             ; yes, so return
WAIT        ENDP
```

Generally, it's wise to avoid using the set clock option, since the clock used by this interrupt is the same clock that you set when you start up your PC. Setting the clock to 0 with this interrupt will reset the system clock to 12:00 a.m.

There is another way to read the time clock. This approach goes through DOS, and returns to you the year, month, day and date, as well as the time in hours, minutes, seconds, and hundredths of seconds. We'll discuss this in the next chapter.

The User Interrupts—INT 1BH and INT 1CH

We touched lightly on the subject of revectoring interrupts in the last chapter. These two interrupts are made expressly to be revectored, but this technique is best left to advanced programmers. Both interrupts normally point to an IRET instruction (one in DOS, one in BIOS). INT 1BH is called whenever the Break key is struck. INT 1CH is called 18.2 times a second by the routine which updates the clock. By revectoring these interrupts, you can divert the computer to your own routine whenever the Break key is struck, or every time the clock is updated; but such methods go beyond the scope of this book.

The Parameter Table Interrupts, 1DH and 1EH

These, too, we'll only touch on. These two interrupt locations do not contain genuine interrupt vector addresses. Instead, they point to data. The vector at interrupt location 1DH points to a table of parameters for the video display. The vector for 1EH points to a table of parameters for the disk drive. Both tables should be left alone, along with their vector pointers. Modifying these tables requires extremely advanced techniques.

The Upper 128 Character Display Data, INT 1FH

This interrupt location also contains a pointer to data. The data pointed to is the character generator graphics that allow the PC to put characters on the screen when in graphics modes, simply by plotting the appropriate pixels on the screen. Advanced programmers can revector this to point to their own tables (in RAM) and thus redefine characters 80H–0FFH. Thus, you could replace character 128 with an alien, character 129 with a spaceship, and so forth. Or you could replace the standard characters with foreign language characters or special scientific symbols relevant to your programs. However, you must be in a graphics mode to use these new symbols; and the use of redefined character sets is a complex subject, better suited to a book devoted to games and graphics or an advanced programmer's manual.

BIOS Interrupt Vectors—Summary Table

In these pages we have covered the most useful BIOS interrupts. You will find that INT 10H and INT 16H are the two most frequently used routines in BIOS (and thus we have discussed them at some length). The other routines are generally of less use. Enough has been said about them here, however, to allow you to understand what is available to you. Further information can, in many cases, be obtained from the commented BIOS listing in the *Technical Reference Manual.* Serious machine language programmers would do well to acquire a copy of this manual. Separate versions exist for the PC, the PC/XT, and the PCjr.

Table 12-11. BIOS Interrupt Vectors

Interrupt vectors listed where identical in PC/XT/jr

Int Num	Name of Routine	DOS or BIOS
8088 predefined interrupts		
0	divide overflow	DOS (IRET)
1	single-step	DOS (IRET)
2	non-maskable	BIOS
3	breakpoint	DOS (IRET)
4	overflow	DOS (IRET)
BIOS interrupts		
5	print screen	BIOS (F000:FF54)
6–7	reserved	BIOS
External 8259A interrupts		
8	8253 clock tick	BIOS (F000:FEA5)
9	keyboard interrupt	BIOS
A–D	reserved	BIOS
E	disk error	BIOS (F000:EF57)
Standard BIOS interrupts		
10	video handler	BIOS
11	equipment determination	BIOS (F000:F84D)
12	memory size determination	BIOS (F000:F841)
13	disk I/O	BIOS (F000:EC59)
14	RS-232 I/O (serial port)	BIOS (F000:E739)
15	cassette I/O	BIOS (F000:F859)
16	keyboard I/O	BIOS
17	printer I/O	BIOS (F000:EFD2)
18	BASIC start vector	BIOS (F600:0000)
19	boot-strap loader	BIOS
1A	time-of-day	BIOS
1B	user keyboard break	DOS (IRET)
1C	user clock interrupt	BIOS (IRET)
1D	video parameters table	BIOS (F000:F0A4)
1E	disk parameters table	DOS (data)
1F	characters 80H–0FFH	BIOS (data)

Interrupt vectors for the unlisted entries can be found by using
DEBUG and examining 0000:0000 through 0000:03FF, but IBM
discourages using ROM addresses directly in your programs.
Note that the BASIC start vector for the PCjr refers to the Cassette BASIC; INT 18H for the Junior's Cartridge BASIC points
to E800:0177.

Program 12-1. Line Draw Procedure

```
video       equ    10h                    ;video I/O interrupt
d_write     equ    12                     ;write dot function

; Line draw procedure
;
; Input --    CX,BL holds X,Y for start of line
;             DX,BH holds X,Y for end of line
;             AL holds palette register to draw line in
;                  0 or 1   for 2-color modes
;                  0 - 3    for 4-color modes
;                  0 - 15   for 16-color modes
;             if high bit of AL set (80H), line will XOR
; Output --   all registers preserved (flags altered)

line        proc   near
            push   ax                     ;save all registers
            push   bx
            push   cx
            push   dx
            push   si
            push   di
            push   bp

; establish the parameters necessary to draw the line:
; AL = color of dot (unchanged since program entry)
```

```
; CX = current dot's x-position (as for write dot function)
; DX = current dot's y-position
; BP = the longer of delta-x, delta-y (for x-, y-incrementing)
; SI = holder for x-incrementing (init. = BP/2), count-up reg.
; DI = holder for y-incrementing (init. = BP/2)
; BX = loop counter (initialize to BP + 1)
;
        push cx                 ;save start position
        push bx                 ; (temporarily)
        mov cs:x_inc+2,-1       ;default: sub 1 from x-position
        sub cx,dx               ;put x-length in CX
        jae x_pos               ;if CX>=DX, CX is positive
        neg cx                  ; else let CX = abs(CX)
x_pos:  neg cs:x_inc+2          ; and let x-position add = 1
        mov cs:x_add+2,cx       ;save x-length at ADD CX,nnnn
        mov cs:y_inc+2,-1       ;default: sub 1 from y-position
        sub bl,bh               ;put y-length in BX
        jae y_pos               ;if BL>=BH, BL is positive
        neg bl                  ; else let BL = abs(BL)
y_pos:  neg cs:y_inc+2          ; and let y-position add = 1
        mov bh,0                ;let BX = BL
        mov cs:y_add+2,bx       ;save y-length at ADD DX,nnnn
        cmp cx,bx               ;longer in CX, shorter in BX
        ja set_bp               ; if CX is above, fine
        mov cx,bx               ; else put BX into CX for BP
set_bp: mov bp,cx               ;BP holds longer length
        pop bx                  ;CX,DX holds pixel X,Y
```

```
        pop  cx               ; CX already init. correctly...
        mov  dl,bl            ; ...now let DX = BL
        mov  dh,0             ; (zero high byte)
        mov  bx,bp            ;BX holds iterations counter
        inc  bx               ; (let BX = BP + 1)
        shr  bp,1             ;init. SI and DI to BP/2
        mov  si,bp            ;SI holds x increment count
        mov  di,bp            ;DI holds y increment count

; handle drawing the line
; write dot function needs (CX,DX) = dot X,Y and (AL) = color
;
draw_line_loop:
        mov  ah,d_write       ;write dot function
        int  video            ; (note AL is preserved)
x_add   label word
        add  si,0ffffh        ;self-modifying 0ffffh
        cmp  si,bp            ;test for overflow
        jb   near ptr y_add   ; no
        sub  si,bp            ; yes- back up x counter
x_inc   label word           ; (self-modifying code)
        add  cx,0ffffh        ; - change x-position
y_add   label word
        add  di,0ffffh        ;also self-modifying
        cmp  di,bp            ;test for overflow
        jb   end_ck           ; no
        sub  di,bp            ; yes- back up y counter
```

229

```
y_inc    label word        ;      (self-modifying code)
         add dx,0ffffh     ;    - change y-position
end_ck:  dec bx            ;next loop
         jnz draw_line_loop ; jump back if not done
;
         pop bp            ;restore all altered registers
         pop di
         pop si
         pop dx
         pop cx
         pop bx
         pop ax
         ret               ;return to caller
line     endp              ;end of LINE procedure
```

13

The DOS Function Interrupt

In the last chapter we discussed the entire range of BIOS interrupts. In this chapter, by contrast, we will focus our attention entirely on one interrupt: the DOS function interrupt, 21H. This single interrupt routine adds enormously to the power of your programs, allowing advanced file-handling, directory control, memory management, and an enormous variety of other functions. There are a variety of other DOS interrupts, summarized in Table 13-1. Most of these, however, will not be discussed here; we'll concentrate our discussion on INT 21H, the DOS function interrupt.

Table 13-1. DOS Interrupts

INT 20H   terminate program
INT 21H   the DOS function call
INT 22H   address for program termination
INT 23H   Ctrl-Break exit address
INT 24H   critical error handler
INT 25H   absolute disk read
INT 26H   absolute disk write
INT 27H   terminate but stay resident

Those curious about the other DOS interrupts can consult DOS 2.00's DOS manual or *DOS 2.10's Technical Reference Manual* (in this chapter, when we refer to the DOS manual, DOS 2.10 users should substitute the *DOS Technical Reference Manual*).

Like BIOS, each function is selected by placing its number in AH. The DOS manual groups these functions into seven broad categories, each including a wide variety of functions. Table 13-2 outlines these categories. Since we will be referring to the DOS functions by their hexadecimal number throughout this chapter, the table below lists the interrupt numbers in hex.

DOS 1.10 users should note that only function numbers 0H through 2EH are available; the others are new to DOS 2.00.

Table 13-2. DOS Breakdown of Functions (in Hex)

0–C	traditional character device I/O
D–24, 27–29	traditional file management group
25–26, 2A–2E	traditional nondevice functions
2F–38, 4C–57	extended function group
39–3B, 47	directory group
3C–46	extended file management group
48–4B	extended memory management group

A list of the DOS functions discussed in this book can be found at the end of this chapter.

Note that all DOS function calls, like BIOS interrupt calls, preserve the registers, unless information is returned in them. AX is sometimes preserved, and sometimes not, depending on the particular function.

Character Device I/O Functions

These functions provide support for those devices which operate on a character-by-character basis, like the screen, the keyboard, or the printer. Most of these functions are carried over to MS-DOS from CP/M. The main group in this category is those functions which deal with the screen and keyboard (together, the console). Also included in this group are the Asynchronous Communications Adapter (modem) support functions, which we won't discuss, and the printer function, which we will.

Redirection of Input and Output with DOS 2.00 and Above

In DOS 2.00 and 2.10, every reference to the keyboard actually means the *standard input device*, and every reference to the screen means the *standard output device*. These names are used because DOS 2.00 has the ability to redirect the normal input and output to disk files instead of to the keyboard and screen. So you can write a DOS-standard file containing all your replies to a program that normally accepts keyboard input. Here we'll use DEBUG as an example:

A>DEBUG < INPUT.FIL

This would *pipe* the contents of INPUT.FIL to DEBUG in lieu of normal keyboard input. The parallel ability to send all of DEBUG's output to OUTPUT.FIL (continuing our example) is also allowed:

A>DEBUG > OUTPUT.FIL

Both can be used at once:

A>DEBUG < INPUT.FIL > OUTPUT.FIL

Furthermore, one program's output can serve as another program's input, using the vertical bar character:

A>PROGRAM1 ¦ PROGRAM2

In this case, all of PROGRAM1's output would become PROGRAM2's input. For more information, see the DOS 2.00 manual; but, for the moment, bear in mind that all these DOS functions can be piped—and remember that BIOS functions can't be. DOS 1.10 users need not concern themselves with piping, since DOS 1.10 doesn't allow for it.

The other unique feature supported by DOS is the printer echo feature. The Echo key (Ctrl-PrtSc on the PC and PC/XT, and Fn-Echo on the Junior) is used to turn this feature on and off. When printer echo is turned on, all output to the screen (for DOS 2.00, the standard output device) will be echoed to the printer. This can be a very useful feature for keeping documented copies of a program's output. For example, you could copy a DEBUG Unassembly to printer simply by typing Ctrl-PrtSc, followed by the U command.

Keyboard Input Functions

In the last chapter we discussed the BIOS keyboard Input command, which allows a key to be read from the keyboard (as ASCII and a scan code). The DOS keyboard input functions add a variety of additional features to this simple BIOS Input command. However, the DOS functions don't handle extended codes well. (Extended codes were discussed in the last chapter.) If the user presses an extended key (such as cursor left), the DOS input routines return 0, and you must call the routine again to get the distinguishing scan code.

Keyboard Input (AH = 1). This DOS command works somewhat like the BIOS Input command; it waits for a key to be pressed and then returns its ASCII code to AL. However, this function also echoes keys to the screen as they are pressed, thus simplifying the programmer's job. Furthermore, function 1 handles Ctrl Break and Ctrl-PrtSc apart from usual keys. If your program uses this function, the user can press Ctrl-Break to return directly to the DOS prompt (aborting from your program), and Ctrl-PrtSc to turn the DOS printer echo feature on and off.

One problem with function 1 is that any extended codes will be printed on the screen, which can be very awkward. As a rule, this function should be avoided if extended codes are to be used.

Console Input Without Echo (AH = 8). Identical to function 1 above, except that this function does not echo back to the screen. This can be useful for "Hit any key" messages, where you don't want random characters to be echoed to the screen. It can also be useful for input routines that are meant to handle extended codes, since DOS doesn't automatically echo the key to the screen.

Direct Console Input (AH = 7). This function is like function 8 above. However, not only does it not echo the character to the screen, it also doesn't handle Ctrl-Break or Ctrl-PrtSc separately. Consequently, the user can't abort back to DOS with this function, nor can he or she turn printer echo on (or off).

Direct Console I/O (AH = 6). A bit more complex, this function neither echoes input back to the screen, nor does it check for Ctrl-Break or Ctrl-PrtSc. Furthermore, this function can handle both input and output. To use it for input, DL must hold FFH (255 decimal). However, rather than waiting for a key to be pressed, this function always returns to the calling program immediately. If a key has been struck, the zero flag will indicate "not zero" and AL will hold the input character's ASCII code. If no key has been struck, the zero flag will return reading 0.

This function can be useful for games in which the keyboard must be checked each turn to see whether a key has been struck. Rather than using BIOS once to check the keyboard status, then again to read the character, you can simply call this function.

If DL holds any value other than FFH, the contents of DL are printed to the screen. We'll discuss the output routines below.

Check Keyboard Status (AH = B hex). This routine checks to see if a character is available from the keyboard. If one is, AL will hold FFH on return. If not, AL will hold 0. Note that this function, like functions 1 and 8 above, makes special checks for Ctrl-Break and Ctrl-PrtSc.

Buffered Keyboard Input (AH = A hex). Similar to BASIC's INPUT statement, this function, rather than returning one character at a time, reads in a whole string of edited characters from the keyboard. To call this function, DS:DX must point to a special *input buffer.* Then, when INT 21H is called, DOS reads characters from the keyboard into the buffer. A final Enter (ASCII 13) from the keyboard marks the end of the input. Here's how the buffer is set up:

Byte 0 This byte contains the maximum number of characters the buffer can hold (including the final Enter). Byte 0 obviously can't hold zero.

Byte 1 On return from the function, DOS loads this byte with the number of characters entered. DOS, inconsistent as always, sets this byte to the number of characters read, excluding the ASCII 13 (Enter).

Byte 2 Starting with this byte, you must have a buffer of the length specified in byte 0.

When the buffer fills to one less than the maximum number of characters (in byte 0), further characters are ignored, and DOS sounds the bell each time a new key is struck. The only character that can be read into the last byte is an Enter. You can, of course, input fewer characters than requested; this will be reflected in byte 1 on return. Here's a program fragment that reads data into a buffer, then loads AL with the first byte of the string. (Note the use of the DUP command below. This command DUPlicates what's inside the parentheses however many times requested. See Chapter 14 for a discussion of DUP.)

```
... in the current data segment
BUFFER  DB 10,?,10 DUP(' ')       ;the DOS input buffer

... in the code segment
        MOV DX,OFFSET BUFFER   ;set DS:DX to buffer address
        MOV AH,0AH             ;DOS function: input string
        INT 21H               ;call DOS function interrupt
        MOV AL,BUFFER+2        ;get first byte of text
```

This function often proves useful for entering filenames, for entering data for a data base program, for entering numeric values (which must be converted to binary), and the like.

Clear Buffer and Call Function (AH = C). This routine first clears the keyboard buffer, then calls one of the other routines described above. To use this option, place 0CH in AH, and one of the other function numbers in AL (only 1, 6, 7, 8, and A allowed). Usually this function is used in conjunction with some message that must be read and acknowledged. Since this routine clears the buffer of any previously typed characters, the user is forced to read any messages previously printed before pressing a key and going on.

Screen Output Functions

We continue our discussion of the use of INT 21H with functions that allow printing to the screen.

Display Output (AH = 2). The counterpart of function 1 above, this function prints the character in DL (not AL) on the screen. It also checks for Break and Echo.

There is one subtle difference between this function and the BIOS teletype function, which we discussed in the last chapter. With BIOS, you can't use the Tab character, ASCII 9; all you get is a graphics character. The DOS function handles the Tab character specially by advancing the cursor to the next tab-column (tabs are set every eight characters).

Direct Console I/O (AH = 6). We discussed this function above. As you may recall, neither Break nor Echo is checked when this function is called. Furthermore, direct console I/O does not perform any Tab expansion, nor does it echo to the printer. However, it will pipe characters to a disk file, under DOS 2.00 and above. To use this function, place the desired character in DL (any character except 255).

Print String (AH = 9). One of the more useful of the DOS console functions, Print String, unlike the previous functions (which print one character at a time), will print an entire string with one function call. To use the function, DS:DX must hold the address of the character string. Oddly (a relic from CP/M), the string must be terminated with a dollar sign ($). Below is an example of how to use this function; there are more examples in the sample DOS program, "DUMP.ASM," in "Sample Programs," Chapter 16. Notice that we use the assembler's OFFSET command to get the address of the start of the string, rather than the contents of the string's first byte.

... in the current data segment
HIT_KEY DB 'Hit any key to begin the program.',13,10,'$'
GET_DISK DB 'Please put your disk in drive A.',13,10,'$'

... in the code segment
```
MOV DX,OFFSET HIT_KEY      ;string's address in DS:DX
MOV AH,9                   ;the print-string function
INT 21H
MOV AH,C                   ;clear buffer and...
MOV AL,8                   ;wait for a key to be struck
INT 21H
MOV DX,OFFSET GET_DISK     ;another string's address
MOV AH,9                   ;the print-string function
INT 21H
```

As you can see, we used the Clear Buffer function, so that the user can't press a key before the program asks him to. Also, note that we used DOS function 8 above (MOV AL,8), not function 1, since we didn't want whatever character was struck to be echoed.

The Printer Function (AH = 5)
This function simply outputs the character in DL to the standard printer device (printer number 0, if you have more than one). As a rule, however, you should use the BIOS printer interrupt (INT 17H) rather than DOS. Function 5 is included in DOS for CP/M compatibility; the printer interrupt, INT 17H, is much more powerful, allowing for multiple printers as well as printer error-checking.

DOS 2.00 File Handling
In this section, we will discuss how to handle files with INT 21H and the newer versions of DOS (2.00 and 2.10). Many of the functions have counterparts in the older DOS 1.10 disk file functions. However, the new functions are, as a rule, simpler and more powerful. Of course, if you're writing a program that must be used both with DOS 2.00 and DOS 1.10, you'll have to use the older file-handling functions.

DOS 2.00 File-Handling Conventions
Handles. DOS 2.00 uses a system of file handles to keep track of all the files that are open. Whenever you open an

existing file or create a new file, DOS assigns a unique *handle*, from 0 to 65,535, to the file. Once this is done, you can read or write to a particular file just by specifying its handle. DOS takes care of the rest. DOS predefines a few handles for your use; these handles are always set up, and no special files have to be opened.

0 standard input device (input can be redirected)
1 standard output device (output can be redirected)
2 standard error output device (always goes to screen)
3 standard auxiliary device (the serial port/modem)
4 standard printer device (printer number 0)

Thus, the first file that your program opens will most likely have a handle of 5, and subsequent files will have higher numbers.

ASCIIZ. You'll find that several of the new DOS functions accept a simple string as a filename. The older version of DOS requires a specific format for the filename. DOS 2.00 accepts a filename just as you would type it at the keyboard, including a drive specifier (such as B:), a directory path (such as \LEVEL1\LEVEL2\), and, of course, a filename (such as FILE1.MSS). The only condition DOS puts on this name is that it must end with an ASCII 0. So, to open, create, delete, or rename a file (for example), you might specify a name like this:

FILE_NAME DB 'B:\WORD\WP\TEST.MSS',0

DOS refers to this sort of string as an *ASCIIZ* string (the Z for the zero byte at the end). Remember, only the filename itself is required; the drive number, the path, and the extension need not be specified if they don't apply.

Errors. Many of the functions can return an error code. On return from these functions, the carry flag will indicate whether or not an error occurred. If the carry flag is clear, the operation was successful. If the carry flag is set, however, there was an error, and AX holds the error code. Only the extended functions return specific error numbers in this fashion. As we discuss each function below, we will note which errors it can potentially return to the calling program. Table 13-3 contains a complete list of the possible error numbers.

Table 13-3. Error Numbers for Extended Functions

1 invalid function number
2 file not found
3 path not found
4 too many open files (no handles left)
5 access denied (general error)
6 invalid handle
7 memory control blocks destroyed
8 insufficient memory
9 invalid memory block address
10 invalid environment
11 invalid format
12 invalid access code
13 invalid data
15 invalid drive was specified
16 attempted to remove the current directory
17 not same device
18 no more files

As a rule, you won't have to worry about errors 7 through 13, which refer to the advanced, extended memory management functions.

DOS 2.00 File-Handling Functions

Open a File (AH = 3D). This call is used to open an already existing file. The name (an ASCIIZ string) must be pointed to by DS:DX, and AL must contain the access code:

AL = 0 file is opened for reading
AL = 1 file is opened for writing
AL = 2 file is opened for both reading and writing

When DOS returns, AX will hold the new handle for the file. This handle should be saved and used for all subsequent reading and writing to the file. If the carry flag is set on return, AX will hold the error number (2, 4, 5, or 12). This function can open any normal or hidden file (like IBMBIO.COM on system disks). It's also possible to open a file to a device (printer 2, for example), a technique best left to advanced programmers.

Create a File (AH = 3C). This call will create a new file in the appropriate directory, or truncate an existing file to zero length, in preparation for writing data to it. To create a file, DS:DX should point to its ASCIIZ name, and CX should hold the file attribute, which is bitwise significant (each bit handles a different function). Normally you will set CX to 0.

bit 0 mark file as read only
bit 1 mark file as hidden
bit 2 mark file as system

Bits 3 and 4 are used by the system to mark the volume name and a subdirectory, respectively.

On return from this function, AX holds the handle for the file, or the error code (3, 4, or 5), depending on the carry flag. Note that error 5, Access Denied, means that you are either trying to truncate a read-only file, or that the directory is full. If the routine is successful, the file is created with a read/write access code (see the Open File function, above).

Close a File (AH = 3E). To close a file, put the file's handle in BX, and call this function. The only possible error you can get (in AX) is number 6, Invalid Handle. It's necessary to close an output file when you're finished so that all the data is written to disk. It's also a good idea to close input files, both for readability and to avoid overloading DOS.

Read from a File (AH = 3F). Use this function to read data from a file that you've opened or created. BX must contain the handle, DS:DX must point to a buffer to hold the data being read, and CX must hold the number of bytes to read. On return, if there was no error, AX holds the number of bytes actually read. If AX is 0, you tried to read past the end of the file. Possible error returns are 5 and 6. This call can also read from devices like the keyboard. If you set BX to 0 (the handle for the standard input device), calling this function will read characters from the keyboard, somewhat like the input function (number A).

Write to a File (AH = 40H). The parameters for writing are the same as for reading. BX holds the handle, DS:DX points to the data to write, and CX holds the number of bytes to write. On return, AX will hold the number of bytes actually written. Note that if AX does not equal CX on return, some error has occurred (the usual cause is a full disk). Possible error returns in AX are 5 and 6. Remember, you can use this call to write to a device, such as the screen or a printer, by using a predefined handle.

Delete a File (AH = 41H). On entry, DS:DX holds the address of the ASCIIZ name of the file to be deleted. The name must not have any global filename characters in it, the asterisk (*) or question mark (?). Error returns from this function are 2 and 5. Note that DOS 1.10 traditional file handling is capable of deleting more than one file at a time, using global filename characters, so you may find that DOS 1.10 can be more useful sometimes.

Rename a File (AH = 56H). To use this function, DS:DX points to the current name of the file; ES:DI points to the file's new name. Both names, of course, are ASCIIZ. The drives specified must be the same, but you can specify different directory paths, allowing the file to be moved from one directory to another and renamed in the process. Error returns are 3, 5, and 17. Again, note that DOS 1.10 can handle multiple file renaming.

Get Disk Free Space (AH = 36H). To use this call, DL must hold the drive: 0 = default, 1 = A:, 2 = B:, and so forth. On return, AX holds FFFFH if the specified drive number was invalid. Otherwise, the registers will be set as follows:

BX the number of available clusters
DX the total number of clusters on the disk
CX the number of bytes per sector (usually 512)
AX the number of sectors per cluster (one or two)

To get the number of bytes remaining on the disk, you have to multiply BX by AX, and then again by CX.

Other DOS Functions

There are a wide variety of other new DOS 2.00 disk functions that we'll just summarize here.

- When dealing with files, you can change your position within the file with function 42H, and can change the file attribute with function 43H. DOS also allows you to scan through a directory searching for filenames that match a global filename (with * and ?). The calls to do this are 4E and 4F for DOS 2.00, and 11H and 12H for DOS 1.10. It's also possible to set and retrieve a file's date and time with function 57.
- Functions 39H through 3BH allow you to handle subdirectories just as do the DOS commands MKDIR (make directory), RMDIR (remove directory), and CHDIR (change directory). You can also have DOS create an ASCIIZ string

containing the full path name of the current directory, using function 47H.

• One very powerful DOS function, 44H, allows you to read and write data, get and set information, and get various status flags for any file or device.

Complete descriptions of all these commands are in the DOS manual. For most normal file-handling uses, however, the functions described in the text will be more than sufficient.

DOS 1.10 File Handling

DOS 1.10's handling of files is more complex and harder to understand than DOS 2.00's. This is understandable, since DOS 1.10 was designed in part for compatibility with the much older CP/M-based systems. Thus, the DOS designers were constrained to use conventions already growing cumbersome at the time DOS 1.10 was written. However, even DOS 2.00 users may find DOS 1.10 useful from time to time (especially for deleting or renaming files).

DOS 1.10 File Control Blocks

Standard FCBs. All file handling is done not with simple ASCIIZ names, but rather with the more complex *file control blocks* (usually referred to as FCBs) that are traditional from CP/M. Each file control block represents one file, and all the data necessary to handle the file is stored with the 37 bytes of the FCB. DOS sets up the file control blocks as shown in Table 13-4.

Table 13-4. FCB Organization

Offset	Size	Description
0	1 byte	drive number (0 = default, 1 = A:, 2 = B:, etc.)
1	8 bytes	filename (padded on the left with spaces)
9	3 bytes	filename extension (also padded with spaces)
12	1 word	current block number (a block is 128 records)
14	1 word	size of one record (normally 128 bytes)
16	2 words	file size, in bytes
20	1 word	date of file, holding year, month, and date
22	10 bytes	<reserved for system use>
32	1 byte	current record (0–127) within block
33	2 words	random file's record number (random files only)

The only information that usually need concern you is the filename (the first 12 bytes), as well as the size of one record (at offset 16 from the start of the FCB), and the current record number (at offset 32). The rest is filled in by DOS.

DOS Initialization of the Program Segment Prefix

Although using this *file control block* may sound extremely cumbersome, in fact there are a few aspects of DOS that make using it easier than you might expect. One of these aspects, a function call to convert a standard human-readable filename to FCB form, is discussed below (the Parse Filename function). The other aspect necessitates a slight diversion into the program loading and initializing techniques of DOS.

The Program Segment Prefix. When any program is loaded, a new segment is assigned to it (the Program Segment). However, the program doesn't start at the beginning of this segment; the first 100H bytes are used by DOS for a variety of purposes. These first 256 bytes are called the Program Segment Prefix, or PSP for short. To accommodate this prefix, .EXE files start off with their code segment 100H above the Program Segment. The data and extra segments, however, point to the Program Segment when your program begins. A large variety of DOS information is placed in the PSP, some important, some advanced and technical. Of particular interest are the following areas within the PSP:

offset 0   The location of an INT 20H command, which is used to end the program.
offset 5CH An FCB area, set up by DOS (filename 1).
offset 6CH Another FCB area set up by DOS (filename 2).
offset 80H The "unformatted parameter area" and default disk transfer area (to be explained).

DOS Default FCBs. Notice that DOS automatically creates an FCB at offset 5CH. This FCB contains the drive, name, and extension of any filename specified after the program name itself. For example, when we invoke DEBUG with PROGRAM.EXE:

A>DEBUG PROGRAM.EXE

DOS creates an FCB at DS:5CH with the name PROGRAM.EXE. In this case, the drive number byte is set to 0 (default). DEBUG can now open the file without any further difficulty. The second FCB area, starting at 6CH, holds the name of the second file that was specified on the initial command line (in the example above we specified only one file). However, since this second FCB area is in the middle of the first one, if you open FCB 1 you'll obliterate FCB 2. It's necessary to move FCB 2 (the formatted name and drive number in particular) somewhere safe before opening FCB 1.

The unformatted parameter area. Yet another area holds the actual characters specified on the command line after the program name. This area, the unformatted parameter area, is located at 80H in the Program Segment Prefix. DOS places anything that you typed after the filename itself in this area.

offset 80H   The number of characters specified, not including the final Enter (ASCII 13).

offset 81H   The characters themselves, terminated with ASCII 13.

So, if you typed

A>MASM TEST.ASM,,,;

the 13 characters (space) TEST.ASM,,; and Enter (ASCII 13) would appear, starting at 81H, and 80H would hold the number 12. DOS 2.00 users should note that piping is transparent to your program, so you'll never see any of the piping characters, <, >, or ¦, nor the filenames that accompany them.

Remember, even programs that don't use disk files at all can read parameters from the unformatted parameter area.

The disk transfer area. The 128 bytes at offset 80H have an additional use. DOS normally uses this area as the *disk transfer area*, or DTA, for DOS 1.10 file handling. In DOS 2.00, you specify the area you wish to read and write disk data to in DS:DX. With DOS 1.10 function calls, by contrast, you must set the address of the disk buffer area (the DTA) with a separate function call. Of course, you can also use the initial DOS DTA default, which is the 128-byte buffer at offset 80H relative to the current DS.

If you use the default FCB at 5CH and the default DTA at 80H, the last byte of the FCB will be overwritten by disk data. However, this is only of significance for random file handling.

We'll discuss the function calls to set the DTA's address below, as well as the technique to set its length. Note that the same DTA is used for all your files, unless you explicitly change it—which you must do if you want to read two files at the same time.

The DOS 1.10 File-Handling Functions

Parse Filename (AH = 29H). This command is very useful if filenames are to be entered from the keyboard. Filenames in an FCB must appear without the usual period between filename and extension, and they must be padded with spaces. Since most people don't enter filenames that way, the *parse filename* routine allows a filename to be *parsed*, or translated, into the format used in an FCB. However, since DOS 1.10 does not allow subdirectories, the parse function does not allow any path names.

To use this command, DS:SI must point to the human-readable version of the filename, and ES:DI must point to the FCB to be filled in. AL is a command byte, bitwise significant:

bit 0 (01)   ignore leading separators (see below)
bit 1 (02)   don't change drive number if drive not specified
bit 2 (04)   don't change filename if filename not specified
bit 3 (08)   don't change extension if extension not specified
bits 4-7   (unused)

The filename separators are (space) (Tab) : . ; , = and +. Filename terminators include all the separators plus   < > ¦ / " [ ] and control characters, including Enter.

Normally, you'll be setting AL = 1, to make the parse routine ignore any initial spaces and so forth. Bits 1–3 are more specialized and normally less useful; they allow parts of the filename (drive, filename, extension) to be already specified at ES:DI, and only have certain parts of it changed. Note that the parse function handles changing the * characters into a string of ? characters.

AL is returned with one of the following:
01 if the ? or * appeared in the filename extension
FF if the drive specifier is invalid
00 drive number valid, no global characters

DS:SI returns pointing to the first character after the filename and ES:DI points to the first byte of the formatted FCB. If no filename was specified, ES:DI+1 will contain a space.

Remember, if filename(s) were specified on the command line, the FCBs at 5C and 6C in the PSP are already formatted, and only need to be opened (though one of the FCBs would have to be moved if you were going to use both of them).

Open File (AH = F). On entry, DS:DX points to an FCB. If the specified file is found, AL will hold 0 on return; otherwise, AL will hold FFH. If the file is found, the FCB will be filled in with the special system data. If no drive was specified (the default drive assumed), DOS replaces it with the actual drive used. However, for some reason DOS does not initialize the current record (the byte at offset 32). It is the programmer's responsibility to set it to 0 before doing any reading or writing.

Create File (AH = 16H). This call works just like the open file call. AL returns 0 if the file was created successfully (either a new file created or an old one set to zero length). If AL returns FFH, there wasn't enough room in the directory.

Close File (AH = 10H). On entry, DS:DX points to the FCB of an already opened file. On exit, AL holds 0 if the file has been properly closed; if the disk has been changed (and thus the file can't be closed), AL returns FFH.

Set Disk Transfer Address (AH = 1A). This call simply puts the DTA at the address in DS:DX. Remember, for multiple files you will have to change the DTA for each file. Use this call to select the appropriate DTA before reading or writing the file's data. This function call takes the place of the (DS:DX) parameter required for DOS 2.00 reads and writes.

To change the size of the DTA from the initial DOS default of 80H, you have to write the appropriate size, as a word value, into offset 14 in the FCB. This is the equivalent of the (CX) parameter for DOS 2.00 reads and writes. Note that you must always set the size *after* opening the file. Remember that you must set the record size in each FCB that uses a given DTA. To set the DTA size to 512 bytes in an example FCB, named FCB_1, do the following:

MOV FCB_1+14, 512 ;address of record size in FCB

The new size of the DTA cannot be larger than the space remaining in its segment. Furthermore, we recommend that you keep the DTA to 512 bytes or less, or DOS may have difficulty reading the file.

Read Sequential Data (AH = 14H). DS:DX must point to the FCB on entry. This call reads the next record from the file and puts it in the DTA. All the FCB variables are updated to point to the next record in the file. AL returns the status:

0   the transfer was completed successfully
1   no more data in the record (end of file)
2   not enough room in the DTA segment to read one record
3   only a partial record read (end of file)

Write Sequential Data (AH = 15H). DS:DX points to the FCB. The information in the DTA is written out to disk. AL returns the status of the operation as follows:

0   transfer completed successfully
1   diskette is full
2   specified DTA size larger than room left in segment

Delete Files (AH = 13H). DS:DX points to an FCB containing the name of the file to be deleted. Multiple entries can be deleted by using global filename characters. If no files are deleted, AL returns FFH; otherwise, it returns 0. Deleting multiple files is not allowed with the DOS 2.00 file-handling functions, so DOS 2.00 users may wish to use this function call on certain occasions.

Rename Files (AH = 17H). For this function, DS:DX points to a modified FCB. The first 12 bytes of the FCB contain the original name, with or without global filename characters. The new name appears at offset 17 within the FCB. Every filename in the directory that matches the first name in the FCB is changed to the second. If ?'s appear in the second name, DOS doesn't change the corresponding character in the filename. AL returns FFH if no match is found, or if the new filename already exists in the current directory; otherwise, AL returns 0.

Get File Size (AH = 23H). One further call can be of some use for DOS 1.10 file handling. To find the file size of a file, set up an FCB, and as usual, point to it with DS:DX. If the specified file isn't found, this function returns FFH in AL; otherwise, 0 is returned. The size of the file is returned in the two words at offset 33–36, in terms of the FCB's record size. You can set the record size (at offset 14) to one byte (MOV FCB_1 + 14,1) to get the length in bytes, or to the length of your DTA to get the number of records (rounded up).

There are a number of other DOS 1.10 disk functions (which can, of course, be used with all versions of DOS). Some of the more useful ones allow you to select or retrieve the current default drive number (functions E and 19H). Also included for DOS 1.10 file handling are routines to read and write random records to a file, or to write and read an entire block of records. You can also retrieve the allocation table information from any disk (including the disk identification byte, the number of clusters, the number of sectors per cluster, and the number of bytes per sector). This parallels the DOS 2.00 Disk Size function.

More DOS Functions Using INT 21H

In the last chapter we discussed the time-of-day interrupt, INT 1AH. We said that there is a method which is often superior for reading the time, and we will describe it here.

Time and Date Handling

Get/Set Date (AH = 2A, 2B). The Get Date function, AH = 2AH, returns information on the year, month, and day. On return from this function, CX and DX are set as follows:

CX holds the year (as a binary number from 1980 to 2099)
DH has the month (1 to 12, January to December)
DL holds the date (1 to 31)

If the time-of-day clock goes past 24 hours, DOS adjusts the date, taking into account the number of days per month and leap years.

The counterpart to this function, for which AH = 2BH, allows you to set the date from within your programs. CX and DX must hold the date, as above. On return, if the date you specified was valid, AL = 0; otherwise, AL = FFH.

Get/Set Time (AH = 2C, 2D). The Get Time function, AH = 2CH, returns the time of day in CX and DX, and the day of the week in AL. Here are the parameters returned:

AL day of the week (0 = Sun, 1 = Mon, etc.) PC DOS 2.10 only
CH hour (0–23)
CL minute (0–59)
DH second (0–59)
DL hundredths of a second (0–99)

Since the time-of-day clock is updated only 18.2 times per second, DL is not, in fact, accurate to within 1/100 second.

The counterpart of this operation is the Set Time function, AH = 2D. To set the time, load CX and DX appropriately. The Set Time function, like the Set Date function, returns AL holding 0 for a valid time or FFH for an invalid time.

Memory-Allocation Functions

A variety of other DOS functions are available. Some of the most powerful DOS functions allow for reallocating portions of memory for various purposes. When your program begins to run, it is allocated all of memory, but there are some DOS functions to change the size of a currently allocated block of memory, to allocate a new block of memory, and to free already allocated memory.

In addition, the very powerful EXEC function call (4BH) allows for loading overlays or for loading and executing another program. (The EXEC function is used in Chapter 10 to load files into BASIC's memory prior to BSAVEing them.) The memory-allocation functions are very useful for advanced programming.

The DOS function interrupt is unquestionably the most powerful single interrupt routine of MS-DOS. The DOS character device I/O functions (keyboard input, screen output, and so forth) are often useful, though the BIOS functions themselves are sometimes best for a job. However, interrupt 21H is useful primarily for its disk- and memory-management functions.

Table 13-5. DOS Functions

(AH) Function Name and Description

Character Device I/O

1   keyboard input (echo, Break/Echo checking)
     output (AL)   = character typed
2   display output, with Break/Echo checking
     input   (DL)   = character to print
5   printer output
     input   (DL)   = character to print
6   direct console I/O (no echo, no wait, no Break/Echo checking)
     input   (DL)   = FFH
     output (ZF)   = 1 if no key was struck
             (ZF)   = 0 and (AL) = character if a key was hit
     input   (DL)   = anything but FFH, character to print
7   direct keyboard input without echo (no echo, no checking)
     output (AL)   = character typed
8   console input without echo (no echo, Break/Echo checking)
     output (AL)   = character typed

9   print string
     input   (DS:DX) = address of string (terminated with $)
A   buffered keyboard input
     input   (DS:DX) = address of DOS input buffer
     output buffer is filled with input line
B   check standard input status
     output (AL)   = 0, no character available
             (AL)   = FF, character waiting
C   clear buffer and invoke a function
     input   (AL)   = 1, 6, 7, 8, A
     in addition to other parameters as appropriate

DOS 2.00 File Handling

36   get disk free space
     input   (DL)   = disk number (0 = default, 1 = A, 2 = B)
     output (AX)   = FFFF if disk number invalid
             (AX)   = number of sectors per cluster
             (BX)   = number of clusters available
             (CX)   = number of bytes per sector
             (DX)   = number of clusters on drive
3C   create a file
     input   (DS:DX) = address of ASCIIZ name of file
             (CX)   = file's attribute
     output (AX)   = handle or error (if CF = 1, AX = error)
3D   open a file
     input   (DS:DX) = address of ASCIIZ name of file
             (AL)   = file access code (0, 1, 2)
     output (AX)   = handle or error
3E   close a file
     input   (BX)   = handle
     output (AX)   = error if CF = 1
3F   read from a file or device
     input   (DS:DX) = address of buffer area
             (BX)   = handle number
             (CX)   = number of bytes to read
     output (AX)   = number of bytes read or error
40   write to a file or device
     input   (DS:DX) = address of buffer area
             (BX)   = handle number
             (CX)   = number of bytes to write
     output (AX)   = number of bytes written or error

41   delete a file
     input   (DS:DX) = address of ASCIIZ name of file
     output (AX)   = error number if CF = 1

56   rename a file
         input   (DS:DX) = address of old ASCIIZ filename
                 (ES:DI)   = address of new ASCIIZ filename
         output (AX)   = error if CF = 1

DOS 1.10 File Handling

F   open file
         input   (DS:DX) = starting address of FCB area
         output (AL)   = 0 if file found, FF if not
10   close file
         input   (DS:DX) = FCB address
         output (AL)   = 0 if file closed, FF if not on disk
13   delete file
         input   (DS:DX) = FCB address
         output (AL)   = FF if no files deleted, 0 otherwise
14   sequential read
         input   (DS:DX) = FCB address
         output (AL)   = 0, 1, 2, 3 depending on read status
15   sequential write
         input   (DS:DX) = FCB address
         output (AL)   = 0, 1, 2, 3 depending on write status
16   create file
         input   (DS:DX) = FCB address
         output (AL)   = 0 if file created, FF if directory full
17   rename file
         input   (DS:DX) = modified FCB address
1A   set disk transfer address (DTA)
         input   (DS:DX) = new DTA address
23   get file size
         input   (DS:DX) = FCB address
         output (AL)   = 0 if file found, FF otherwise
         random record field = number of records in file
29   parse filename
         input   (DS:SI)   = address of command line to parse
                 (ES:DX)   = starting address of area for a new FCB

Time and Date Handling

2A   get date
     output (CX)   = year (1980–2099)
              (DH)   = month (1–12)
              (DL)   = day (1–31)

2B   set date
     input parameters as above for get date
     output (AL)   = 0 for valid date, FF otherwise

2C   get time
     output (CH)   = hours (0–23)
              (CL)   = minutes (0–59)
              (DH)   = seconds (0–59)
              (DL)   = hundredths of seconds (0–99)
              (AL)   = day of the week (0 = Sun), PC DOS 2.10
                    only

2D   set time
     input parameters as above for get time
     output (AL)   = 0 for valid time, FF otherwise

4

Using the
Assembler

14
Basic Assembler Control

This chapter is the first of two introducing the assembly language programmer to the *IBM Macro Assembler.* In previous chapters, you have been introduced to some of the commands, or *pseudo-ops,* used by the assembler. In this section, we will examine the entire range of pseudo-ops used by the assembler, and you will encounter a variety of new commands as well as learning more about the ones you already know.

This chapter was written to describe the features (and flaws) of IBM's *Macro Assembler* Version 1.00. Certain pseudo-ops are defective in this implementation. Version 2.00, released in the fall of 1984, has fixed certain errors (the XOR, SHL, and SHR pseudo-ops work in Version 2.00, for example), and has increased the speed of assembly by a factor of four or five.

We recommend that you read the material in each chapter first, and then use the *Assembler Reference Manual* to review what you have learned. In many cases the manual will tell you more than you want to know; just skip over material that doesn't immediately make sense. Occasionally, we've made a note of an assembler manual error; more often, however, we have simply documented the actual behavior of the assembler, and not made a note of the manual's error.

In this chapter we will discuss the more often used commands of the *Macro Assembler.* The chapter is divided into four sections: program structure commands, arithmetic operators and numeric format, assembler operators, and listing control pseudo-ops. For reference, the pseudo-ops appearing in this chapter are listed in Table 14-1.

Table 14-1. Pseudo-ops

SEGMENT	ENDS	ASSUME
PROC	ENDP	END
EQU	=	DB
DW	DT	DQ
.RADIX	PAGE	TITLE
SUBTTL		

In addition, we will be discussing in this chapter most of the assembler operators, given below in Table 14-2.

Table 14-2. Assembler Operators

DUP	+,−,*,/,MOD	SHL,SHR
relational operators	OFFSET	
SEG	TYPE	SIZE
LENGTH	seg. override	PTR

Program Structure Pseudo-ops

We'll begin by reviewing the pseudo-ops used for structuring programs and data. All of these have been discussed earlier, but here we'll discuss them in a little more detail.

The SEGMENT and ENDS Pseudo-ops

In the sample programs presented in this book, SEGMENT and ENDS have been used primarily for three purposes: setting up an area for data, for code (the actual program), or for the stack. These separate areas are addressed by the DS register, the CS register, and the SS register, respectively. When using string commands, or addressing the screen directly, you've set the ES register to point to the appropriate segment as well.

The SEGMENT command precedes each segment that you set up, and the ENDS pseudo-op serves to mark its end. The format of the SEGMENT command is as follows:

segname **SEGMENT** [*align type*][*combine type*][*'class'*]

(Note that the brackets, here and later, are meant to show that the item is optional. Don't actually put brackets in your program.)

The *segname* (CSEG, DSEG, or what have you) simply identifies the segment you've defined. Each segment must have a legal assembler name. The name serves to identify the

segment for the ASSUME statement or for any segment overrides. Both the ASSUME statement and the use of segment
overrides will be discussed further in this chapter.

The items following SEGMENT are optional; none, all, or
any of them can be specified. The *align type* is usually used
only when linking object modules together, so we won't discuss it here. In our sample programs, the align type is left un-
specified.

The *combine type* is also optional. For most segments you
will be working with, it too is left out. The combine type indicates in what fashion the segment can combine with other
segments of the same name (in other object modules, typically). Leaving this option out means the segment won't be
combined with other segments of the same name in other
modules. For single modules such as the ones we are working
with, it doesn't matter how the segments can be combined, so
generally we leave this option out.

However, there are two common and useful combine
types. The combine type STACK serves to define a segment as
the program stack area. Only one stack segment per program
should be defined. Another useful SEGMENT combine type is
AT expression, which functions somewhat like the DEF SEG
command in BASIC. This combine type tells the assembler to
place the segment at the address specified by an expression (a
segment value, not an absolute address). This option is normally used to locate variables in the interrupt vector area, the
BIOS ROM, the DOS data area, or the screen. You can't actually place data or code in a segment defined with AT expression. The following definition sets up a segment at the
color/graphics screen on the PC series:

SCREEN SEGMENT AT 0B800H
SCREEN ENDS

This is equivalent to the BASIC statement

DEF SEG = &HB800

Finally, the SEGMENT *'class'* name (also optional), specified with single quotes, is used to group segments together
when the program is LINKed. For our purposes, the class
name is useful as a note to the purpose of the segment; thus a
segment named CSEG might be put in the class 'CODE'.

The ENDS pseudo-op is placed at the end of each segment. Its format is simply:

segname **ENDS**

The *segname*, of course, must be the same name as the one specified for the matching SEGMENT command. If a SEGMENT and the following ENDS have different segnames, the assembler will return

0:Block nesting error

Note that one of the more complex data storage pseudo-ops, STRUC, also uses the ENDS command as a terminator, so don't always assume ENDS marks the end of a segment.

The ASSUME Pseudo-op

The ASSUME pseudo-op can, in some ways, be difficult to understand. The usual format for the ASSUME command is

ASSUME *segment register:segment name,segreg:segname* **,etc**

This tells the assembler what to expect from each segment reference. A typical ASSUME command might be

ASSUME CS:CSEG,DS:DSEG,SS:SSEG

where CSEG, DSEG, and SSEG had already been defined by the SEGMENT command.

Without the ASSUME command (or if ASSUME NOTHING has been specified), the computer doesn't know which segment register to use (CS, DS, SS, or ES) when it needs to make a reference to a segment in your program. For the assembler to assemble a MOV from some data in DSEG, it has to know which segment register should be used for DSEG. Normally, DS is used for data, but if ES is the only segment register pointing to DSEG, the assembler has to be informed (with ASSUME ES:DSEG), so it can insert the appropriate segment register override. Similarly, it has to know which segment is being used for the current program area. In other words, whenever you reference a location in a segment, the assembler has to know what segment register to use for that segment.

If you don't tell the assembler what to ASSUME, you have to use a segment override every time you address memory. Often the assembler errors 62 (No or unreachable CS) and 68 (Can't reach with segment reg) indicate some problem with your use of the ASSUME statement (and it's easy to forget the ASSUME command altogether).

However, one irritating problem for programmers is that telling the assembler what to ASSUME doesn't mean that the segment registers will automatically point to the correct segments. When your program begins, DS and ES always point to the Program Segment Prefix (discussed in the DOS Interrupts chapter). So, even if you've told the assembler to ASSUME that DS is to be used for DSEG, your program still has to be responsible for putting the location of DSEG into DS:

MOV AX,DSEG   ;note: MOV DS,DSEG is illegal
MOV DS,AX

The PROC and ENDP Pseudo-ops

PROC (PROCedure) and ENDP surround a section of code in much the same way that SEGMENT and ENDS surround a segment. The PROC command establishes whether a routine is NEAR or FAR for CALLs, JMPs, and RETurns. The format for PROC is

procedure-name **PROC [NEAR]**

or

procedure-name **PROC FAR**

The NEAR attribute is the default for a procedure, so it doesn't need to be specified (as the brackets above indicate). The attribute of the procedure (NEAR or FAR) determines if a RET encountered in the code is a far RETurn (inter segment) or a near RETurn (intra segment). It also sets the type (NEAR or FAR) of the PROC label.

As with SEGMENT, PROC requires an END pseudo-op to mark the end of the procedure. Simply place the ENDP command at the end of the procedure, with the following format:

procedure-name **ENDP**

DOS requires a far RETurn, so the main program is defined as a FAR procedure and the appropriate far return address is pushed onto the stack at the beginning of the program. Therefore, most assembly programs have the following structure:

```
segname   SEGMENT
          ASSUME CS:segname, etc.
program   PROC FAR
          PUSH DS               ;set up far return for CS
          MOV AX,0
```

259

```
        PUSH AX              ;set up IP = 0 for return
... program code...
        RET                  ;pop CS:IP as a far return
program ENDP
segname ENDS
        END program
```

Note that we push DS, not CS, since only DS and ES are guaranteed to point to the Program Segment Prefix, which contains the INT 20H command (discussed in the chapter on MS-DOS interrupts) at location DS:0000. You could simply place an INT 20H at the end of your program, but the far RETurn is standard for the assembler.

By contrast, procedures called from the main program (subroutines) are declared NEAR. Since these subroutines are in the same segment as the main program, the PROC should be NEAR. Sometimes object module subroutines are defined as FAR PROCs in different segments, but as a rule, your subroutines should be NEAR PROCs.

The END Pseudo-op

This command is required at the end of the source program. An optional expression can follow the command:

END [expression]

The expression tells the assembler where the computer should begin executing your program. A typical example is END BEGIN. If you don't use the expression, your program will begin at the beginning of the code segment. But sometimes it's useful to start your program at some other address than the start of the code segment. (For example, if your program has a lengthy section of initialization code, and you need as much data storage space as possible, you can put the initialization code at the end of the program and then overwrite it during the course of the main program.)

Symbols

A label is a name that marks a location in your program code. You have already encountered and used labels many times in your programs. A label is limited to code (you can't define a label with data, for example), and a label is usually used only as the operand of a jump or CALL.

All of the labels must end with a colon. This tells the

assembler that the label should always be used with NEAR commands, thus JMPs and CALLs to those labels will be intra-segment. The exception to the colon rule is the PROC pseudo-op, in which the NEAR or FAR attribute is explicitly stated, and thus using a colon is prohibited.

A FAR attribute means that JMPs and CALLs to that label will specify the segment as well as the offset value. In other words, they will be inter-segment. A label can be FAR only if it is the name of a FAR procedure, or if it has been defined with the LABEL pseudo-op, discussed in the next chapter. FAR labels, however, are not particularly useful for most small assembly language tasks.

Variables are the counterpart to labels. Rather than defining a location in code, they define a location in data. The type of a label is always NEAR or FAR; a variable, by contrast, can have a type of WORD, BYTE, DWORD, or one of the less common types. A variable gets its type from the data pseudo-op it's associated with; for example, a variable with a DB pseudo-op is a BYTE variable. We will discuss the data pseudo-ops in a moment.

SMALL   DB 13,14,15,16   ;SMALL is a BYTE variable
LARGE   DW 1314,1516   ;LARGE is a WORD variable

Remember that a *label* is defined as a symbol with NEAR or FAR type, whereas a *variable* is a symbol with type BYTE, WORD, and the like.

A *constant* is a number without any attribute or type; usually it's just a value. Constants are typically used to replace hard to remember values, such as interrupt function numbers. They're also used for the sake of clarity and documentation. A constant can be defined either with the EQU (equate) pseudo-op, or with the = (equal sign) pseudo-op. Normally, constants are defined with the EQU pseudo-op; the = pseudo-op is ordinarily used for macros and conditionals (advanced programming techniques found in the next chapter). The format for the EQU pseudo-op is

name **EQU** *expression*

The *expression* can be one of five things—a number (a signed or unsigned word), an EQU symbol (if your expression is some other symbol, plus or minus some quantity), an alias (another name for some other symbol), an opcode (thus allowing you to rename 8088 instructions), or text of any kind. The constant *name* can then be used anywhere the expression is valid. But once defined with EQU, it cannot then be redefined. The following are all legitimate uses of the EQU pseudo-op:

VIDEO	**EQU 10H**	;a constant numeric value
BNE	**EQU JNZ**	;an opcode
STACK2	**EQU [BP+6]**	;an index reference (text)
LOCATN	**EQU ES:[DI]**	;a segment prefix and operand (text)
ALIAS_1	**EQU LABEL_1**	;an alias for a symbol
LABEL_2	**EQU LABEL_1+5**	;an EQU symbol
TEXT_1	**EQU WORD PTR [BX]**	;simple text

Now, having defined BNE as EQUal to JNZ, we could legally write:

BNE LABEL_2 ;this would assemble to a JNZ

However, by far the most common use of EQU is for constant numeric values, such as VIDEO above.

Data Storage Commands

In this section we turn to the structure of data. Most of the commands discussed here should be familiar to you from earlier chapters.

Data storage pseudo-ops. The DB (Define Byte) and DW (Define Word) pseudo-ops are the most commonly used data storage commands. The DB command allows you to store byte values. (As you will recall, a byte is any value from 0 to 255 unsigned, including character data, or -128 to 127 signed.) The DW command stores words (values from 0 to 65535 unsigned or -32768 to 32767 signed). The DW command can also be used to store the offset of a variable or label. Most DB and DW areas are used as variables, as we discussed above. The DB pseudo-op gives its associated variable the type BYTE; DW, the type WORD.

There are three other, less common types of data storage pseudo-ops. These include DD, Define Doubleword (type DWORD), which can store values from 0 to almost 4.3 billion. Additionally, DD can store variables and labels in *segment:offset* four-byte form (refer to Chapter 5). The DQ command, Define Quadword, is used for storing quad words (type QWORD), 64 bits long (if you ever need to store values of up to 18 billion billion . . .). The DT pseudo-op, Define Tenbytes, is used for storing 10-byte, 18-digit BCD numbers, type TBYTE (see Chapter 8). Note that with the *Small Assembler*, DD can store only symbol *segment:offset* values, not numbers, and DQ and DT can't be used.

An entry after a data storage pseudo-op can take many forms:

- a simple number or a constant, signed or unsigned. The range of the number depends, of course, on the particular pseudo-op.
- a variable or label. For DW, the symbol's offset is stored; for DD, the full *segment:offset* form. DB, DQ, and DT cannot be used to store variable or symbol addresses.
- a string of ASCII characters, with the DB pseudo-op only. These characters must be enclosed with single or double quotes.
- a question mark, ?, meaning that the assembler places no value there, but reserves that location for use by the program.

All of the following are valid expressions:

NUM_BASE	DB 16	
FILLER	DB ?	;initialize with indeterminate value
NAMES	DB 'STEVE JOHN MARY'	
LARGE_NMS	DW 3498,−4590,20000,0,−32767,10	
OFFSETS	DW FILLER,NAMES,LARGE_NMS	;2-byte offsets here
SEG_OFFS	DD FILLER,NAMES,LARGE_NMS	;4-byte segment:offset form
PI_BCD	DT −314159265357989324	;10-byte BCD format (MASM)
HUGE_NUM	DQ 18446744073709551615	;max. number with DQ (MASM)

Any combination of these forms is legal:

BUFFER   DB 10,?,'

The DUP command. One very useful command for all of the above storage pseudo-ops is the DUP command. In a situation where you would like to initialize a 1000-byte table with the value 73, it's clearly not very practical to type out 1000 DB entries of value 73. Instead, using the DUP command, you can simply specify

DB 1000 DUP(73)

and the assembler will create the appropriate table. The DUP command can be used with any of the data pseudo-ops, and with more than one operand:

```
DW 512 DUP(-5467,993)          ;creates 1024 words
DT 2 DUP(764851298612348971)   ;2 10-byte BCD numbers (MASM)
DD 5 DUP(ADDRESS1,ADDRESS2,ADDRESS3)
                               ;creates 5 copies of three 4-byte
                               addresses
```

The DUP command can be nested:

```
TABLE1   DB 2 DUP(4,2 DUP(2,3),12)
         ;i.e., 4,2,3,2,3,12,4,2,3,2,3,12
TABLE2   DB 10 DUP(16,?,16 DUP(' '))
         ;10 copies of a 16-byte DOS input buffer
```

Two assembler operators are used with DUP: SIZE and LENGTH. These will be discussed later. For some of the more esoteric uses of the DUP command (for example, creating an uninitialized block of data), see your assembler manual.

Arithmetic Operators and Numeric Format

In this section we will discuss the arithmetic operators, such as +, −, /, and *, as well as all the different ways of entering numeric quantities: decimal, hexadecimal, characters, and others.

Arithmetic Operators

The most common of these operators, and the easiest to use and understand, are the standard arithmetic operators, +, −, *, and /. Of these, the addition operator is the most commonly used. So if, using MASM, you had a two-word variable in the data segment:

LONG_WORD DD 12345678H

you could get the first word with a MOV AX,LONG_WORD and the second word with a MOV DX,LONG_WORD+2. Similarly, elements in a table are often accessed with the + operator:

BYTABLE DB 67,68,77

To get the second element, you specify BYTABLE+1.

The subtraction operator is also frequently used: sometimes to make a negative offset (LONG_WORD−2, perhaps), and sometimes to find the offset difference between two variables. For example, if we had these messages in the data area:

MESSAGE_1 DB 'Place disk in drive.
MESSAGE_2 DB 'Thank you!'

the command

MOV CX,MESSAGE_2–MESSAGE_1

would subtract the offset of MESSAGE_1 from that of MESSAGE_2, returning the value into CX; that difference would be the length of MESSAGE_1.

The multiplication (*) and integer division (/) operators are used for a variety of reasons: sometimes to access an element in a table, sometimes simply to create an entry for a constant or data item. One example mentioned above gives the idea:

INCHES_PER_MILE DW 5280*12

What is crucial to bear in mind when using arithmetic operators is that they are calculated when the program is assembled, not when it is executed. So, specifying

MOV AX,TIME/60

would not return the value of TIME divided by 60. In fact, the assembler would return error 42 (Constant expected).

Only in one situation is an arithmetic operator calculated when the program executes: when you use positive or negative offsets to an address, such as MOV AX,[DI+2]. The offset is calculated when the program is executed. See Chapter 6 for a full description of these offsets.

A number of other arithmetic operators are available. Most of these are not used very frequently, so we'll just skim through them. The first of these is MOD. This returns the remainder of an integer division, much as the / operator returns the quotient. The following example should help to make the use of MOD clearer:

PI_QUOT   DW 31416 / 10000   ;this equals 3
PI_REM   DW 31416 MOD 10000   ;this equals 1416

There is another class of arithmetic operators, the logical operators, which consist of the Boolean AND, OR, NOT, and XOR functions. These are used in precisely the same way as the other operators. For example:

COMMAND_BYTE EQU LOW_NYBBLE OR HIGH_NYBBLE

This sets COMMAND_BYTE to the logical OR of LOW_NYBBLE and HIGH_NYBBLE. The NOT operator, however, takes the format NOT value. It's the only arithmetic operator that takes only one operand:

BIT_5_MASK EQU NOT 20H

Remember that these arithmetic operators are quite different from the 8088 opcodes of the same name. These operators are all calculated at the time of assembly; the opcodes are executed at runtime. (Assembler Version 1.00 owners note that the XOR operator doesn't work properly.)

Several other operators do exist. There are the two shift operators, SHL and SHR, but these are defective in Version 1.00 of the assembler, so we won't discuss them here. The final class of operators is the relational operators. These are, however, fairly complex, and not often used. In brief, they are used to compare two operands for greater than, less than, equal, and the like. They return only true (0) or false (0FFFFH). These operators are so obscure that the IBM manual doesn't even discuss them, and we shall follow its lead.

Operator Precedence

One question that users of BASIC and Pascal may ask concerns operator precedence. *Operator precedence* refers to the order in which the computer performs the operators. The concept of precedence should be familiar to users of high-level languages. It means simply that the computer selects the most important operators and calculates them first, rather than performing each operation in left to right order. For example, the expression

14 + 2 * 3

evaluates out to 14 + (2 * 3) = 14 + 6 = 20, since * has a higher precedence than +, not simply to 14 + 2 * 3 = 16 * 3 = 48. However, also like BASIC and Pascal, it is possible to use both parentheses (like this) and square brackets [like this] to establish precedence. For example, to force the expression above to be equal to 48 instead of 20, you would specify

(14 + 2) * 3

The *IBM Assembler Manual* has an extensive precedence list, some of which concerns terms we have not yet discussed. A simplified order of precedence is given below in Table 14-3; the complete table is given on pages 4-20 and 4-21 of the assembler manual.

Table 14-3. Operator Precedence

1. entries within parentheses and square brackets
2. the assembler operators (to be discussed)
3. multiplication and division: *, /, MOD; SHL, SHR
4. addition and subtraction: +, −
5. relational operators
6. logical NOT
7. logical AND
8. logical OR, XOR

Entries at the same level are calculated left to right, but always before lower-level entries. However, for the most understandable code, it's always best to use parentheses to indicate explicitly the desired order of precedence.

Alternate Forms of Numeric Entry

At different points in the book we have put numbers in hex or binary directly into the program. Now, let us look systematically at the different forms of entering numeric values with the *Macro Assembler*. Any of these can be either positive or negative (you can even have negative characters).

- Decimal is usually the default for entering numbers, but when necessary (see the .RADIX command below), the suffix D is used to identify the number as decimal. For example, 65 and 65D are both legitimate decimal numbers.
- Hexadecimal is frequently used. The hexadecimal number must begin with one of the digits 0–9 and end with the letter H for hex (thus 0H, 45H, 9AH, 0A1H, and 0FFH are legal; FF, 0FF, and FFH are not).
- Binary is also used, primarily for I/O and graphics purposes. A valid binary number consists of a sequence of 1's and 0's followed by the letter B, as in 01101001B.
- Character entries are also legal; they are enclosed within single or double quotes. More than two characters are legal for DB only. "$", 'Testing . . .', and "It's time" are all legal. If you wish to put single quotes in your string, surround the string with double quotes; the reverse is true for double quotes. However, you cannot use both in one string.

Other options are available from the assembler, but are infrequently used. Octal can be entered with a suffix of O or Q. Decimal Scientific Real numbers, used with the DD pseudo-op, can be entered as floating-point decimal digits

(2.997E+8), which are stored in four-byte format, like IBM's BASIC. Hexadecimal Real numbers, which are identical to standard hexadecimal, can be entered with a suffix of R. The last two types above are available only with MASM and are intended to support the 8087 numeric coprocessor. Some information on all of these types is available in the *Assembler Reference Manual*, pages 4-4 and 4-5.

We mentioned above that decimal is usually the default base for entering numbers. It's possible to use the .RADIX command to change the default to another number base. (.RADIX never affects DD, DQ, or DT, which always default to decimal.) For example, to use hexadecimal as your default base (perhaps to practice thinking in hex), you would begin your program with

.RADIX 16

(the operand of .RADIX is always in decimal). Once you have done this, all numbers without a suffix would be interpreted by the assembler as hexadecimal (base 16). If you were writing an I/O-intensive program, you might use

.RADIX 2

for binary (base 2).

Any radix between 2 and 16 is allowed.

You can change the default base back to decimal at any point in your program by inserting the .RADIX 10 command in your program. However, if you change the base to something other than decimal, remember to use the D suffix when you want base 10.

Assembler Operators

At this point we begin to look at the more detailed and complex assembler commands. First let us recall how the IBM assembler keeps track of all its variables and labels (collectively called symbols) in a source program. Each symbol is associated with a segment, an offset (how many bytes it is from the beginning of the segment), and a type. For a label, the type refers to whether the label was specified as NEAR or FAR, and for a variable, whether the variable addresses DB, DW, DD, DQ, or DT data, or one of the advanced data pseudo-ops. All assembler symbols are defined by segment, offset, and type.

Value-Returning Operators

The *value-returning operators* can be very useful. You have already encountered and used one of them: the OFFSET command. In this section we will discuss the OFFSET command, as well as the two commands that are its counterparts, SEG and TYPE, and two commands useful with variables defined with DUP: LENGTH and SIZE.

The OFFSET command. IBM allows the access to each of the defined characteristics of a symbol separately. The OFFSET command returns the offset of a variable within its segment. Normally, when you specify the name of a variable (for example, as an operand of the MOV command), the assembler assumes you want the contents of the variable. However, if you want to reference the variable indirectly, it is necessary that you know its offset. For example,

```
DSEG    SEGMENT
VAR_1   DW 303
VAR_2   DW 450
  .
  .
  .
DSEG    ENDS
CSEG    SEGMENT
        ASSUME CS:CSEG,DS:DSEG
BEGIN:  MOV DI,VAR_2
        MOV SI,OFFSET VAR_2
  .
  .
  .
```

When this program fragment is executed, DI will hold 450 (the value stored at VAR_2), but SI will hold 2, the location (or offset) of the variable VAR_2 within the DSEG segment.

For more information about, and examples of, the OFFSET command, see Chapters 9 and 13.

The SEG operator. The next operator, SEG, is used less often. It returns the segment value of the symbol (variable or label). Thus, in the above example, MOV AX,SEG VAR_1 would put the segment register value for DSEG into AX. Likewise, MOV BX,SEG BEGIN would put the value for CSEG into BX. However, these same operations can be done with MOV BX,CSEG and MOV AX,DSEG. The SEG operator is used mainly for self-documenting code (as below):

269

MOV AX,SEG VAR_2   ;equivalent to MOV AX,DSEG
MOV ES,AX
MOV DI,OFFSET VAR_2

The TYPE operator. The last operator, TYPE, is useful for making code more easily modified (as we shall see in a moment), as well as more self-documenting. The TYPE operator returns different values for variables and for labels. For variables, TYPE returns a value equal to the number of bytes in the variable's type (1 for BYTE, 2 for WORD, 4 for DWORD, and so forth). The possible values are given in Table 14-4. For labels, TYPE returns NEAR or FAR as appropriate; this is not usually very useful.

Table 14-4. Values Returned with TYPE

BYTE = 1 (with DB)   **WORD = 2 (with DW)**
DWORD = 4 (with DD)   **QWORD = 8 (with DQ)**
TBYTES = 10 (with DT)

Advanced data ops return TYPE as appropriate to their definition. Constants and segment names always return 0.

A common use of TYPE is to access elements in a table without explicitly using the number of bytes per entry. If we declare a table of numbers as below:

TABLE DB 0,1,8,27,64,125,216

containing the cubes of numbers from 0 to 6, we can access, for example, the cube of 3 with

MOV AL,TABLE + 3

But if we wanted to extend the table to include the cubes of 7 to 10, we would have a problem; the values 343, 512, 729, and 1000 don't fit into bytes. The solution is to redeclare TABLE as a WORD table, then double all the offset references within it (for example, to get the cube of 3, we now need MOV AX,TABLE + 6). If we had specified the instruction as

MOV AL,TABLE + 3 * TYPE TABLE

changing the type of TABLE from DB to DW would automatically change the offset from 3 to 6 above. It is thus easier to change from byte entries to word entries.

The other reason to use TYPE for variables is that it greatly improves the readability of the program. If you saw, for example,

INC TABLE+4

you could have no way of knowing whether it referred to the third word entry, the fifth byte entry, or the second double-word entry, without going back to the definition of TABLE itself. Using the form

INC TABLE+4*TYPE TABLE

however, makes it clear that what is referred to is the fifth entry in the table, regardless of the actual type.

The SIZE and LENGTH operators. The SIZE and LENGTH operators can also prove useful in a program. They return values for variables defined with the DUP command. The LENGTH operator returns the length of a DUP table is, that is, how many DUPlicates were made. If the variable wasn't created with the DUP command, LENGTH returns one. Thus, for this entry, LENGTH returns 16:

TABLE_16 DW 16 DUP(DUMMY_RETURN)
  ;16 of DUMMY_RETURN's offset

SIZE tells you how long the table is in bytes. So, for the above entry, SIZE returns 32. For this entry, TYPE returns 2 (for a WORD); and, as a rule, the assembler always uses LENGTH * TYPE to calculate SIZE. This means that the SIZE and LENGTH operators are useful when there's only one entry for DUP. Entries such as

DB 10 DUP(16,?,16 DUP(' '))

will not return the correct SIZE value; since LENGTH is 10 and TYPE is 1 SIZE will be 10 * 1, or only 10.

Attribute Operators

The counterpart of the variable-returning operators is the attribute operators. Instead of returning the segment, offset, or type identification of a symbol, they allow you to override the segment or type of the symbol.

Segment override. The segment identification of a variable can be overridden by use of a segment prefix. As well as overriding a variable or label, the segment override operator can also be used to override an address expression, such as ES:[BX+SI]. Bear in mind that the ASSUMEd segment prefix can be overridden not only by the segment registers (CS, DS, ES, and SS), but also by the names of the segments (CSEG,

DSEG, or whatever). Remember, if you don't tell the assembler what to ASSUME, you must use a segment override operator for each variable.

The PTR command. The type identification of a variable or label can also be overridden with PTR. Its format is

type **PTR** *expression*

The *expression* is a variable or label, and the *type* should be BYTE, WORD, or DWORD for variables; for labels, NEAR or FAR. If, for example, you want to jump to a procedure that has been defined as FAR, but you're in the same segment, you can say:

JMP NEAR PTR procedure-name

Or, if you should wish to access a WORD array in memory by BYTE (for example), you could use the form

MOV AL,BYTE PTR table_name + 4

to get the fifth byte of the table. (See the next chapter, LABEL and THIS, for another way to do this.)

Sometimes PTR is required. When you reference some indirect memory address, you must tell the assembler whether you are dealing with a byte or a word. For example,

MOV [DI+BX],100

In this expression, [DI+BX] could be pointing to a byte or a word with equal ease. The assembler has no way of knowing (so you get an error message, 35:Operand must have size). For this sort of expression you must specify the type explicitly:

MOV WORD PTR [DI+BX],100

The offset cannot be overridden (a strange idea that would be), but a few more attribute operators exist (SHORT, THIS, HIGH, and LOW). THIS will be discussed in the next chapter along with the LABEL command; the other attribute operators are abstruse, and unnecessary for most programming.

Common Listing Pseudo-ops

A few of the assembler pseudo-ops give the assembler instructions about the format of the list file. Three of these in particular are quite useful and will be discussed below.

The PAGE Pseudo-op

This pseudo-op is used to control the length and width of a logical page in the assembler .LST file. In addition, the command can be used to force a new page. The first command in a file will often be

PAGE *[operand 1][,operand 2]*

The first operand is the number of lines per page. Normally, this is 66 (the default for six lines per inch for 11-inch paper). However, if you have especially long or short paper, this operand can take any value from 10 to 255. Usually it's not specified, and left to default to 66 lines per page.

The second operand is used more often. It controls the width of the page. The assembler defaults to the normal 80-column width of most printers, but any number from 60 to 132 can be specified. Wide, 132-column printers should set the page width to 132 with

PAGE ,132

Typically, 80-column dot-matrix printers can set character widths to 10 cpi (characters per inch), 12 cpi, or about 17 cpi. For our work, we use the

PAGE ,96

command, and set the printer to print in 12 cpi. If you need more room for comments, however, PAGE ,132 and 17 cpi may be better.

The PAGE command can also be used without any operands, in which case the printer advances to the next page and the listing continues from there. If you use the format PAGE + , the chapter number is incremented and the page number is reset to one.

The TITLE and SUBTTL Pseudo-ops

The TITLE pseudo-op is often specified immediately after the PAGE ,width command. It takes the format

TITLE *text*

and the specified text (up to 60 characters) becomes the title, going at the top of each page in the listing, below the assembler title and page number. This command can be used only once in the source file.

The SUBTTL command is similar to TITLE, but defines a subtitle, which appears below the title. The format is SUBTTL *text*. As many subtitles as you wish can be defined in a single file. The new subtitle takes effect on the following page, so the SUBTTL command is often used in conjunction with the PAGE command:

SUBTTL (whatever subtitle you wish goes here)
PAGE　　;make subtitle immediately effective

Once you understand these commands, you can write quite complex assembly language programs. In the next chapter, you will be introduced to some even more powerful assembler commands, including macros, conditionals, and cross-referencing.

CHAPTER

15
Advanced Assembler Control

In this chapter we will discuss the more advanced commands available with IBM's assembler. Most of our discussion will be centered on the use of *macros*, as well as on the use of the conditional assembly pseudo-ops. At the end of this chapter, we will discuss the use of the cross-referencing facility CREF, which comes with the assembler, as well as the assembler pseudo-ops that control it.

Not all of the remaining assembler commands will be discussed in this chapter. Some of the commands are very obscure; some of them are powerful but useful only at the most advanced level. In this latter category, for the curious, fall the advanced data-structuring commands, STRUC and RECORD, as well as the very powerful external assembly pseudo-ops. A brief description of the excluded material appears at the end of the chapter.

In Table 15-1 below is a list of those commands discussed in this chapter. Appendix C has a table briefly describing all the assembler pseudo-ops discussed in this book.

Table 15-1. Assembler Commands

MACRO	ENDM	LOCAL
&,%,;;	INCLUDE	REPT
IRP	IRPC	.XALL
.LALL	.SALL	IF<condition>
ELSE	ENDIF	SHORT
THIS	LABEL	ORG
.CREF	.XCREF	

MACROS

One of the most versatile commands available on the *Macro Assembler* is the MACRO command (not available with the

275

Small Assembler). A *macro*, generally speaking, is any utility that allows you to execute a series of standard commands with only one macro command. Users of some of the newer word processors may be familiar with this concept; *WordPerfect*, for example, allows the user to key in a single macro command, such as Alt-L, that signals the program to execute a series of predefined commands.

For those who know DOS well, the DOS batch files are also similar to assembler macros. First, you set up a file containing all the commands you want to have executed. Then, to execute them, you simply type the name of the batch file. Macros work the same way: Specify the commands that make up the macro, then to use those commands in your program, just specify the name of the macro.

Thus, the *Macro Assembler* allows you to define a single command (with a name of your choosing) in terms of other *Macro Assembler* commands and opcodes. One simple macro might be used to print an often used message in your program. The code to print this message might be as follows:

```
MOV DX,OFFSET MSG_1   ;address of message start
MOV AH,9              ;DOS print string command
INT 21H              ;invoke the DOS function interrupt
```

This fragment of code could be defined, by the MACRO statement, to be the PRINT_MESSAGE command. Defining a macro is really quite simple: The name of the command-to-be, followed by the MACRO pseudo-op, is placed before the code (the code is the body of the macro). The ENDM command (for END Macro) is placed at the end of the code. To define PRINT_MESSAGE, then, we would place the following in our source code:

```
PRINT_MESSAGE   MACRO
                MOV DX,OFFSET MSG_1
                MOV AH,9
                INT 21H
                ENDM
```

(Note that, unlike ENDS and ENDP, you don't specify the name of the macro with ENDM.) Once the macro command has been defined in this way, it can be used later at any point in the program, and as often as you wish, simply by specifying PRINT_MESSAGE.

However, *a macro does not function in the same way as a subroutine*. It is critical to understand the difference. The code of a subroutine appears in the final object code in only one location. Whenever you need to use the subroutine, you CALL it, then RETurn from it. A macro, by contrast, is not called by the main program when it is used. Instead, every time the name of the macro appears in the program, the code constituting the macro is substituted directly for the name.

As an example, if PRINT_MESSAGE_2 were a subroutine, the assembler statements

CALL PRINT_MESSAGE_2
CALL PRINT_MESSAGE_2

would appear in a DEBUG list as, perhaps,

091C:0200 E84201   CALL   0345
091C:0203 E83F01   CALL   0345

However, the parallel macro statements

PRINT_MESSAGE
PRINT_MESSAGE

(assuming the macro PRINT_MESSAGE had been defined as above) would appear in DEBUG as

091C:0200 BA1000   MOV   DX,0010   (offset of MSG_1)
091C:0203 B409   MOV   AH,09   (print function)
091C:0205 CD21   INT   21   (DOS call)
091C:0207 BA1000   MOV   DX,0010   (and again)
091C:020A B409   MOV   AH,09
091C:020C CD21   INT   21

Macros are not, however, limited to repeating the same sequence of instructions each time they're invoked. A macro can be given a list of operands, much as regular 8088 opcodes are given operands. These operands are then substituted into the expansion of the macro according to its initial definition.

To allow a macro to have operands, the first line of the macro definition must be enlarged to include a list of so-called dummy parameters. These dummy parameters appear immediately following the MACRO statement, separated by commas. There can be as many of them as fit on one line. For example:

SAMPLE_MACRO MACRO P1,P2,P3,P4

You might invoke SAMPLE_MACRO with

SAMPLE_MACRO AX,BX,ADD,SUM

Now, when the macro is expanded by the assembler, the operands (AX, BX, ADD, and SUM in this case) will be substituted for the dummy parameters (P1, P2, P3, and P4):

P1 is replaced with AX
P2 is replaced with BX
P3 is replaced with ADD
P4 is replaced with SUM

So, if we code SAMPLE_MACRO like this:

```
SAMPLE_MACRO  MACRO P1,P2,P3,P4
              P3 P1,P2
              MOV P4,P1
              ENDM
```

and called it with

SAMPLE_MACRO AX,BX,ADD,SUM

the assembler would expand it as follows:

```
ADD AX,BX
MOV SUM,AX
```

As you can see, each of SAMPLE_MACRO's operands has been substituted for the corresponding dummy parameter. If SAMPLE_MACRO were invoked elsewhere in the program, with, perhaps,

SAMPLE_MACRO DX,DSEG,MOV,DS

the assembler would expand it as

```
MOV DX,DSEG
MOV DS,DX
```

Dummy parameters have to follow the usual rules for variables; they don't have to be named P1, P2, P3, and so forth, but can take more descriptive names if your macro has a more specific purpose than the one above. Also, as you have seen, the dummy parameters can play any role in the macro definition, from variables, labels, and registers to opcodes and pseudo-ops.

Another macro might use these dummy parameters more usefully—for example, to handle the multiply operation. This macro would be defined in terms of moving data to the AX register, multiplying it by some other data, then placing the answer in a specified register or variable.

MULTIPLY MACRO VAR_1,VAR_2,TARGET_REG

```
        PUSH DX                 ;DX is changed by word
                                ;multiply
        MOV AX,VAR_2            ;AX = VAR_1 * VAR_2
        MUL VAR_1
        MOV TARGET_REG,AX       ;TARGET_REG can be
                                ;register or variable
        POP DX
        ENDM
```

This could be called with any of the following:

MULTIPLY BX,3,CX   ;this gives CX = BX * 3
MULTIPLY TRACKS,SECTORS_PER_TRACK,BLOCKS_PER_DISK
                              ;this might be only variables, no
                              ;registers or constants
MULTIPLY SEG_SIZE,17,DS   ;DS = 17 * SEG_SIZE

There is an additional feature involved in macro parameter passing that makes the process even more flexible. Although a certain number of parameters are defined on the first line of the macro definition, it is possible, in fact, to pass the macro as few or as many parameters as you like. If fewer parameters are specified than there are dummy parameters, the remaining parameters are simply made blank (see the IFB conditional below). If more parameters are specified than are defined in the macro, the extra ones are simply ignored. Thus, you can have a multipurpose macro which accepts a different number of parameters, depending upon (let's say) the value of the first parameter. (See the sample macro program at the end of this chapter.) How to change the expansion of the macro, however, is a subject we shall cover later, in the section on Conditionals.

Now let us look over some of the reasons for you to use macros in your programs. Generally, macros are not useful for making object code as efficient as possible. Instead, they are used because:

- Macros are dynamic. As we have seen, parameters can be passed to a macro in a much more all-encompassing fashion then parameters passed via the stack or registers to a subroutine.
- Macros usually help to streamline and simplify the program source code by making it more understandable both for the initial programmer and for later readers.

- Macros, as we shall see, can be entered into a macro library that can be stored on disk and easily accessed.
- Macros are, in general, faster. Since the subroutine is placed directly in the object code by a macro expansion, the computer is not delayed by CALL and RETurn. Typically, the delay is all of 35 clock cycles, or well over 0.000007 seconds.

The LOCAL Special Macro Operator

One problem with invoking the same macro in several places occurs when there is a label in the macro. You might, for example, define a short macro that incremented a double word.

```
INC_DWORD    MACRO DWORD_VAR
             INC DWORD_VAR
             JNZ NO_INC
             INC DWORD_VAR+2
NO_INC:
             ENDM
```

The macro as written will serve to increment a double word. (There are simpler methods, but the above example illustrates the point at hand.) However, consider what happens when we use this macro command twice in the same program:

```
INC_DWORD DWORD_1
INC_DWORD DWORD_2
```

This will result in the following macro expansion by the assembler:

```
             INC DWORD_1
             JNZ NO_INC
             INC DWORD_1+2
NO_INC:
             INC DWORD_2
             JNZ NO_INC
             INC DWORD_2+2
NO_INC:
```

As you can see, the same label name is being used in two places. When the assembler tries to assemble this code, quite a few errors will be generated:

```
Error  ——  4:Redefinition of symbol
Error  ——  26:Reference to multidefined
Error  ——  5:Symbol is multidefined
```

However, there is a macro command that allows this problem to be circumvented: the LOCAL pseudo-op. This command tells the assembler which labels would be multidefined (like NO_INC above), and the assembler renames them to avoid the problem. The format of the command is

LOCAL label_1,label_2,label_3, etc.

You can specify as many label names as can fit on one 132-column assembler line. But one warning about this command: The LOCAL command must be the very first command after the MACRO command, preceding even any comments.

In our example above (INC_DWORD), the LOCAL pseudo-op would be used as follows:

```
INC_DWORD  MACRO DWORD_VAR
           LOCAL NO_INC
           INC DWORD_VAR
           JNZ NO_INC
           INC DWORD_VAR+2
NO_INC:
           ENDM
```

Now, each time INC_DWORD is invoked and expanded by the assembler, the assembler will assign a new name to NO_INC. The assembler's naming system is simply to create label names of the format ??0000 to ??FFFF. This gives us over 65,000 possible labels for use with LOCAL macro labels. Note that the manual erroneously states that LOCAL labels start with ??0001.

Program 15-1 is a listing from the *Macro Assembler* of the appropriate sections of a program which uses INC_DWORD.

Notice that expanded macro code has a plus sign (+) on column 31 of the listing to help you tell it apart from normal code. Also, there is an additional entry in the SYMBOLS section of the assembler. This entry, *Macros*, lists each defined macro in alphabetical order.

The Ampersand (&) Macro Special Operator

A variety of further operators are provided for use with the MACRO command. The ampersand (&) operator allows you to concatenate symbols together with text or with other symbols. (More technically, it serves as a flag to warn the assembler that the following name is a dummy parameter where there wouldn't normally be a parameter.)

For example, we can make a macro which allows us to conditionally CALL a subroutine:

```
BAD_COND   MACRO COND,ROUTINE
           LOCAL DO_CALL,SKIP
           JCOND DO_CALL
           JMP SKIP
DO_CALL:   CALL ROUTINE
SKIP:      ENDM
```

Unfortunately, the COND parameter in the macro above won't be replaced by our macro parameter when the macro is expanded. The assembler sees the expression JCOND as entirely different from the dummy parameter COND (and, in fact, a syntax error). The ampersand operator allows you to concatenate the COND operand onto the J:

```
CALL_COND   MACRO COND,ROUTINE
            LOCAL DO_CALL,SKIP
            J&COND DO_CALL
            JMP SKIP
DO_CALL:    CALL ROUTINE
SKIP:
            ENDM
```

Now, the assembler will recognize the COND in the macro as the dummy parameter. When CALL_COND is invoked,

CALL_COND NZ,READ_KEYBOARD

it will be expanded by the assembler to

```
        JNZ ??0000
        JMP ??0001
??0000: CALL READ_KEYBOARD
??0001:
```

The ampersand operator is also needed with some of the conditionals, since the parameters that conditionals use are sometimes embedded in other text.

The Percent (%) Operator

There is another useful macro special operator, the percent operator. Until now all of the parameters we have passed to macros have been simply names. It is also possible to pass the value of a constant to a macro. For example, if we had the following code:

```
BDOS          EQU 21H
;
MAKE_MSG  MACRO MSG_NUM
              DB 'This is interrupt number &MSG_NUM'
              ENDM
```

we could invoke the macro with MAKE_MSG BDOS. However, that would expand to

DB 'This is interrupt number BDOS'

This is not what we intended. To make the macro create a message with the actual number (21H in this case), it is necessary to use the percent operator. Invoking the macro with

MAKE_MSG %BDOS

gives us

DB 'This is interrupt number 33'

Note that the percent operator returns the number in the current radix (see the .RADIX command), no matter whether the number was defined as decimal, hexadecimal, binary, or anything else.

The INCLUDE Pseudo-op

When dealing with a large number of macros, it is often convenient to keep them separate from the main program. The macros can then be included in the file at assembly time by the INCLUDE pseudo-op. This command takes the format

INCLUDE *filename.ext*

where the *filename.ext* is the DOS filename of the file in which the macros are stored. Thus if you have a file containing nothing but six or eight of your favorite macros (a macro library), you can use them in another program. For example, you can put an INCLUDE at the beginning of your program, using the traditional name for a macro library, MACRO.LIB:

INCLUDE MACRO.LIB

(Usually the INCLUDE pseudo-op is used with the IF1-ENDIF construction that we'll be discussing shortly.) Note, by the way, that this is only one use for the INCLUDE command. It can be used to include anything into your source file, and the included file will be assembled at the point that the INCLUDE statement appeared.

Listing of Macros in the Assembler's List File

Normally, when a macro is invoked within a program, all that appears in the assembler list output is the lines that create actual 8088 code. Thus, assembler directives, equates, and the like will not appear except in the original definition of the macro. Separate comment lines will likewise not appear, although comments appended to the ends of lines will appear as usual.

However, this can be changed with some of the macro listing pseudo-ops, .XALL, .LALL, and .SALL. .XALL is the default state of the assembler for macro listing: list only lines that create valid code (discussed above). When a .LALL command is encountered, all the macro expansions following the command appear in full: all comments, assembler directives, and so forth, appear in the list file each time the macro is invoked and expanded.

Even in .LALL mode, however, it is possible to suppress the listing of certain comments with the use of the "two semicolons" operator. If you use two semicolons (;;) instead of one (;) for a comment in a macro, the comment will not appear in the expanded macro in the assembler list file. Use two semicolons when the comment is meant to appear only in the definition of the macro or when it contains extra descriptive detail not needed in the usual macro expansion.

The other macro list mode is .SALL (Suppress ALL). This has the effect of suppressing the listing of the entire macro expansion. All that appears in the assembler list file is the invocation of the macro, not the expansion. This can be useful when large macros are involved, or when you want to shorten the listing.

Bear in mind that these three commands don't affect the object file at all, only the list file. Also note that these commands can be sprinkled as you wish throughout the source file; each affects only the macros following it.

With all of these commands (plus a few others that are very obscure), you can control powerful functions very simply with the macro operator. One fairly powerful macro, for example, appears in the sample listing at the end of this chapter. Our treatment of macros has stopped short of some of the more esoteric aspects of the macros. For example, macros can be nested one within the other if you so desire. Or (even worse) a macro can redefine itself during the course of its expansion (for an example of this confusing technique, see page 5-52 in the assembler manual). But without going to these extremes, macros can be easy to use and good for your programming style. Now we'll turn from macros to a related set of commands, the repeat commands.

The Repeat Commands

The *Macro Assembler* includes three additional macro commands. These commands appear directly in the source code and serve to repeat the given expression.

The REPT (REPeaT) pseudo-op is the most straightforward. To use it, simply put

REPT *expression*

before the statements to be repeated, and ENDM after them. Thus,

REPT 4
SHL AL,1
ENDM

repeats the shift left command four times, generating

SHL AL,1
SHL AL,1   .
SHL AL,1
SHL AL,1

The repeat commands need not be within a macro. It was evidently in the interests of conciseness (as well as of confusing the programmer) that IBM chose to use the ENDM command to end both macros and the repeat commands.

The second repeat command is IRP, for Indefinite Repeat. This command is closer in spirit to a macro than REPT. The format is

IRP *dummy,<argument list>*

The *dummy* plays the same role as the dummy parameters in a MACRO, but the IRP dummy takes its values from the IRP command's *argument list*. An example will serve to make this clear:

IRP REGISTER,<AX,BX,CX,DX,DI,SI,BP,ES,DS>
PUSH REGISTER
ENDM

REGISTER takes on the values AX, BX, CX, etc., repeating until the last argument is used. Note that the argument list *must* be enclosed in the so-called *angle brackets*, known to most of us as the less than (<) and greater than (>) signs. The example above will generate the following object code:

PUSH AX
PUSH BX
PUSH CX
PUSH DX
PUSH DI
PUSH SI
PUSH BP
PUSH ES
PUSH DS

This, as you can see, can prove useful when you have to make quite sure that no registers are changed by a subroutine.

The final repeat command is IRPC. This is similar to the IRP command, but instead of a list of arguments within angle brackets, the format is simply

IRPC *dummy,string*

The *string* is a string of characters, not enclosed in quotes, although you may, if you wish, enclose it in angle brackets. The repeat loop begins by assigning the first character of the string to the *dummy*, then the second on the next pass, until the entire string is finished. This is, perhaps, the least useful of the repeat commands. One example of its use might be:

IRPC X,0123456789
DW X*X*X
ENDM

This would create a WORD table of the cubes of 0 to 9.

The EXITM Pseudo-op

One final macro command exists, EXITM. This command allows you to exit from a macro or repeat structure early, aborting the macro expansion. The EXITM command cannot, however, take the place of ENDM. Every macro must have one and only one ENDM. EXITM can occur anywhere within the macro, as often as necessary. However, we will put off its discussion until we have mastered the concept of conditionals, without which EXITM has very little use.

Conditionals

Conditional pseudo-ops can, in many respects, be considered an extension of the macro commands (most conditionals appear within macros). Conditional pseudo-ops allow for different paths to be taken at assembly time by the assembler. They are similar to the conditional jumps, which control what part of the program to execute under what conditions. The conditional pseudo-ops, however, control what part of the program to assemble. As you may imagine, this is primarily useful with macros: different sections of one macro can be expanded depending on one (or more) of the parameters of the macro. However, a few uses exist outside of macros, and these will be described in due course. *Small Assembler* users should note that most of the conditional pseudo-ops can be used both with *Small Assembler* and the *Macro Assembler*.

The Structure of a Conditional

First let's discuss the structure of a conditional pseudo-op. All conditionals begin with the IF statement or some variation of it (for example, IF1, IFDEF, IFIDN, etc.). Furthermore, all conditionals must end with the ENDIF statement. An optional ELSE statement can also be included.

The syntax is similar to BASIC, but with some differences. For example, the IF statement does not, with the assembler, go at the beginning of a line of commands. Instead, the IF statement, with any operands, goes separately on the first line of the conditional structure. The body of the IF-clause (statements to be executed should the IF be true) follows. Then, if desired, comes the ELSE statement, on a line by itself, followed by the body of statements in the event the IF is false. Finally, on yet another line comes the (required) ENDIF statement to mark the end of the conditional. So, where BASIC requires that the IF clause be held entirely on one line, the assembler insists that every statement be on a separate line. The format is therefore:

IF\<condition\>

```
        .
        .           ;body of statements IF true
        .
ELSE                ;(optional)
        .
        .           ;(optional statements IF false)
```

ENDIF   ;required terminator

It's often necessary to insure that two or more conditions be true before taking one path or another in the assembly. For this reason, *nested conditionals* are allowed to any depth. You'll see some examples of nested conditionals in Program 15-2 below.

The Conditional Pseudo-ops

The first and most elementary IF command is simply the word IF itself:

IF *expression*

The IF is true if the *expression* is not 0. This, incidentally, corresponds with the relational operators, discussed briefly in the last chapter, for which true is 0FFFFH and false is 0. There is an example of the IF command in Program 15-2.

The counterpart to the IF pseudo-op is the IFE command, which is true if the *expression* is 0 (IF Equal). In effect, this statement reverses the logic of the IF command.

Two other IF statements are used to control conditional assembly on pass 1 and pass 2. These statements are IF1 and IF2, and are true on, respectively, pass 1 and pass 2. The IF1 statement often occurs with the INCLUDE statement, described above. The statements

IF1

        INCLUDE MACRO.LIB   ;or whatever name
ENDIF

will read in the library on the first pass only, thus saving time (the disk drive is accessed only once) and list file space (since source code is printed only on pass 2). The INCLUDE statement is usually seen in this format.

There are four IF statements of roughly similar use which we will summarize briefly. These fall into pairs. First is the IFDEF/IFNDEF pair: These take one operand (a symbol) and are true if, respectively, the symbol is DEFined (IFDEF) or Not DEFined (IFNDEF).

IFDEF *symbol*

or

IFNDEF *symbol*

Second is the IFB/IFNB pair. The operand for these conditionals is an argument enclosed in angle brackets:

IFB *<symbol>*

or

IFNB *<symbol>*

These commands return true if the argument is Blank (IFB) or Not Blank (IFNB), respectively. Their primary use is to detect the blank parameters that occur when a parameter is not specified in a macro expansion. If a macro is designed to accept a variable number of parameters, an IFB <dummy_parameter> test can be made to assemble different sections of code. These four conditionals are the only ones not supported by the *Small Assembler*.

In general, the most useful IF commands are the IFIDN (IF IDeNtical) and IFDIF (IF DIFferent) commands. These take two operands and compare them:

IFIDN *<argument 1>,<argument 2>*

or

IFDIF *<argument 1>,<argument 2>*

As with the IFB/IFNB conditionals, the *arguments* for IFIDN and IFDIF must be enclosed in angle brackets. As you have no doubt guessed, these commands return true if (for IFIDN) the arguments are identical or if (for IFDIF) they are different. These commands are almost always used within a macro. Typically, one of the arguments is a parameter for the macro, and the other is a constant to compare the parameter with. There are examples of both of these conditionals in Program 15-2.

The Equal Sign (=) Pseudo-op

The equal sign pseudo-op is often useful in conjunction with the IF and IFE conditionals. A constant may be defined with the = command much as with the EQU command, but only numeric values may be used with the = command (the EQU command, you may recall, accepted almost anything as an operand). The flexibility and usefulness of the = command lies in the fact that a constant can be defined and then redefined, and what's more, redefined in terms of its previous value. (The use of the word *constant* to refer to a changeable quantity is amusing, but follows assembler naming conventions.) The following, therefore, are all valid uses of the = pseudo-op:

```
CONST    = -3
CONST    = 0
CONST    = CONST + 1
FALSE    = 0
TRUE     = NOT FALSE      ;this is a logical NOT
DE_BUG   = TRUE
```

If you need to define constants for use with a macro, it's convenient to define them with the = pseudo-op, rather than EQU. That way, you can avoid the assembler Redefinition of symbol error each time the macro is expanded.

One of the possible uses for the = pseudo-op outside a macro is to choose whether or not debugging sections of the program are to be included. For example, you might write a subroutine that displays the values of the registers, and call it periodically during the course of the program. Naturally, this would be less than desirable during actual trial runs of the program, so it should operate only when you were attempting to debug the program.

Here is one way to execute a routine only part of the time. We would write the debugging subroutine as follows:

```
DUMP_REGISTERS PROC NEAR  ;procedure
IFE DE_BUG                ;true if debug is 0 (false)
RET                       ;don't dump the registers
ELSE                      ;else, if debug is true
 .
 .                        ;execute the main body
 .                        ;to dump the registers
 .
RET                       ;then return
ENDIF                     ;end of condition
DUMP_REGISTERS ENDP       ;end of procedure
```

When you want to assemble the program with a register dump, you would set DE_BUG = 1 (or TRUE above); to disable register dump, you would reset it to 0, or FALSE. Other uses of the = pseudo-op exist for use with conditionals, but these are rather obscure.

EXITM, Again

Before we plunge into the sample program, let's review the EXITM command. Normally the EXITM command occurs only with conditionals, and serves as a way to abort the macro quickly if the parameters are misspecified. For example, if a macro with several parameters was invoked with none, you might wish to abort the macro expansion early. To do so, you might code:

IFB <*parameter_1*>
EXITM
ENDIF

If parameter 1 is blank (not specified), the macro would abort. Unfortunately, as far as the assembler is concerned, the IF statement opened with IFB was never closed with an ENDIF. We aborted out of the middle of a conditional. There's no way around this problem, however, so when a macro aborts conditionally from a macro expansion, you will be stuck with an Open conditionals message from the assembler. However, the Open conditionals message is usually not important (unless you didn't use the EXITM command, in which case some of your conditionals really are open). Bearing all this in mind, examine Program 15-2, the sample macro program.

More Commands

A few more operators are of use to the advanced assembler user. We will discuss first the SHORT operator, and then LABEL and THIS, which are logically connected.

The SHORT Operator

The SHORT operator is used to instruct the assembler that the label of a forward JMP command is within 127 bytes:

JMP SHORT *label*

This may appear at first as rather confusing, since we know that the assembler is responsible for making jumps short or near. However, the assembler has to make assumptions about the labels and variables it encounters on its first pass through the source code. For example:

      JMP LABEL_1
        .
        .

                ;intermediate code

        .
LABEL_1:

The assembler has no way of knowing whether a jump ahead (like the JMP to LABEL_1 above) is going to need a two-byte offset (if it's further than 127 bytes), or whether one byte will do. So it simply sets up two bytes for the offset. When it makes its second, code-generating pass, it gives the JMP a one-byte offset if possible, and then puts a NOP in the other, unused byte. (NOP is one of the 8088's simpler instructions: It's a do-nothing command, No OPeration.) You can see the NOP in the DEBUG unassembly, as well as in hex form in the assembler list file (90H).

Using the SHORT prefix merely tells the assembler that the JMP will need only one byte as an offset. If the jump is more than 128 bytes, you get an assembler error message. This operator need never occur in your own programs, unless for some reason one program must be particularly short; however, many DOS and BIOS routines use this command, so it is useful to be familiar with it.

The LABEL and THIS Operators

These two assembler commands play virtually identical roles. They are, however, different types of instructions. The command THIS falls under the category of Attribute Operators, along with PTR, segment overrides, and the SHORT command above. LABEL, however, is a pseudo-op in its own right.

Normally, the assembler knows the type of a symbol: Variables are defined with DB, DW, DD, and the like, while labels are either NEAR or FAR. LABEL and THIS provide a method of declaring a variable without a data pseudo-op, or a label without PROC or a colon. You can therefore put a symbol wherever you please, then instruct the assembler what its type should be. Although their formats are different

name **LABEL** *type*
name **EQU THIS** *type*

both set *name* equal to the type specified, at the current segment and offset. The LABEL pseudo-op creates a standard label or variable; the THIS operator creates a symbol marked with an E (an EQU symbol) in the symbol table. The *type* can be any of the standard label or variable types (NEAR, FAR, BYTE, WORD, DWORD, QWORD, or TBYTE).

A few uses for these commands are given below:

```
BYTE_TABLE    EQU THIS BYTE
WORD_TABLE    DW 5678,4321,50000,123,0
```

Here the table can be accessed either as *words* (with WORD_TABLE) or as *bytes* (with BYTE_TABLE). This eliminates the need for the rather clumsy form:

MOV AH,BYTE PTR WORD_TABLE+4

For those adventuresome enough to write self-modifying programs, the ability to set a symbol to a different type comes in very handy:

MOV CMP_VALUE+1,AL   ;modify the 0 in CMP AL,0

.
.
.

CMP_VALUE EQU THIS BYTE
CMP AL,0   ;this 0 is modified above

The LABEL command is often used to make locations in program code FAR so they can be JMPed to from other object modules (this is another advanced technique).

Cross-Referencing

One feature of the assembler can prove very useful when you begin to write long programs. You will no doubt find that remembering where each of your labels and variables is referenced can be a hassle. As a solution to that problem, the assembler comes with a cross-reference utility. When you start MASM, the prompt comes up for Cross-reference; until now you have always hit Return. To create the cross-ref file, enter the name for the file and hit Return. Below, we have included a sample from the "Switch" program from the first programming chapter.

A>MASM [or ASM depending on which assembler you are using]
The IBM Personal Computer MACRO Assembler
Version 1.00 (C)Copyright IBM Corp 1981

Source filename [.ASM]: SWITCH [name of the source file]
Object filename [SWITCH.OBJ]: [Enter if you want object code]
Source listing [NUL.LST]: SWITCH if you want a source listing
Cross-reference [NUL.CRF]: SWITCH for the cross-reference

Note that whenever you select the cross-reference option, the assembler will automatically include line numbers in the .LST file.

One would not generally make a cross-reference of a program this short, but we will, just so you can see how it's done.

The cross-reference file (with .CRF extension) produced by the assembler is not in human-readable form. We must run a translation program on the .CRF file. This utility is named CREF and is discussed in Chapter 3 of the *Assembler Reference Manual*. Type CREF from the DOS prompt and answer the questions as shown below, assuming that the name of the .CRF file is SWITCH.CRF:

A>CREF
Cref filename [.CRF]: SWITCH [The name of the .CRF file]
List filename [SWITCH.REF]: [Enter/ default to SWITCH.REF]

When CREF is done, the DOS prompt will return. You can examine the cross-reference file by entering the command:

A>TYPE SWITCH.REF

A cross-reference file which looks like the one printed as Table 15-2 should scroll up your screen. As you know, you can use Ctrl PrtSc to get a hard copy of the cross-reference; or you can specify PRN at the "List filename" prompt.

Table 15-2. Cross-Reference of SWITCH

Symbol Cross-reference	(# is definition)		Cref-1	
CODE	26#	28	50	
DATA	12#	17	28	34
DEST	15#			
MOVE_BYTES	39#	45		
SOURCE	13#			
STACK	19#	24	28	
SWITCH	27	49		

A cross-reference for a program this short is not terribly useful; however, with longer programs, you may find it indispensable. The cross-reference tells you where each symbol is used, and where it is defined. The names of the symbols are along the left, in alphabetical order. The line numbers are in ascending order from left to right and refer to the source listing produced by the assembler. The line numbers with the number signs (#) after them are the lines in which the symbol is defined (remember, with = pseudo-op a constant can be redefined as often as you like). For example, SOURCE was first defined in line 13 of the source file.

The assembler provides pseudo-ops to turn the output to

the .CRF file on and off. If your program is in two almost separate halves, for example, with few references between them, you might want to get a cross-reference only of the first half. To do so, put the .CREF command (enable .CRF output) at the beginning of the program, and the .XCREF command (disable .CRF output) at the appropriate midpoint. The assembler defaults to .CREF unless specifically overridden.

With the contents of this chapter under your belt, you will be able to program for a long time without recourse to any of the further capabilities of the *IBM Macro Assembler*. This material is ample to provide a full understanding of almost all source code, as well as to allow you to utilize much of the power of the assembler.

However, the assembler has much more to it than what we have gone through in the last two chapters. Many powerful and useful commands still remain to master (as well as a scattering of less important commands). A brief outline will suffice to give you an idea of what else remains:

- The ability to link together two or more assembly files, as well as optionally combining two or more logical segments together into a GROUP. Normally, one program is contained in one source file, but if you have some general-purpose subroutines, or if parts of your program are error-free, you can assemble them separately and combine them only at LINK time, in object-module form. A master program might call an external subroutine by specifying

  EXTRN *subroutine:***NEAR**

  while the subroutine specified PUBLIC subroutine. At LINK time you would simply respond master+subroutine.
- The ability to link not only to other machine language programs, but to high-level languages like Pascal and Compiled BASIC. Linking to high-level languages allows you to combine the breadth of a high-level language with the speed and compactness of machine language.
- The possibility of compacting your data (bit packing). The RECORD pseudo-op allows you to define, for example, three variables in a single word. To access one of these variables, you load the appropriate word, mask off unwanted bits with the MASK operator, and shift it right *shift count* times, leaving the data ready to be used.

• The use of structured data. The STRUC command allows you to specify a variable in terms of subvariables; for example, a STRUC variable named TEMPERATURE might have a subvariable named HIGH, and the assembler allows you to access the subvariables with TEMPERATURE.HIGH. This feature is very much like the powerful Pascal RECORD command.

All these commands are enough to provide continuing pleasure as you master them and put them to use. The diversity and power of the assembler, however, are such that it will be a long time before using it becomes a chore.

Program 15-1. BITS.LST

```
                      ;sample listing 15-1
                      ;
                              page ,96
                              title This program counts the on and off bits in DS
                      ;
                      ; BITS.ASM
                      ;
                      inc_dword macro dword_var
                              local no_inc        ;let Assembler generate ??nnnn
                      ; this macro increments a doubleword
                              inc dword_var       ;increment low word
                              jnz no_inc          ;no overflow wraparound, end
                              inc dword_var+2     ;if zero, increment high word
                      no_inc:
                              endm
                      ;
0000                  dseg    segment para 'DATA'
0000  00 00 00 00     offbits dd 0                ;here we store the number or 1s
0004  00 00 00 00     onbits  dd 0                ;and here the number of 0s
0008                  dseg    ends
                      ;
0000                  sseg    segment para stack 'STACK'
0000  10 [            db 16 dup('STACK   ')   ;16 copies of 'STACK   '
        53 54 41 43
        4B 20 20 20
      ]
0080                  sseg    ends
                      ;
0000                  cseg    segment para 'CODE'
                              assume cs:cseg,ds:dseg,ss:sseg
                      ;
0000                  counter proc far
```

297

```
0000    1E              push ds                 ;set up far RETurn to DS:0000
0001    B8 0000         mov ax,0
0004    50              push ax
0005    B8 ---- R       mov ax,dseg             ;load DSEG into DS
0008    8E D8           mov ds,ax

                    ;
000A                initialize:
000A    BB 0000         mov bx,0                ;BX will be the indirect reg.
000D                main_loop:
000D    8A 07           mov al,[bx]             ;get a byte from segment
000F    B9 0008         mov cx,8                ;we will loop through 8 bits
0012                bit_loop:
0012    D0 E8           shr al,1                ;push low bit into Carry flag
0014    73 0D           jnc off                 ;if no carry, low bit was zero
0016                on:     inc_dword onbits     ;use macro to increment count
0016    FF 06 0004 R  +     inc onbits          ;increment low word
001A    75 04         +     jnz ??0000          ;no overflow wraparound, end
001C    FF 06 0006 R  +     inc onbits+2        ;if zero, increment high word
0020                +   ??0000:
0020    EB 0B 90            jmp end_loop

0023                off:    inc_dword offbits    ;increment count of off bits
0023    FF 06 0000 R  +     inc offbits         ;increment low word
0027    75 04         +     jnz ??0001          ;no overflow wraparound, end
0029    FF 06 0002 R  +     inc offbits+2       ;if zero, increment high word
002D                +   ??0001:
002D                end_loop:
002D    E2 E3           loop bit_loop           ;complete 8 SHRs
002F    43              inc bx                  ;go to next byte
0030    75 DB           jnz main_loop           ;if BX is non-zero, keep going
                                                ;otherwise, BX gone past 0FFFFh
0032    CB              ret                     ;back to DEBUG, leaving values

                    ;
0033                counter endp                ;end of procedure
```

0033

```
cseg    ends              ;end of segment
        end counter       ;end of program
```

The IBM Personal Computer MACRO Assembler 01-01-80   PAGE   Symbols-1
This program counts the on and off bits in DS

Macros: N a m e   Length

INC_DWORD.   0005

Segments and groups:

N a m e	Size	align	combine	class
CSEG	0033	PARA	NONE	'CODE'
DSEG	0008	PARA	NONE	'DATA'
SSEG	0080	PARA	STACK	'STACK'

Symbols:

N a m e	Type	Value	Attr	
BIT_LOOP	L NEAR	0012	CSEG	Length =0033
COUNTER.	F PROC	0000	CSEG	
END_LOOP	L NEAR	002D	CSEG	
INITIALIZE	L NEAR	000A	CSEG	
MAIN_LOOP.	L NEAR	000D	CSEG	
OFF.	L NEAR	0023	CSEG	
OFFBITS.	L DWORD	0000	DSEG	
ON	L NEAR	0016	CSEG	
ONBITS	L DWORD	0004	DSEG	
??0000	L NEAR	0020	CSEG	
??0001	L NEAR	002D	CSEG	

Warning Severe
Errors Errors
0   0

Program 15-2. INPUT.LST

```
        page ,96
        title This macro simplifies your console input requests

; INPUT.ASM

input   macro string_mode,string,string_len
        local query,skip

; Two formats are available with this macro:
;
;       (1) input string_mode,string
;       or
;       (2) input string_mode,string,string_len

; STRING will be interpreted in light of STRING_MODE. If
; STRING_MODE is 'immediate' the STRING must be a quoted string
; (either "string" or 'string'). If STRING_MODE is 'indirect'
; then STRING must be a valid variable name in the current data
; segment. In either case, the string must end with '$'.

;       The first format above utilizes DOS function call 1 to
; read a single character. Input: string. Output: AL, holding
; the character read.  AH, DX destroyed, all else preserved.

;       The second format allows for a full line of input to be
; returned to the calling program via DOS function call 0Ah.
; The program is required to specify the length of the string
; needed (not including the final carriage return). The value
; of STRING_LEN must not be zero.  For this format only, an
; area in the current data segment must be set up, named
; INPUT_BUFFER. Input: STRING, STRING_LEN. Output: DS:SI
; points to string text; AL holds length; DX destroyed.
```

```
; Now we define our constants (with = to avoid redefine)
bdos    = 21h           ;DOS function interrupt
con_in  = 1             ; get one character from CON:
print_s = 9             ; print string function
input_s = 10            ; input a string from CON:
;
; First we test to see if parameters were passed at all.
;
        ifb <string_mode>       ;no parameters passed
        .lall                   ; allow us to return a comment:
no parameters specified for INPUT macro!  Macro aborted
        .xall                   ; resume standard list state
        exitm                   ; abort from macro with EXITM
        endif
;
; Now we test for 'immediate' or 'indirect' and set up DS:DX
; according to results.  If STRING_MODE is neither, we abort.
; If indirect we check to see if STRING is defined; else abort.
; Finally, we print either STRING or QUERY.  The ampersands
; below are needed so the Assembler can recognize a parameter.
;
        ifidn <&string_mode>,<indirect>
        ifndef string          ; make sure STRING is defined
        .lall
STRING must be a defined variable for indirect mode!
        .sall
        exitm
        endif
        mov dx,offset string   ; if it is defined, then ...
        else                   ; set up DS:DX for STRING
        ifdif <&string_mode>,<immediate>
        .lall                  ; pass this message to program
Must specify "immediate" or "indirect" as parm. #1!
        .xall                  ; resume standard list mode
        exitm                  ; abort macro
```

```
        else                             ; ELSE STRING_MODE is immediate
        jmp skip                         ; skip over DB area
query   db string
skip:   push ds                          ; string is in mem; save DS
        push cs                          ; transfer CS to DS ...
        pop ds                           ; ... via the stack!
        mov dx,offset query              ; set up DS:DX for QUERY
        endif                            ; end the IFIDN
        endif                            ; end the IFDIF
        mov ah,print_s                   ; DOS function 9 = print string
        int bdos                         ; DOS function call int.
        ifidn <&string_mode>,<immediate>
        pop ds                           ; if we pushed it, pop it back
        endif

; Test here for STRING_LEN.  If it's blank, we do format one.
;

        ifb <&string_len>                ; if STRING_LEN blank: format #1
        mov ah,con_in                    ; get a character into AL
        int bdos                         ; and that's that

; If it's not blank, and STRING_LEN > 0, we do format two.
;

        else                             ; STRING_LEN nonblank: format #2
        ife string_len                   ; if STRING_LEN is zero ...
        .lall                            ; allow a comment to program:
query string printed; can't input a string of length 0!
        .xall                            ; resume normal list mode
        exitm                            ; abort from macro
        endif                            ; STRING_LEN valid, > 0
        mov dx,offset input_buffer       ; DS:DX addr.s INPUT_BUFFER
        mov input_buffer,string_len+1    ; set byte 0 to # of chars
        mov ah,input_s                   ; DOS function to input string
        int bdos                         ; go input it
        mov al,input_buffer+1            ; get length of input
```

```
                         mov si,offset input_buffer+2  ;get address of text
                         endif                          ;end of IFB <&STRING_LEN>
                         endm                           ;end of INPUT macro

0000                     ;
0000                     dseg            segment para 'DATA'
                         ;note for INPUT_BUFFER no need to set it longer than necessary
0000 ?? 19 [             input_buffer    db ?,?,25 dup(?)  ;our macro's input buffer
        ??
     ]
001B ??                  name_len        db ?
001C ??                  family_size     db ?
001D 48 6F 77 20 6F 6C   age             db 'How old are you (0 to 999)? $'
     64 20 61 72 65 20
     79 6F 75 20 28 30
     20 74 6F 20 39 39
     39 29 3F 20 24
003A ??                  age_digits      db ?
003B 54 79 70 65 20 74   height          db 'Type the digit for your height in feet: $'
     68 65 20 64 69 67
     69 74 20 66 6F 72
     20 79 6F 75 72 20
     68 65 69 67 68 74
     20 69 6E 20 66 65
     65 74 3A 20 24
0064 ??                  height_answer   db ?
0065                     dseg            ends
0000                     ;
0000 10 [                sseg            segment para stack 'STACK'
        53 54 41 43                      db 16 dup('STACK   ')
        4B 20 20 20
     ]
```

```
0080                    sseg    ends
0000                    ;
                        cseg    segment para 'CODE'
                                assume cs:cseg,ds:dseg,ss:sseg
0000                    input_test proc far
0000    1E                      push ds                 ;set up return address
0001    B8 0000                 mov ax,0
0004    50                      push ax
0005    B8 ---- R               mov ax,dseg             ;and DSEG into DS
0008    8E D8                   mov ds,ax

                                subttl Actual testing of macro occupies rest of program
                        ;;

                                page

                        ;;
                                input                   ;test error for no parameters
                                .lall                   ; allow us to return a comment:

                        ;;      no parameters specified for INPUT macro! Macro aborted

                                input immediate,'What is your name? $',20 ;imm./buffer
000A    EB 15 90        +       jmp ??0003              ; skip over DB area
000D    57 68 61 74 20 69  + ??0002  db 'What is your name? $'
0021    1E              + ??0003: push ds               ; string is in mem; save DS
0022    0E              +       push cs                 ; transfer CS to DS ...
0023    1F              +       pop ds                  ; ... via the stack!
0024    BA 000D R       +       mov dx,offset ??0002    ; set up DS:DX for QUERY
0027    B4 09           +       mov ah,print_s          ;DOS function 9 = print string
0029    CD 21           +       int bdos                ;DOS function call int.
002B    1F              +       pop ds                  ;if we pushed it, pop it back
002C    BA 0000 R       +       mov dx,offset input_buffer ;DS:DX addr.s INPUT_BUFFER
002F    C6 06 0000 R 15 +       mov input_buffer,20+1   ;set byte 0 to # of chars
0034    B4 0A           +       mov ah,input_s          ; DOS function to input string
0036    CD 21           +       int bdos                ; go input it
```

```
0038  A0 0001 R              mov al,input_buffer+1          ; get length of input
003B  BE 0002 R              mov si,offset input_buffer+2   ;get address of text
003E  A2 001B R              mov name_len,al                ;use length returned in AL
                       +     input immediate,'How many in your family:$'  ;single
0041  EB 1B 90               jmp ??0005                     ; skip over DB area
0044  48 6F 77 20 6D 61  ??0004  db 'How many in your family:$'   ; string is in mem; save DS
005E  1E               +  ??0005: push ds                   ; transfer CS to DS ...
005F  0E               +     push cs                        ; ... via the stack!
0060  1F               +     pop ds
0061  BA 0044 R        +     mov dx,offset ??0004           ; set up DS:DX for QUERY
0064  B4 09            +     mov ah,print_s                 ;DOS function 9 = print string
0066  CD 21            +     int bdos                       ;DOS function call int.
0069  1F               +     pop ds                         ;if we pushed it, pop it back
006B  B4 01            +     mov ah,con_in                  ; get a character into AL
006B  CD 21            +     int bdos                       ; and that's that
006D  A2 001C R              mov family_size,al             ;save ASCII input character
                       +     input indirect,age,3           ;indirect/buffered
0070  BA 001D R        +     mov dx,offset age              ; set up DS:DX for STRING
0073  B4 09            +     mov ah,print_s                 ;DOS function 9 = print string
0075  CD 21            +     int bdos                       ;DOS function call int.
0077  BA 0000 R        +     mov dx,offset input_buffer     ;DS:DX addr. s INPUT_BUFFER
007A  C6 06 0000 R 04  +     mov input_buffer,3+1           ;set byte 0 to # of chars
007F  B4 0A            +     mov ah,input_s                 ; DOS function to input string
0081  CD 21            +     int bdos                       ; go input it
0083  A0 0001 R              mov al,input_buffer+1          ; get length of input
0086  BE 0002 R              mov si,offset input_buffer+2   ;get address of text
0089  A2 003A R              mov age_digits,al              ;use length returned in AL
                       +     input indirect,height          ;indirect/single
008C  BA 003B R        +     mov dx,offset height           ; set up DS:DX for STRING
008F  B4 09            +     mov ah,print_s                 ;DOS function 9 = print string
0091  CD 21            +     int bdos                       ;DOS function call int.
0093  B4 01            +     mov ah,con_in                  ; get a character into AL
```

```
0095  CD 21              +     int bdos                       ; and that's that
0097  A2 0064 R          +     mov height_answer,al           ;save ASCII
                         +     input immediate,'Thank you.',0 ;test err. for length 0
                         +     jmp ??000B                     ; skip over DB area
009A  EB 0B 90           + ??000A:
009D  54 68 61 6E 6B 20    ??000A  db 'Thank you.'
00A7  1E                 + ??000B:  push ds                   ; string is in mem; save DS
00A8  0E                 +     push cs                        ; transfer CS to DS ...
00A9  1F                 +     pop ds                         ; ... via the stack!
00AA  BA 009D R          +     mov dx,offset ??000A           ; set up DS:DX for QUERY
00AD  B4 09              +     mov ah,print_s                 ;DOS function 9 = print string
00AF  CD 21              +     int bdos                       ;DOS function call int.
00B1  1F                 +     pop ds                         ;if we pushed it, pop it back
                         +     .lall                          ; allow a comment to program:
                         +;
                         +;  query string printed; can't input a string of length 0!
                         +;
                         +     input 'Thank you'              ;test for wrong STRING_MODE
                         +     .lall                          ; pass this message to program
                         +;
                         +;  Must specify "immediate" or "indirect" as parm. #1!
                         +;
                         +     input indirect,question        ;test for undefined indirect
                         +     .lall                          ;test for undefined indirect
                         +     STRING must be a defined variable for indirect mode!
                         +;
00B2  CB                 +     ret                            ;done
00B3              input_test endp
00B3              cseg   ends
                         end input_test

Open conditionals: 7
```

The IBM Personal Computer MACRO Assembler 01-01-80   PAGE   Symbols-1
This macro simplifies your console input requests

Macros:

Name	Length
INPUT.	0073

Segments and groups:

Name	Size	align	combine	class
CSEG	00B3	PARA	NONE	'CODE'
DSEG	0065	PARA	NONE	'DATA'
SSEG	0080	PARA	STACK	'STACK'

Symbols:

Name	Type	Value	Attr	
AGE	L BYTE	001D	DSEG	
AGE_DIGITS	L BYTE	003A	DSEG	
BDOS	Number	0021		
CON_IN	Number	0001		
FAMILY_SIZE.	L BYTE	001C	DSEG	
HEIGHT	L BYTE	003B	DSEG	
HEIGHT_ANSWER.	L BYTE	0064	DSEG	
INPUT_BUFFER	L BYTE	0000	DSEG	
INPUT_S.	Number	000A		
INPUT_TEST	F PROC	0000	CSEG	Length =00B3
NAME_LEN	L BYTE	001B	DSEG	
PRINT_S.	Number	0009		
??0002	L BYTE	000D	CSEG	

```
??0003 . . . . . . .   L NEAR   0021   CSEG
??0004 . . . . . . .   L BYTE   0044   CSEG
??0005 . . . . . . .   L NEAR   005E   CSEG
??000A . . . . . . .   L BYTE   009D   CSEG
??000B . . . . . . .   L NEAR   00A7   CSEG

Warning  Severe
Errors   Errors
0        0
```

5
Sample Programs

16
Sample Programs

The first sample program, "DUMP.ASM" (Program 16-1) is a utility that allows you to examine a file as a hexadecimal listing (like DEBUG's D command). It's a good example of simple disk input/output handling with DOS 2.00 (DOS 1.10 programmers should convert it to DOS 1.10 file handling; it will be good practice). To use this program once it's assembled, simply type "DUMP filename.ext" and the file will be displayed in hexadecimal. Any errors that occur will be displayed, with the appropriate error number, and the program will stop.

The second sample program, "REBOUND.ASM" (Program 16-2), uses only BIOS functions to control the screen, so it should be usable on any PC-DOS computer. Note that, as printed, the program will work best in a PC with color/graphics board. One set of modifications should be made if you're using a PCjr. Another set should be made if you're using a PC with a monochrome board. Any version will work in any computer, but speed or color use varies.

To use the program, simply type "REBOUND" from the DOS prompt. The game will prompt you to hit the Enter key; when you do, the game begins. Use the Shift keys to move the paddle back and forth; the goal is to knock down all the bricks forming the wall. However, you have a limited number of balls. A few convenience features were added to the game; the space bar will pause the game until another key is hit, and the Esc key will reset to the initial message. You can add a variety of improvements to the game. For example, you can allow the player to pick a level of difficulty, or to select the number of balls or the number of rows of bricks.

The third sample program, called "LIFE.ASM" (Program 16-3), is a BIOS version of the game of Life. It uses many macros (see Chapter 15) and provides some examples of how macros can be used in the normal course of programming. The game of Life allows you to watch the generations of a one-celled life form pass across the screen. Each cell on the screen can, in each turn, die, remain stable, or give rise to new cells. The changing patterns formed by the successive generations can be an intriguing sight if the initial pattern of cells is chosen carefully.

To begin the game, type "LIFE" from the DOS prompt. To enter the initial pattern of cells, hit any key wherever you want a cell to be. The space bar is used to erase mistaken entries, the cursor keys to maneuver the cursor around the screen, and the Enter key to end the entry of cells.

Program 16-1. DUMP.ASM

```
        page   ,96
        title .This program dumps the contents of a file in hex and chr.
;
; DUMP.ASM
;
dseg      segment  para public 'DATA'
number    dw ?                            ;how many bytes in block
handle    dw ?                            ;handle number for input
noopen    db cr,lf,'The file could not be opened.$'
noread    db cr,lf,'Error while reading a data sector.$'
done      db cr,lf,'BDOS code on exit: $'
buffer    db 64 dup ('BUFFER  ')
bufflen   equ $-buffer
dseg      ends
;
psp       segment  at 0                   ;used for program prefix
          org 80h
upa       label byte
psp       ends
;
sseg      segment  para stack 'STACK'
          db 16 dup ('STACK   ')
sseg      ends
;
          page
```

313

```
cseg    segment para public 'CODE'
;
bdos    equ 21h          ;interrupt number
prints  equ 9            ;print a string to console
open    equ 3dh          ;open file named at DS:DX
close   equ 3eh          ;close file
read    equ 3fh          ;read next sequential block
;
video   equ 10h          ;video interrupt
setcrs  equ 2            ;set cursor position
readcrs equ 3            ;read cursor position
outchar equ 14           ;write character, advance
readvid equ 15           ;read video state
;
lf      equ 10           ;line feed character
cr      equ 13           ;carriage return character
;
        assume cs:cseg,ss:sseg
program proc far
        push ds
        mov ax,0
        push ax
;
        assume ds:psp
        mov bl,upa
        mov bh,0
        mov upa+1 [bx],0    ;convert to ASCIIZ
;
```

```
        mov  dx,offset upa+2      ;open file
        mov  ah,open              ;open the file
        mov  al,0
        int  bdos
        assume ds:dseg            ;(set DS to DSEG)
        mov  dx,dseg
        mov  ds,dx
        jnc  init                 ;no error
        mov  dx,offset noopen     ;no file, so print and RET
        call print
        jmp  endprg
;
init:   mov  handle,ax            ;store handle
        mov  number,bufflen
        mov  cx,0                 ;init count and buffer pointer
        mov  bx,bufflen
;
main:   cmp  bx,number           ;any more data?
        jne  moredat
        call readnx
        jc   error                ;no, so get more
        jz   lastchr              ; c=1 indicates error
        mov  number,ax            ; z=1 indicates end of file
        mov  bx,0
moredat:test bx,000fh            ;reset buffer-pointer
        jnz  inline               ;at start of line?
        call newlin               ;yes, so crlf and output cx
```

315

```
inline: mov al,' '                          ;ouput a separator
        call chrout
        mov al,buffer [bx]
        call hexout                         ;print the number
        inc cx                              ;increment the count
        inc bx                              ;increment pointer for buffer
        test bx,000fh                       ;at end of line?
        jnz main                            ;no, so repeat loop
        call chars                          ;display characters
        jmp main
;
error:  mov dx,offset noread                ;indicate data read error
        call print
        jmp endprg
;
lastchr:test bx,000fh
        jz endprg                           ;no chrprint if already done!
        push ax
        call chars                          ;do last chars and fall through
        pop ax
;
endprg: mov dx,offset done                  ;print "final BDOS code:"
        call print
        call hexout                         ;print error
        mov bx,handle                       ;close file
        mov ah,close
        int bdos
        ret                                 ;back to DOS or DEBUG
```

```
; program endp
subs    proc near
;
; read next sector, return z=0 if no more data
; if c=1, AL holds the error number and z=?
; otherwise return number of bytes in new sector in AX
;
readnx: push cx
        push bx
        mov ah,read         ;get next sector
        mov bx,handle
        mov cx,bufflen
        mov dx,offset buffer
        int bdos
        pop bx
        pop cx
        jc readend
readok: cmp ax,0            ;if error (c=1) return
readend:ret                 ;set z=0 if no more data
;
; print the character values for the numbers
;
chars:  call tab            ;position at col.55
        dec bx              ;go back to start of line
        and bx,0fff0h
chrlp:  mov al,buffer [bx]  ;get value
```

```
        cmp al,32         ;if less than 32 ...
        jb period         ;... or greater than 127
        cmp al,128
        jb printc
period: mov al,'.'        ;set character to a period
printc: call chrout       ;output it
        inc bx
        cmp bx,number     ;test for early end
        je endchr
        test bx,000fh     ;test for 16 bytes output
        jnz chrlp
endchr: ret

; set column = 55, preserve BX, CX
;
tab:    push bx           ;save reg.s
        push cx
        mov ah,readvid    ;get active page
        int video
        mov ah,readcrs    ;get cursor r,c in DH,DL
        int video
        mov dl,55         ;set column = 55
        mov ah,setcrs     ;set cursor
        int video
        pop cx
        pop bx
        ret
```

```
; do a cr-lf sequence and print CX (file byte count)
;
newlin: mov al,cr               ;end of line: return
        call chrout
        mov al,lf
        call chrout
        mov al,ch               ;print the count
        call hexout
        mov al,cl
        call hexout
        mov al,' '              ;extra separator
        call chrout
        ret
;
; output byte in AL in hex
; preserve BX and CX
;
hexout: push ax                 ;print high nybble
        shr al,1
        shr al,1
        shr al,1
        shr al,1
        call nybout
        pop ax                  ;get low nybble, fall through
nybout: and al,0fh
        add al,'0'              ;adjust to ASCII
        cmp al,'9'
        jbe chrout              ;fall through
```

319

```
        add al,'A'-'9'-1        ;adjust to A-F, fall through
;
; do a safe CONOUT from AL
;
chrout: push bx
        push cx
        push ax
        mov ah,readvid          ;save CX,BX
        int video               ;get active page into BH
        pop ax
        mov bl,15
        mov ah,outchar          ;print in bright white
        int video
        pop cx                  ;restore CX,BX
        pop bx
        ret
;
; print the string at DS:DX, and save AX
;
print:  push ax
        mov ah,prints
        int bdos
        pop ax
        ret
;
subs    endp
cseg    ends
end     program
```

Program 16-2. REBOUND.ASM

```
        page ,96
        title REBOUND.ASM -- monochrome and color/graphics

;
; REBOUND.ASM
;
; interrupts and functions used in the program

video    equ 10h    ;video I/O interrupt number
setmode  equ 0      ; set current video mode
settype  equ 1      ; set cursor size
setpos   equ 2      ; set cursor position
readpos  equ 3      ; read cursor position
scrolup  equ 6      ; scroll active page up
scroldn  equ 7      ; scroll active page down
readchr  equ 8      ; read attribute/character
writeac  equ 9      ; write attribute/character
ttype    equ 14     ; write teletype to page
;
keybd    equ 16h    ;keyboard I/O interrupt
keyread  equ 0      ; wait and read next key
status   equ 1      ; check if any keys pressed
shift    equ 2      ; read shift status into AL
;
timeday  equ 1ah    ;time of day clock
readtim  equ 0      ; read the current time
```

```
; other constants used in the program
;
brick_1  equ  219        ;filled blocks
brick_2  equ  219        ; (note: monochrome board
brick_3  equ  219        ; has different block values)
brick_4  equ  219
;
att_1    equ  1          ;attribute for brick_1: blue
att_2    equ  2          ; for brick_2: green
att_3    equ  4          ; for brick_3: red
att_4    equ  6          ; for brick_4: brown
backgnd  equ  7          ; for background: light grey
frame    equ  15         ; for game frame: white
balls_r  equ  12         ; for "Balls remaining": pink
break    equ  15         ; for "REBOUND: white
paddle   equ  9          ; for paddle: light blue
ballatt  equ  3          ; for ball: cyan
;
delay_1  equ  4000       ;delay LOOP to slow game down
delay_2  equ  10         ;multiply factor for diff.
;
l_mar    equ  3          ;left margin of field
r_mar    equ  76         ; right margin
t_mar    equ  3          ; top margin
top_row  equ  t_mar+3    ;row of top of bricks
rows     equ  5          ;number of rows of bricks
```

```
; program data
;
dseg        segment  para  'DATA'
ball_pos         dw ?  ;column, row of ball (low byte/high byte)
old_ball_pos     dw ?  ;last col, row at which ball was plotted
direction        db ?  ;direction of ball: 0=NW, 1=NE, 2=SW, 3=SE
ball_wait_count  db 0  ;BALL delay before move (overflow counter)
speed            db ?  ;general game speed (127-255)
move_y_flag      db 0  ;flag to move ball up/down not
plot_ball_flag   db ?  ;toggle for draw/erase ball vs move ball
paddle_pos       db ?  ;position of player's paddle
bricks_number    db ?  ;number of bricks remaining on field
hit_key_flag     db 0  ;0 = do HIT_KEY query before game
;
; lists of the objects the ball can hit
;
bricks  db  brick_1,brick_2,brick_3,brick_4   ;list for SCASB
v_obst  db  179,218,191                        ;vertical objects
h_obst  db  196,205,218,191,213,184            ;horizontal objects
;
; each string starts with row,column & ends with a zero
;
header   db  l_mar+1,1,'Balls remaining: '
balls    db  ?,39 dup(' '),'R E B O U N D',0   ;note BALLS var.
mvict    db  27,2,'Congratulations! You win!',0
mdefeat  db  25,2,'Triumph! Nothing can stop me!',0
```

```
mhitkey db 31,16,'Hit Enter to Begin',0

; each line is composed of fields of three bytes each:
; +0: the number of times to repeat the character (CX)
; +1: the attribute to use when printing the character (BL)
; +2: the actual character to be printed (AL)
; each string is terminated with a zero-byte
;
chrs_1   db 4,att_1,brick_1,4,att_2,brick_2,0
chrs_2   db 2,att_3,brick_3,4,att_4,brick_4,2,att_3,brick_3,0
top_att  db 36,balls_r,' ',36,break,' ',0
pad_chr  db 1,paddle,' ',1,paddle,213
         db 6,paddle,205,1,paddle,184,1,paddle,' ',0
pad_clr  db 79,paddle,' ',0
hit_clr  db r_mar-l_mar-1,backgnd,' ',0
;
dseg     ends
;
sseg     segment para stack 'STACK'
         db 16 dup('STACK   ')    ;stack 128 bytes deep
sseg     ends
;
cseg     segment para 'CODE'
         assume cs:cseg,ds:dseg,es:dseg,ss:sseg
rebound  proc far
;
         push ds                    ;set up far RETurn
```

```
        mov ax,0
        push ax
        mov ax,dseg        ;initialize DS,ES to DSEG
        mov ds,ax
        mov es,ax

;
initialize: mov al,3        ;set color/graphics to 80 col.
        mov ah,setmode     ;... and active page to zero
        int video
        mov cx,0           ;clear screen to backgnd attr.
        mov dh,24
        mov dl,79
        mov al,0
        mov bh,backgnd
        mov ah,scrolup
        int video
        mov ch,20h         ;disable cursor
        mov ah,settype     ; by calling set cursor type
        int video          ; with CH = 20H

; draw top line of playfield area
;
        mov dh,t_mar       ;row (fourth row)
        mov dl,l_mar       ;column (fifth column)
        mov bh,0           ;page zero
        call set_cursor    ;set cursor position
```

```
        mov   al,218            ;right angle single line
        mov   bl,frame          ;get frame attribute
        call  write_1_ac        ;write attribute/character
        mov   dl,l_mar+1        ;column four
        call  set_cursor
        mov   al,196            ;horiz. single line
        mov   cx,r_mar-l_mar-1  ;write 72 copies
        call  write_ac
        mov   dl,r_mar          ;last column
        call  set_cursor
        mov   al,191            ;right angle
        call  write_1_ac

;
; draw sides of playfield outline
;
draw_sides:
        mov   dh,t_mar+1        ;fifth row

        mov   dl,l_mar          ;second column
        call  set_cursor
        mov   al,179            ;vertical line
        call  write_1_ac        ;write one copy
        mov   dl,r_mar          ;jump to right-hand side
        call  set_cursor
        mov   al,179            ;another vertical line
        call  write_1_ac        ;output it
        inc   dh                ;go to next row
        cmp   dh,24             ;check if on last row
```

```
        jb  draw_sides              ;if not, go repeat

;
; draw header (balls remaining/REBOUND
; initialize BALLS, BRICKS_NUMBER, SPEED, PLOT_BALL_FLAG
;

        mov  dl,l_mar+1             ;initialize top row to correct
        mov  dh,1                   ; attributes (held in TOP_2)
        mov  si,offset top_att      ; for header
        call print_fields
        mov  balls,'5'              ;initialize number of balls
        mov  si,offset header
        call print_string           ;print the header
        mov  bricks_number,92       ;92 bricks in 5 rows of 18/19
        mov  speed,128              ;paddle moves 2 x ball
        mov  plot_ball_flag,0       ;begin by drawing ball

;
;; draw in the rows of bricks using different block characters
;; data for the rows of bricks is stored in CHRS_1 and CHRS_2
;; once a field is read into CX,BL,AL the WRITE_AC routine
;; is called and we advance the cursor by (CX) characters
;; at the end of each line, we scroll the window and DEC DI;
;; when DI is zero, all rows have been printed
;

        mov  di,rows               ;DI holds 5
bricks_row_loop:
        mov  dh,top_row-1          ;do all work on seventh row
        mov  dl,l_mar+1            ;--- on fifth column
```

```
        mov bh,0                ;... and on screen zero
        mov si,offset chrs_1    ;default to CHRS_1 (first row)
        test di,1               ;check if even or odd row
        jnz brl_1               ;if odd, default is correct
        mov si,offset chrs_2    ;otherwise, use CHRS_2 (row 2)
brl_1:  mov cx,9                ;9 copies of each pattern
brl_2:  call print_fields       ;print pattern once
        loop brl_2              ;loop back and print it again
        call scroll_window      ;scroll window one line down
        dec di                  ;decrement rows-count
        jnz bricks_row_loop     ;if not zero, loop back
        cmp hit_key_flag,0      ;test for display message
        jnz new_ball            ; no, so skip to NEW_BALL
        mov hit_key_flag,1      ; yes, so set flag
        call hit_key            ; and wait for go-ahead

; here begins the game proper;
; we come here whenever we lose a ball
;
new_ball:
        dec balls               ;we're starting one ball now
        cmp balls,'0'           ;check if any balls still left
        jae nb_1                ;0 or more balls waiting
        jmp defeat_handler      ;otherwise, player loses
        mov si,offset header    ;print balls/REBOUND
        call print_string       ; (thus updating BALLS display)
nb_1:   mov dh,24               ;clear bottom row so we can
```

```
        mov dl,0                         ; start with paddle in center
        mov si,offset pad_clr            ; (blank to background attrib.)
        call print_fields
        mov paddle_pos,35                ;center paddle
        mov ah,readtim                   ;get time (as a random number)
        int timeday                      ;take low word and ...
        mov ax,dx                        ;... put in AX for DIV op-code
        and ax,0fffh                     ;strip high four bits
        mov dl,20                        ;get time MOD 20 in AH
        div dl
        add ah,l_mar+1                   ;correct to left margin
        test ah,1                        ;half chance for right margin
        jz nb_2                          ; no, skip
        add ah,r_mar-l_mar-21            ; yes, put at right margin
nb_2:
        mov dl,ah                        ;put in DL so we can store DX
        mov dh,top_row+rows              ;ball starts under bottom row
        mov ball_pos,dx                  ;store col,row in BALL_POS
        mov direction,2                  ;assume ball's at right (go SW)
        cmp ah,39                        ;test assumption
        ja main_loop                     ; yes, keep default
        mov direction,3                  ; no, reverse direction (go SE)

;
; beginning of main loop for one ball-round
; here we handle moving the paddle back and forth
;
main_loop:
        mov ah,shift                     ;check shift status of keyboard
```

```
        int keybd
        and al,3          ;mask off all but shift keys
        jz do_draw        ;if neither key pressed no move
        cmp al,3          ;both keys pressed?
        je do_draw        ; yes, so don't move
        cmp al,1          ; 1 = move one right
        je ml_1           ; if so, 1 = move right
        mov al,-1         ; 2 = move one left
ml_1:   add al,paddle_pos ;get new position in AL
        cmp al,i_mar-1    ;test if beyond left edge
        jl do_draw        ; if so, no movement
        cmp al,r_mar+1-9  ;test if at right edge
        jg do_draw        ; if so, no movement
        mov paddle_pos,al ;AL is valid, so put in PADDLE_POS

do_draw:
        call draw_paddle  ;redraw paddle every turn

; handle the movement of the ball
;
; first we wait (with LOOP) for a delay (from SPEED)
; to slow the game down so it can be played
; we also check BALL_WAIT_COUNT to see if we move ball
;
move_ball_test:
        mov al,speed      ;calculate loop from SPEED:
        sub al,127        ; AX = 4000 - 10 * (AL - 127)
        mov cl,delay_2    ;DELAY_2 is a constant (10)
```

```
        mul cl                         ; at min speed, delay 4000
        neg ax                         ; at max, delay 2720
        add ax,delay_1                 ;DELAY_1 is a constant (4000)
        mov cx,ax                      ;set up for LOOP
mb_1:   loop mb_1                      ;17 machine cycles per loop
        mov al,ball_wait_count         ;test for overflow
        add al,speed                   ; with BALL_WAIT_COUNT
        mov ball_wait_count,al
        jc move_ball                   ;overflow, so move
        jmp check_keyboard

; here we find the ball's next position into DL,DH
; loop back here until no obstacles ahead of ball
;
move_ball:
        mov dx,ball_pos                ;DL = old column, DH = old row
        mov al,direction               ;get direction byte
        and al,1                       ;get horizontal component
        shl al,1                       ;multiply by two
        sub al,1                       ;convert 0,1 to -1,+1
        add dl,al                      ;DL holds new column
        mov al,direction               ;direction byte
        and al,2                       ;get vertical component
        sub al,1                       ;convert 0,2 to -1,+1
        xor move_y_flag,1              ;only move y every other turn
        jnz off_check                  ;if MOVE_Y_FLAG was zero, move
        mov al,0                       ; ... else don't move y
```

```
; check if ball is off-screen (lost the ball)
; if not, check spaces or bricks
;
off_check:
        add dh,al                       ;finally, we adjust DH
        cmp dh,24                       ;check if off-screen
        ja off_screen                   ;DH > 24, so ball is lost
        mov bh,0                        ;set page zero
        call set_cursor                 ;set cursor to next position
        mov ah,readchr                  ;function 8, read character
        int video                       ;get character ahead of ball
        cmp al,' '                      ;if next spot is empty,
        je no_obstacles                 ; skip over obstacle checking
        mov di,offset bricks            ;start at start of BRICKS
        mov cx,4                        ;check four bricks
        cld                             ;scan upwards through BRICKS
        repne scasb                     ;check for AL in BRICKS
        jne vertical_obstacles          ;if (ZF)=0, AL not in BRICKS
        call remove_brick               ;handle erasing the brick
        xor direction,2                 ;reverse y-direction
        mov move_y_flag,0               ;make ball bounce next turn
        jmp move_ball                   ;go back and try to move it

;
; execute this code if the ball has gone off the screen
;
off_screen:
        mov dx,old_ball_pos             ;the ball could be at old pos
```

```
        call erase_ball          ;(so erase it there)
        mov dx,ball_pos          ;or at new pos (BALL_POS)
        call erase_ball          ;(so erase it there too)
        call draw_paddle         ;in case we erased part of it
        mov ah,ttype             ;set up for teletype output
        mov al,7                 ;beep when you miss
        int video                ;go do beep
        jmp new_ball             ;loop back, check for no balls

; the ball has something in front of it
; it's not a space or a brick, so bounce off it
;
vertical_obstacles:
        mov di,offset v_obst     ;check if it's a vert. obstacle
        mov cx,3                 ;corners & vertical side bar
        repne scasb              ;scan table
        jne horizontal_obstacles ;if not a vertical obstacle
        xor direction,1          ;if it is, flip horiz component
horizontal_obstacles:
        mov di,offset h_obst     ;scan horizontal obstacles
        mov cx,6                 ;corners, top bar, paddle
        repne scasb              ;scan table
        je ho_1                  ;if equal, then horiz. obstacle
        jmp move_ball            ;if vertical, skip ahead
ho_1:   xor direction,2          ;otherwise, flip vert component
        jmp move_ball            ; and skip ahead
;
```

```
; go to no_obstacles if only a space in front of the ball
; here we alternately draw/erase the ball, and move it without
;
no_obstacles:
        xor  plot_ball_flag,1      ;come here on space
        jnz  no_show               ;test for plot ball/move ball
                                   ;if NZ, then move, else plot
plot_ball:
        push dx                    ;erase and re-plot the ball
        mov  dx,old_ball_pos       ;save new col,row on stack
        call erase_ball            ;get old ball's position
        pop  dx                    ;and erase there
        call draw_ball             ;recover new position
        mov  ball_pos,dx           ;and draw there
        jmp  check_keyboard        ;now save new position
                                   ;and skip to keyboard check
no_show:
        xchg dx,ball_pos           ;don't plot ball, just move it
        mov  old_ball_pos,dx       ;get POS = new pos, DX = old
                                   ;store old pos in OLD_BALL_POS
;
; check if anything requested at keyboard
; Esc restarts, Space pauses, Ctrl-Break terminates
;
check_keyboard:
        mov  ah,status             ;check buffer status
        int  keybd
        jz   check_win             ;skip checks if buffer empty
        mov  ah,keyread            ;otherwise get character
        int  keybd
        cmp  ah,1                  ;check for ESCape scan code
```

```
        jne   sp_chk                    ;no, skip over Esc handler
        mov   hit_key_flag,0            ;restart with "Hit Key" message
        jmp   initialize                ;go back and start over
sp_chk: cmp   al,' '                    ;test ASCII for space
        jne   brk_ck                    ;not space, keep checking
        mov   ah,keyread                ;get any key
        int   keybd
        jmp   check_win

brk_ck: or    al,ah                     ;.. and continue on
        jne   check_win                 ;test for AL=0,AH=0, Ctrl-Break
abort:  mov   al,3                      ;no, skip keyboard checking
        mov   ah,setmode                ;yes: set 80 x 25 b/w ...
        int   video
        ret                             ;  ... and drop out into DOS

;
; check to see if we've won the game yet
;
check_win:
        cmp   bricks_number,0           ;check if no bricks left
        jz    victory_handler           ;brick subroutine BRICKS_NUMBER
        jmp   main_loop                 ;if BRICKS_NUMBER zero, victory
                                        ;otherwise, loop back ...
;
; these two routines handle defeat and victory
;
victory_handler:
        mov   si,offset mvict           ;get victory message, fall to..
end_game:                               ;.. handle end of game
```

335

```
        call  print_string          ;print whichever message
        mov   dx,old_ball_pos        ;erase the ball at old position
        call  erase_ball
        mov   dx,ball_pos            ;erase the ball at new position
        call  erase_ball
        call  draw_paddle            ;then redraw the paddle in case
        call  hit_key                ;call "Hit Key" message
        jmp   initialize             ;... and go play again
defeat_handler:
        mov   si,offset mdefeat      ;get defeat message,
        jmp   end_game               ;... and go handle end of game

;
rebound endp                         ;and that's it!
;
; this routine draws a paddle at PADDLE_POS
; (incidentally erasing fragments to the sides)
;
draw_paddle proc near
        mov   dh,24                  ;paddle always on bottom line
        mov   dl,paddle_pos          ;PADDLE_POS holds row position
        mov   si,offset pad_chr      ;data for paddle printing
        call  print_fields           ;print it where requested
        ret                          ;and back to main routine

draw_paddle endp

;
; the following routines handle drawing and erasing the ball
; ball's position is taken from current DL,DH
```

```
; AX and BX are destroyed on output
;
ball_routines proc near         ;note two sub.s in one proc.
draw_ball:                      ;draw ball at BALL_POS
    push dx                     ;save DL,DH (col,row)
    mov bh,0                    ;set page zero
    call set_cursor            ;set cursor to X,Y
    mov al,9                    ;print a circle ..
    mov bl,ballatt             ;... with attribute BALLATT
    call write_1_ac           ;call function 9, write att/chr
    pop dx                     ;restore DL,DH
    ret                        ;and back to main program
erase_ball:                     ;write space at BALL_POS
    push dx                     ;save DL,DH (col,row)
    mov bh,0                    ;set page zero
    call set_cursor            ;set the cursor
    mov al,' '                  ;blank with space
    mov bl,backgnd             ;use background attribute
    call write_1_ac           ;write att/character
    pop dx                     ;restore DL,DH
    ret                        ;back to main program
ball_routines endp
;
; this routine erases the brick the ball is touching
; input: (DL,DH) is row,col within the brick to be removed
; output: brick erased, AX destroyed, SPEED set as necessary
;..
```

```
remove_brick proc near
    dec bricks_number        ;one less brick
    push bx                  ;save used registers
    push cx
    push dx

    mov bh,dh                ;save actual brick row
    sub dh,top_row           ;top row = 0
    and dh,1                 ;even row = 0, odd = 1
    shl dh,1                 ;even 0, odd 2
    sub dl,l_mar+1           ;left column = 0
    sub dl,dh                ;adjust to even brick
    and dl,11111100b         ;go to start of brick
    add dl,dh                ;re-adjust to real bricks
    mov cx,4                 ;assume a whole brick
    jns rb_1                 ;if positive a good value, else
    mov dl,0                 ;it's a left half-brick
    mov cx,2                 ;so assume only a half-brick
rb_1:
    add dl,l_mar+1           ;re-adjust to real columns
    mov dh,bh                ;and real rows
    cmp dl,r_mar-2           ;check for right half-brick
    jb rb_2                  ;no, so skip
    mov cx,2                 ;only delete half a brick
rb_2:
    mov bh,0                 ;page zero
    call set_cursor          ;put cursor at start of brick
    mov al,' '               ;blank brick to a space ...
    mov bl,backgnd           ;... with BACKGND attribute
```

```
        call write_ac          ;write as many blanks as (CX)

        sub dh,top_row         ;get row number again
        mov cl,5               ;shift value (mult. by 32)
        shl dh,cl              ;get 32 * brick number
        not dh                 ;DH = 255 - 32 * row
        cmp dh,speed           ;test current speed value
        jb rb_3                ; already faster
        mov speed,dh           ; no, set a higher speed
;
rb_3:   pop dx                 ;restore altered registers
        pop cx
        pop bx
        ret                    ;and back to program

remove_brick endp
;
; scroll the area within the outline down one row
; AX, BX, CX destroyed
;
scroll_window proc near
        push dx                ;save cursor row,column
        mov al,1               ;scroll window one line
        mov ch,top_row-1       ;top line = row 6
        mov cl,l_mar+1         ;don't scroll left border
        mov dh,23              ;scroll all the way to bottom
        mov dl,r_mar-1         ;don't scroll right border
        mov bh,backgnd         ;clear to standard bakgnd
```

```
        mov ah,scroldn        ;function 7, scroll window down
        int video             ;restore cursor position
        pop dx
        ret
scroll_window endp
;
; print the string at DS:SI terminated with a zero-byte
; all strings are printed at the col,row in their first 2 bytes
;
print_string proc near
        push bx               ;save altered register
        lodsw                 ;get row,column in AL,AH
        mov dx,ax             ;copy to cursor register
        mov bh,0              ;page zero
        call set_cursor       ;and put cursor there
print_loop:
        lodsb                 ;get a message ASCII byte
        cmp al,0              ;is it the end flag?
        jz print_done         ;yes, so go POP/RET
        mov ah,ttype          ;no, so print it
        int video
        jmp print_loop        ;and loop back again
print_done:
        pop bx                ;restore altered reg.
        ret                   ;and RETurn
print_string endp
;
```

```
; this routine prints the num,att,chr -field string pointed to
; by DS:SI starting at cursor position (DL,DH)
; on return, AX and BX destroyed, DL updated
;
print_fields proc near
        push cx                          ;save useful registers
        push si
        mov bh,0                         ;use active page (page zero)
pf_1:   call set_cursor                  ;set cursor to DL,DH
        lodsb                            ;get first byte of field
        cmp al,0                         ;if length=0, string ended
        jz pf_2                          ; so jump to the RETurn
        mov cl,al                        ;set CX = byte 1 (count)
        mov ch,0                         ; set high byte = zero
        lodsb                            ;get second byte of field
        mov bl,al                        ;set BL = byte 2 (attribute)
        lodsb                            ;set AL = byte 3 (character)
        call write_ac                    ;write (CX) copies of (AL,BL)
        add dl,cl                        ;move cursor over (CX) times
        jmp pf_1                          ;loop back for more data
pf_2:   pop si                           ;restore useful registers
        pop cx
        ret
print_fields endp
;
; this subroutine displays the string at MHITKEY
; then waits for a key to be struck
```

341

```
;
hit_key   proc near
          call hk_1                         ;call set-attrib subroutine
          mov si,offset mhitkey             ;print "Hit Key" message
          call print_string
hk_0:     mov ah,keyread                    ;read a key from keyboard
          int keybd
          cmp ah,28                         ;scan code of Enter
          jne hk_0                          ; not, so go wait some more
hk_1:     mov dx,word ptr mhitkey           ;get col,row of "Hit Key"
          mov dl,l_mar+1                     ;set row to start of area
          mov si,offset hit_clr             ;point at blanking field
          call print_fields                 ;and print it
          ret                               ;RET to HIT_KEY or main program
hit_key   endp
;
; the subroutines within this procedure allow the program to
; use the video functions somewhat more easily,
; simply by CALLing them, rather than specifying AH and INT.
;
video_procs proc near
set_cursor:
          push ax
          mov ah,setpos                     ;put cursor at DL,DH
          int video                         ; no registers altered
          pop ax
          ret
```

```
write_1_ac:                 ;write att/chr, only once
        mov cx,1            ; (repeat counter = 1)
write_ac:                   ;write att/chr (CX) times
        mov ah,writeac
        int video
        ret
video_procs endp
;
cseg    ends
        end rebound
```

Program 16-2A. REBOUND Monochrome Modifications

```
;
; other constants used in the program
;
brick_1   equ 176        ;1/4-filled block
brick_2   equ 177        ;1/2-filled block
brick_3   equ 178        ;3/4-filled block
brick_4   equ 219        ;filled block
;
att_1     equ 15         ;attribute for brick_1: white
att_2     equ 7          ; for brick_2: light grey
att_3     equ 15         ; for brick_3: white
att_4     equ 7          ; for brick_4: light grey
backgnd   equ 7          ; for background: light grey
frame     equ 15         ; for game frame: white
balls_r   equ 7          ; for "Balls remaining": grey
break     equ 15         ; for "REBOUND: white
paddle    equ 7          ; for paddle: light grey
ballatt   equ 15         ; for ball: white
```

Program 16-2B. REBOUND PCjr Modifications

```
delay_1   equ 2500       ;delay LOOP to slow game down
delay_2   equ 6          ;multiply factor for diff.
```

Program 16-3. LIFE.ASM

```
; LIFE
;
        page ,96
        .sall
;
; This program plays the game of life
; The user sets up the screen as he would like it to start
; then presses RETURN and the program goes
; until he presses a key.
;
;
UP_scan      equ 48H        ;up
DOWN_scan    equ 50H        ;down
LEFT_scan    equ 4BH        ;left
RIGHT_scan   equ 4DH        ;right
SPACE_scan   equ 39H        ;space
RET_scan     equ 1CH        ;return
;
cell         equ 15         ;cell character (large star)
space        equ ' '        ;blank character
normal       equ 7          ;normal attribute
;
video        equ 10H        ;VIDEO I/O int number
DOS_func     equ 21H        ;DOS function call
;
```

```
locate  macro row,column              ;set cursor position
        mov ah,2
        mov dh,row
        mov dl,column
        mov bh,0
        int video
        endm
;
check   macro coord,value,offset      ;special macro for setup
        local no_change
        cmp coord,value
        je no_change
        add coord,offset
no_change:
        ret
        endm
;
output  macro character,attribute     ;put character on screen
        mov ah,10
        mov bh,0
        mov cx,1
        mov al,character
        int video
        endm
;
place   macro matrix,xpos,ypos,character ;put char in matrix
        mov bx,ypos
```

```
        shl bx,1
        mov bx,row_addr[bx]
        mov si,xpos
        mov &matrix[bx+si],character
        endm
;
peek    macro matrix,xpos,ypos  ;look into matrix
        mov bx,ypos
        shl bx,1
        mov bx,row_addr[bx]
        mov si,xpos
        mov al,&matrix[bx+si]
        endm
;
clear   macro matrix            ;clear matrix
        mov cx,2000
        mov al,space
        lea di,es:matrix
        rep stos matrix
        endm
;
data    segment
matrix_1        db 2000 dup (?)
matrix_2        db 2000 dup (?)
;
population      dw ?            ;number of cells
generation      dw ?            ;number of generations
```

```
;
row_byte     equ this byte    ;row counter
row_pos      dw ?
col_byte     equ this byte    ;column counter
col_pos      dw ?
;
legal_keys   db UP_scan,DOWN_scan,LEFT_scan,RIGHT_scan  ;command keys
             db SPACE_scan,RET_scan
                              ;matching routines
key_routines dw do_up,do_down,do_left,do_right
             dw era_cell,do_ret
;
                              ;title messages
title_mes    dw game,cr,cr,author,cr,date,cr,cr,key_mes,0H
;
game         db 'The game of LIFE.$'  ;name of game
cr           db 13,10,'$'             ;cr-lf
author       db 'Implemented by Marc Sugiyama$' ;author
date         db 'September 12, 1984$'  ;date
key_mes      db 'Press any key to continue:$'
ins_mes      db 'Press any key to create a cell;'
             db " erase with space; start with return.$" ;instructions
gen_mes      db 'Generation:'         ;info
             db 'Population:$'         ;info
again_mes    db 'Play life again (y/n)? $'   ;play again?
spaces       db 79 dup(' '),'$'
```

```
;
row_addr      dw 0        ;table of 80s to find row address
              irp row,<1,2,3,4,5,6>
              dw &row*80
              endm
              irp row,<7,8,9,10,11,12>
              dw &row*80
              endm
              irp row,<13,14,15,16,17,18>
              dw &row*80
              endm
              irp row,<19,20,21,22,23,24>
              dw &row*80
              endm
;
;offsets for 8 directions
direction     dw -81,-80,-79,-1,1,79,80,81
data    ends
;
stack   segment stack              ;set up the stack segment
        db 1024 dup (?)
stack   ends
;
code    segment                    ;our code segment
program proc far
        assume es:data,ds:data,cs:code,ss:stack
        push ds                    ;for FAR return
```

349

```asm
        mov ax,0
        push ax
        mov ax,data       ;set up our data segs
        mov ds,ax
        mov es,ax
        call do_title     ;print the title page
;
runagain:
        clear matrix_1    ;put spaces in matrices
        clear matrix_2
        mov population,0  ;zero population
        mov generation,1  ;set generation to one
        call do_setup     ;set up screen
        jc done           ;if CF=1 then leave program
        call play         ;play the scenario
        call again        ;ask to play again
        jc runagain       ;if CF=1 then play again
        call cls          ;clear screen
;
done:   ret               ;return to DOS
program endp
;
; Again asks if the player wants to play again, if so, CF set
; Otherwise, CF=0
; All registers should be considered destroyed.
;
again   proc near
```

```
        locate 0,39             ;put cursor top line
        mov dx,offset again_mes ;set DS:DX to message
        call print              ;print message
check_key_again:
        call press_key          ;get key press
        and al,0DFH             ;AND out lower case bit
        cmp al,'Y'              ;play again
        je playagain
        cmp al,'N'              ;don't play again
        jne check_key_again
not_again:
        clc                     ;CF=0 means return to DOS
        ret
playagain:
        stc                     ;CF=1 means play again
        ret
again   endp
; Title clears the screen and prints the name of the program
; Consider all registers destroyed.
;
do_title proc near
        call cls                ;clear screen
        locate 1,0              ;set cursor to print message
        mov si,offset title_mes ;print messages one by one
print_title:
        mov dx,[si]             ;set DS:DX to message
```

351

```
        cmp dx,0            ;if message offset is zero, then done
        je wait_for_key
        add si,2            ;point to next message
        call print         ;print message
        jmp print_title    ;get next message to print
;
wait_for_key:
        call press_key     ;wait for key press
        ret                ;return to caller

do_title endp
;
; Set up the cells on the screen using user input.
; Consider all registers destroyed.
;
do_setup proc near
        call cls           ;clear screen
        locate 0,0         ;home cursor
        mov dx,offset ins_mes  ;print instructions
        call print
;
        mov row_pos,12     ;put cursor at center screen
        mov col_pos,39
;
poscrs: locate row_byte,col_byte  ;set to center of screen
        mov ah,0           ;get a key stroke
        int 16H
        cmp ax,0           ;program interrupted
```

```
        jne check_keys              ;return with error
        stc
        ret
;
check_keys:
        mov bx,0                    ;check for which key
checkloop:
        cmp ah,legal_keys[bx]
        je do_key                   ;if legal key, execute routine
        inc bx
        cmp byte ptr legal_keys[bx],0  ;last possible key?
        jne checkloop
        call set_cell               ;possible alternative
        jmp poscrs
;
do_key: shl bx,1                    ;2X for word table
        call key_routines[bx]       ;call routine
        jmp poscrs                  ;do the next key
;
do_up:    check row_pos,1,-1        ;process up
do_down:  check row_pos,24,1        ;down
do_left:  check col_pos,0,-1        ;left
do_right: check col_pos,79,1        ;right
                                    ;put new cell down
set_cell: peek matrix_2,col_pos,row_pos ;check if cell there
        cmp al,cell
        je noset
```

```
        output cell,normal            ;if new cell, put on screen
        place matrix_2,col_pos,row_pos,cell ;add to matrix
        inc population                ;set population
noset:  ret                           ;return to process next key
                                      ;remove cell from matrix
era_cell: peek matrix_2,col_pos,row_pos ;check if cell there
        cmp al,space
        je noera
        output space,normal           ;put space in spot
        place matrix_2,col_pos,row_pos,space ;clear matrix spot
        dec population                ;reduce population
noera:  ret                           ;return to process next key
do_ret: pop ax                        ;pop up one level
        clc                           ;continue with main program
        ret                           ;return to main level
do_setup endp

; Play, does the actual game, printing the generation at the
; top of the screen, as well as the number of cells living.
; Consider all registers destroyed.
;
play    proc near
        locate 0,0                    ;clear the first row
        mov dx,offset spaces
        call print
        locate 0,0                    ;print counters at top
        mov dx,offset gen_mes
```

```
        call print             ;print info messages
;
        cld                    ;work up (string ops)
;
play_loop:
        mov ah,1
        int 16H                ;pressing key interrupts play
        jz cont                ;if key pressed, stop
stopplay:
        ret
cont:
        call print_data        ;print gen and pop
        cmp population,0       ;if no living cells, exit game
        je stopplay
;
        mov cx,2000
        lea si,ds:matrix_2
        lea di,es:matrix_1
        rep movs matrix_1,matrix_2   ;move matrix two to one
;
        clear matrix_2         ;clear matrix two
;
loop1:  mov row_pos,1          ;start with row one
loop2:  mov col_pos,1          ;and column one
        peek matrix_1,col_pos,row_pos
```

```
        call look_around            ;look around
        cmp al,cell                 ;check for cell (peek op)
        jne nocell                  ;jump if no cell
        cmp cl,2                    ;cells survives if surrounded by
        je survive                  ;two or three other cells
        cmp cl,3
        je survive
        locate row_byte,col_byte    ;set cursor pos
        output space,normal         ;kill on screen
        place matrix_2,col_pos,row_pos,space  ;kill in matrix
        dec population              ;reduce population by one
        jmp next

;
survive:
        place matrix_2,col_pos,row_pos,cell  ;put in matrix
        jmp next

;
nocell: cmp cl,3                    ;give birth of new cell
        jne next
        inc population              ;new cell born
        locate row_byte,col_byte    ;set cursor pos
        output cell,normal          ;make it bright
        place matrix_2,col_pos,row_pos,cell  ;put in matrix

;
next:   inc col_pos                 ;do next column
        cmp col_pos,79              ;done all?
        jnb skip1                   ;conditional jump too far
```

```
skip1:    jmp loop2
          inc row_pos            ;do next row
          cmp row_pos,23         ;done all?
          jnb skip2              ;short jump problem again
          jmp loop1
skip2:    inc generation         ;have finished next generation
          jmp play_loop          ;do again
play      endp
;
; look around checks to see how many cells are around a space
; only BX,CX,DI,SI are used
;
look_around proc near
          mov bx,row_pos          ;find row
          shl bx,1                ;get address from table of 80s
          mov bx,row_addr[bx]
          add bx,col_pos          ;add column to it
          add bx,offset matrix_1  ;add offset into data seg
          mov di,14               ;set DI to last dir offset
          mov cl,8                ;set CL to all cells
look_loop:
          mov si,direction[di]           ;get direction offset
          cmp byte ptr [bx][si],cell     ;see if cell
          je look_next
          dec cl                  ;if not cell, reduce CL by one
look_next:
          sub di,2                ;get next direction offset
```

16
Sample Programs

```
          jns  look_loop              ;done them all?
          ret                          ;return to caller
look_around endp
;
; print data outputs the population and the generation
; consider all registers lost.
;
print_data proc near
          locate 0,11
          mov ax,generation            ;position for generation
          call decimal_out             ;pass generation to DECIMAL_OUT
          locate 0,30                  ;position for population
          mov ax,population            ;pass population to DECIMAL_OUT
          call decimal_out
          ret                          ;return to caller
print_data endp
;
; Output a hex word in decimal
; AX, DX, BP destroyed
;
decout    proc near
;constants for binary to ASCII conv
tens      dw 1,10,100,1000,10000
leading_zero  db 0    ;leading zero flag
;
decimal_out:
          mov leading_zero,1           ;set leading zero flag
```

```
        mov bp,8                    ;set BP to end of ten table
;
decout1:
        mov dx,0                    ;prepare to divide
        div tens[bp]               ;divide by power of ten
        add al,'0'                 ;convert to ASCII
        push dx                    ;store remainder
        cmp al,'0'                 ;is byte a zero?
        jne send_char              ;no, so print it
        cmp bp,0                   ;is is the last character?
        je send_char               ;yes, so print it
        cmp leading_zero,1         ;is it a leading zero?
        je send_space              ;yes, so don't print it
send_char:
        mov leading zero,0
        call chrout                ;print it
        jmp next_digit
send_space:
        mov al,' '                 ;pad with spaces
        call chrout
next_digit:
        pop ax                     ;get remainder back
        sub bp,2                   ;point to next lower ten
        jns decout1                ;if still in table, do again
        ret
decout  endp
;
```

```
chrout    proc near
          mov ah,14           ;function call to output
          int video           ;print character
          ret

chrout    endp
;
routines proc near            ;misc routines
;
; Print message pointed to by DS:DX
;
print:    push ax             ;save AX
          mov ah,9            ;set function call nine
          int DOS_func        ;print the message
          pop ax              ;restore AX
          ret

; wait for key to be pressed
;
press_key:
          mov ah,0CH          ;function 0CH (clear buffer)
          mov al,7            ;set to no echo, wait for key
          int DOS_func        ;execute
          ret

; clear the screen
cls:      mov ah,0
          mov al,2            ;set 80x25 (clears page)
```

```
        int video
        mov ah,5        ;select page zero
        mov al,0
        int video
        ret             ;return to caller
;
routines endp
code    ends
        end
```

The 8088 Instruction Set

We will discuss two aspects of the 8088 instruction set here. First we will present a table of the execution times for each instruction to execute, then a table of what flags each instruction sets when it executes.

Execution Time

If you are trying to write a time-efficient program, it can be very helpful to know how long each instruction takes to execute. The time is given in *clock cycles*. The microprocessor paces itself with clock pulses at a rate of 4.77 million per second (or 4.77 megahertz, 4.77 MHz). However, on some computers, such as the PCjr, the computer's RAM is shared with the video controller, so it takes extra clock cycles to read the program from memory, thus slowing everything down.

There are a few strange notations in Table A-2. Every time the 8088 reads data from memory, it takes an additional quantity of time depending on the addressing mode. This extra time is called EA, for Effective Address, and adds the number of clock cycles to memory addressing, as shown in Table A-1.

Notice that it takes longer to use [BP] with [SI] or [DI] than it does to use [BX]. Also, you must add yet another two clock cycles if your operand takes a segment override.

On the 8088, words often take a different length of time to handle than bytes. This is shown below by putting the time for a word in parentheses after the time for a byte. Notice also that for string commands, the time to execute once is followed by the time to execute using the REP prefix. Additionally, notice that when rotating or shifting a value by CL, it takes four cycles per bit (as shown in the table).

For example, if you program

MOV AX, CS:TABLE [BP]

you must first find the time to move memory into a register. Table A-2 gives the time for MOV register, memory as 8(12)+EA. Since AX is a word register, we take the 12-cycle value. The addressing mode is base with displacement, so the Effective Address calculation time is 9 clock cycles. To this we add 2 clock cycles for the segment override, to get 12+9+2, or 23 clock cycles in all.

Table A-1. Effective Address Calculation Time

Addressing Mode	Operands	Clock Cycles
displacement addressing	label	6
base/index addressing	[BX]	5
	[BP]	
	[DI]	
	[SI]	
base/index with displacement	[BX]+disp	9
	[BP]+disp	
	[DI]+disp	
	[SI]+disp	
base and index	[BX][SI]	7
	[BX][DI]	
	[BP][SI]	8
	[BP][DI]	
base, index, displacement	[BX][SI]+disp	11
	[BX][DI]+disp	
	[BP][SI]+disp	12
	[BP][DI]+disp	

Table A-2. Execution Time for 8088 Instructions

Instruction		Clock Cycles
AAA		4
AAD		63
AAM		80
AAS		4
ADC, ADD	accumulator,data	4
	register,data	4
	register,register	3
	register,memory	9(13)+EA
	memory,data	17(25)+EA
	memory,register	16(24)+EA
CALL	near	23
	far	36
	indirect register near	24
	indirect memory near	29+EA
	indirect memory far	57+EA
CBW		2

Instruction		Clock Cycles
CLC		2
CLD		2
CLI		2
CMC		2
CMP	accumulator,data	4
	register,data	4
	register,register	3
	register,memory	9(13)+EA
	memory,data	10(14)+EA
	memory,register	9(13)+EA
CMPS		22(30) / 9+22(30) per rep
CWD		5
DAA		4
DAS		4
DEC	register	3(2)
	memory	15(23)+EA
DIV	register	80 to 90 (144 to 162)
	memory	86 to 96 (154 to 172)+EA
ESC	number,register	2
	number,memory	8(12)+EA
HLT		2
IDIV	register	101 to 112 (165 to 184)
	memory	107 to 118 (175 to 194)+EA
IMUL	register	80 to 98 (128 to 154)
	memory	86 to 104 (138 to 164)+EA
IN	accumulator,port	10(14)
	accumulator,DX	8(12)
INC	register	3(2)
	memory	15(23)+EA
INT	number	51
INT	3	52
INTO		53 or 4
IRET		32
JCXZ	short label	18 or 6
Jcond	short label	16 or 4
JMP	direct	15
	indirect register near	11
	indirect memory near	18+EA
	indirect memory far	24+EA
LAHF		4
LDS	register,dword memory	24+EA
LEA	register,word memory	2+EA
LES	register,dword memory	24+EA
LOCK		2
LODS		12(16) / 9+13(16) per rep

Instruction		Clock Cycles
LOOP	short	17 or 5
LOOPZ	short	18 or 6
LOOPNZ	short	19 or 5
MOV	accumulator,memory	10(14)
	memory,accumulator	10(14)
	register,data	4
	register,register	2
	register,memory	8(12)+EA
	memory,data	10(14)+EA
	memory,register	9(13)+EA
	segment,word register	2
	segment,word memory	12+EA
	word register,segment	2
	word memory,segment	13+EA
MOVS		18(26) / 9+17(25) per rep
MUL	register	70 to 77 (118 to 133)
	memory	76 to 83 (128 to 143)+EA
NEG	register	3
	memory	16(24)+EA
NOP		3
NOT	register	3
	memory	16(24)+EA
OR	accumulator,data	4
	register,data	4
	register,register	3
	register,memory	9(13)+EA
	memory,data	17(25)+EA
	memory,register	16(24)+EA
OUT	port,accumulator	10(14)
	DX,accumulator	8(12)
POP	register	12
	segment	12
	memory	25+EA
POPF		12
PUSH	register	12
	segment	12
	memory	24+EA
PUSHF		14
RCL, RCR	register,1	2
	register,CL	8 + 4 per bit
	memory,1	15(23)+EA
	memory,CL	20(28)+EA + 4 per bit
REP		2
REPE		2
REPNE		2

RET	(near)	20
	(far)	32
	pop (near)	24
	pop (far)	31
ROL, ROR	register,1	2
	register,CL	8 + 4 per bit
	memory,1	15(23)+EA
	memory,CL	20(28)+EA + 4 per bit
SAHF		4
SAL, SAR	register,1	2
	register,CL	8 + 4 per bit
	memory,1	15(23)+EA
	memory,CL	20(28)+EA + 4 per bit
SBB, SUB	accumulator,data	4
	register,data	4
	register,register	3
	register,memory	9(13)+EA
	memory,data	17(25)+EA
	memory,register	16(24)+EA
SCAS		15(19) / 9+15(19) per rep
SHL, SHR	register,1	2
	register,CL	8 + 4 per bit
	memory,1	15(23)+EA
	memory,CL	20(28)+EA + 4 per bit
STC		2
STD		2
STI		2
STOS		11(15) / 9+10(14) per rep
SUB	(see SBB)	
TEST	accumulator,data	4
	register,data	5
	register,register	3
	register,memory	9(13)+EA
	memory,data	11+EA
WAIT		3 + wait period
XCHG	AX,register	3
	register,memory	17(25)+EA
	register,register	4
XLAT		11
XOR	accumulator,data	4
	register,data	4
	register,register	3
	register,memory	9(13)+EA
	memory,data	17(25)+EA
	memory,register	16(24)+EA

Opcodes and Flags

As a rule, most instructions either set all of the arithmetic flags, or else don't set any of them. The following instructions set all the arithmetic flags:

ADD, ADC, SUB, SBB, NEG, CMP, CMPS, SCAS

All of the flags are set in accordance with the result of the operation (remember, the comparisons—CMP, CMPS, and SCAS—are really subtractions). For a discussion of how the flags are set, see the discussion of conditional jumps in Chapter 5.

Some instructions don't set any of the flags. Basically these instructions fall into two categories: move instructions and jump instructions. Neither of these alters any flags.

Move instructions:
MOV, LEA, LODS, STOS, MOVS, PUSH, POP, IN, OUT, XCHG, XLAT, LDS, LES

Jump instructions:
JMP, jump-on-condition, LOOP, CALL, RET

There are also a handful of other opcodes that are very specialized and don't have any effect on the flags:

CBW, CWD, ESC, HLT, LAHF, PUSHF, LOCK, NOP, NOT, REP, WAIT

Take special note of CBW, CWD, and NOT, since these instructions might well be expected to set flags, but in fact do not.

Several instructions affect the flags in a self-apparent fashion. The CLC, STC, and CMC instructions, for example, clearly affect only the carry flag; likewise for CLI and STI, and CLD and STD.

The following table lists other opcodes that affect the flags in different ways. The asterisk (*) means that the flag is changed purposefully by the instruction, the question mark (?) means the flag is randomly changed, and the dash (−) means not changed. Where there's a zero (0), the instruction always clears the flag.

ZF = zero flag, result is 0
SF = sign flag, result is negative (high bit is 1)
CF = carry flag, unsigned result too large
OF = overflow flag, signed result too large

AF = auxiliary carry flag
PF = parity flag
DF = direction flag, clear = increment string pointer
IF = interrupt flag, enable external interrupts
TF = trap flag, enable interrupt 1 after each instruction

Bit-Positions of Flags in Flags Register

15	14	13	12	11	10	9	8	7	6	5	4	3	2	1	0
–	–	–	–	OF	DF	IF	TF	SF	ZF	–	AF	–	PF	–	CF

Table A-3. Flag Setting

Instruction	ZF	SF	CF	OF	AF	PF	DF	IF	TF
ADC, ADD, CMP, CMPS, NEG, SBB, SCAS, SUB	*	*	*	*	*	*	–	–	–
CALL, CBW, CWD, ESC, HLT, IN, JMP, jump-on-condition, LAHF LDS, LEA, LES, LOCK, LODS, LOOP, LOOPE, LOOPNE, MOV, MOVS, NOP, NOT, OUT, POP, PUSH, PUSHF, REP, REPE, REPNE, RET, STOS, WAIT, XCHG, XLAT	–	–	–	–	–	–	–	–	–
DEC and INC	*	*	–	*	*	*	–	–	–
AND, OR, XOR, TEST	*	*	0	0	?	*	–	–	–
SHR, SHL, SAL, SAR	*	*	*	*	?	*	–	–	–
ROL, ROR, RCL, RCR	–	–	*	*	–	–	–	–	–
DIV and IDIV	?	?	?	?	?	?	–	–	–
MUL and IMUL †	?	?	*	*	?	?	–	–	–
AAA and AAS	?	?	*	?	*	?	–	–	–
AAD and AAM	*	*	?	?	?	*	–	–	–
DAA and DAS	*	*	*	?	*	*	–	–	–
INT and INTO ‡	–	–	–	–	–	–	–	0	0
IRET	restores all nine flags from stack								
POPF	restores all nine flags from stack								
SAHF	restores ZF, SF, CF, AF, PF from AH								
CLC, STC, CMC, STD, CLD, STI, CLI	affects one flag, as appropriate								

† The MUL instruction sets CF and OF if the result of the multiplication is larger than a byte (for byte multiplication) or a word (for word multiplication).

‡ INT and INTO clear the trap and interrupt flags so that interrupts won't interrupt each other. However, the IRET instruction at the end of the interrupt routine restores IF and TF.

Addressing Modes
and Possible Register Arrangements

Addressing Mode Name	Possible Arrangements
Direct mode	(label)
	displacement
Register Indirect mode	[BX]
	[BP]
	[SI]
	[DI]
Based mode	[BX+n]
	[BP+n]
Indexed mode	[SI+n]
	[DI+n]
Based Indexed mode	[BX+SI]
	[BX+DI]
	[BP+SI]
	[BP+DI]
Based Indexed mode with Displacement	[BX+SI+n]
	[BX+DI+n]
	[BP+SI+n]
	[BP+DI+n]

where n represents a signed 8- or 16-bit displacement.

Table of Registers

The 8088 has 14 word-sized registers. There are four general-purpose accumulators, four index registers, four segment registers, one program counter, and one status register. The four general-purpose accumulators are named as follows:

Primary accumulator	: AX
Base register	: BX
Counter	: CX
Data register	: DX

Each of these word-sized accumulators can be referred to as two separate byte-sized accumulators:

AX = AH,AL
BX = BH,BL
CX = CH,CL
DX = DH,DL

BX is the only general-purpose register that can be used in register indirect addressing. The AX:DX pair is frequently used to store double words. CX, the counter, is used to hold the number of iterations for the LOOP command, the number of times to repeat a string command. CL is also used to hold the number of times to perform a shift or rotate command.

The four word-sized index registers are as follows:

Stack Pointer   : SP
Base Pointer   : BP
Source Index   : SI
Destination Index : DI

The four segment registers are as follows:

Code Segment : CS
Data Segment : DS
Stack Segment : SS
Extra Segment : ES

The instruction pointer (IP) and the status registers are the remaining two registers. The IP points to the current instruction in the machine language program. It is an offset value from the CS register.

The status register can be broken down into the following bits:

bit	use	bit	use
00H	carry flag	08H	interrupt enable/disable
01H	parity flag	09H	flag
02H	unused	0AH	direction flag
03H	auxiliary carry flag	0BH	overflow flag
04H	unused	0CH	unused
05H	zero flag	0DH	unused
06H	sign flag	0EH	unused
07H	trap mode (single-step)	0FH	unused
	flag		unused

MASM Pseudo-ops

Brief Descriptions of MASM Pseudo-ops

Pseudo-ops marked with a star (*) can't be used with ASM.

*%	use value of constant, not name
*&	force assembler to recognize next word as parameter
.CREF	turn on Cross REFerence output at this point
.LALL	list complete macro/repeat expansions
.RADIX	set default base to decimal number following .RADIX
.SALL	suppress all output of macro/repeat expansions
.XALL	only output code-producing lines of macros/repeat blocks
;	comment line: the assembler ignores everything following
*;;	macro comment, never expanded into the list file
=	dynamic assignment pseudo-op for constants
ASSUME	which segment registers are pointing at which segments
DB	define a byte value
DD	define a double word value (four bytes)
*DQ	define a quad word value (eight bytes)
*DT	define a ten-byte value for packed decimal format
DUP	duplicate the operand the specified number of times
DW	define a word (two bytes)
ELSE	precedes a block of code to be executed if an IF is false
END	marks the end of the source file; can specify start
ENDIF	marks the end of a conditional block of statements
*ENDM	marks the end of a macro (don't precede with macro name)
ENDP	marks the end of a procedure (preceded with PROC name)
ENDS	marks the end of a segment (preceded with SEG-MENT name)
EQU	equate a symbol to a value, a symbol, an alias, or text
*EXITM	abort a macro early
IF	assemble following statements if operand <> 0
IF1	assemble following statements if assembler on pass 1
IF2	assemble following statements if assembler on pass 2
*IFB	assemble following statements if operand is blank
*IFDEF	assemble following statements if operand is defined

IFDIF	assemble following statements if operand 1 <> operand 2
IFE	assemble following statements if operand = 0
IFIDN	assemble following statements if operand 1 = operand 2
***IFNB**	assemble following statements if operand is not blank
***IFNDEF**	assemble following statements if operand is not defined
INCLUDE	include the "filename.ext" file in the assembly process
***IRP**	repeat loop once for each parameter specified
***IRPC**	repeat loop once for each character in specified string
LABEL	define the symbol preceding LABEL as the type following it
LENGTH	return the length in units (bytes, words, etc.) of the operand
***LOCAL**	macro operator to make assembler rename operand labels
***MACRO**	define a macro with specified name and operands
OFFSET	return the offset of the symbol from the start of its segment
PAGE	define the length and width of a page, or force a new page
PROC	begin a procedure with the specified name and type
PTR	override the type of the expression with the specified type
***REPT**	repeat the specified block of codes "operand" times
SEG	return the segment address of the specified segment
SEGMENT	define the start of a segment with the specified name
SHORT	make the jump statement assume a forward jump is short
SIZE	return the size in bytes of a DUPlicated entry
SUBTTL	specify a new subtitle for the list file
THIS	used with EQU to define a symbol with specified type
TITLE	specify the title of the list file
TYPE	return the type (that is, length in bytes) of the operand

Binary Information

Hex Number	Binary Number	Decimal X000	0X00	00X0	000X
0	0000	0	0	0	0
1	0001	4096	256	16	1
2	0010	8192	512	32	2
3	0011	12288	768	48	3
4	0100	16384	1024	64	4
5	0101	20480	1280	80	5
6	0110	24576	1536	96	6
7	0111	28672	1792	112	7
8	1000	32768	2048	128	8
9	1001	36864	2304	144	9
A	1010	40960	2560	160	10
B	1011	45056	2816	176	11
C	1100	49152	3072	192	12
D	1101	53248	3328	208	13
E	1110	57344	3584	224	14
F	1111	61440	3840	240	15

X is the hex digit

ASCII Values

Hex	ASCII	Character	Hex	ASCII	Character
0	000	(null)	20	032	(space)
1	001	☺	21	033	!
2	002	●	22	034	''
3	003	♥	23	035	#
4	004	♦	24	036	$
5	005	♣	25	037	%
6	006	♠	26	038	&
7	007	(beep)	27	039	'
8	008	■	28	040	(
9	009	(tab)	29	041	)
A	010	○	2A	042	*
B	011	♂	2B	043	+
C	012	(form feed)	2C	044	,
D	013	(carriage return)	2D	045	-
E	014	♫	2E	046	.
F	015	☼	2F	047	/
10	016	►	30	048	0
11	017	◄	31	049	1
12	018	↕	32	050	2
13	019	‼	33	051	3
14	020	¶	34	052	4
15	021	§	35	053	5
16	022	▬	36	054	6
17	023	↨	37	055	7
18	024	↑	38	056	8
19	025	↓	39	057	9
1A	026	→	3A	058	:
1B	027	←	3B	059	;
1C	028	∟	3C	060	<
1D	029	↔	3D	061	=
1E	030	▲	3E	062	>
1F	031	▼	3F	063	?

Hex	ASCII	Character	Hex	ASCII	Character
40	064	@	60	096	`
41	065	A	61	097	a
42	066	B	62	098	b
43	067	C	63	099	c
44	068	D	64	100	d
45	069	E	65	101	e
46	070	F	66	102	f
47	071	G	67	103	g
48	072	H	68	104	h
49	073	I	69	105	i
4A	074	J	6A	106	j
4B	075	K	6B	107	k
4C	076	L	6C	108	l
4D	077	M	6D	109	m
4E	078	N	6E	110	n
4F	079	O	6F	111	o
50	080	P	70	112	p
51	081	Q	71	113	q
52	082	R	72	114	r
53	083	S	73	115	s
54	084	T	74	116	t
55	085	U	75	117	u
56	086	V	76	118	v
57	087	W	77	119	w
58	088	X	78	120	x
59	089	Y	79	121	y
5A	090	Z	7A	122	z
5B	091	[	7B	123	{
5C	092	\	7C	124	¦
5D	093	]	7D	125	}
5E	094	∧	7E	126	~
5F	095	–	7F	127	⌂

Hex	ASCII	Character	Hex	ASCII	Character
80	128	Ç	A0	160	á
81	129	ü	A1	161	í
82	130	é	A2	162	ó
83	131	â	A3	163	ú
84	132	ä	A4	164	ñ
85	133	à	A5	165	Ñ
86	134	å	A6	166	ª
87	135	ç	A7	167	º
88	136	ê	A8	168	¿
89	137	ë	A9	169	⌐
8A	138	è	AA	170	¬
8B	139	ï	AB	171	½
8C	140	î	AC	172	¼
8D	141	ì	AD	173	¡
8E	142	Ä	AE	174	≪
8F	143	Á	AF	175	≫
90	144	É	B0	176	▒
91	145	æ	B1	177	▓
92	146	Æ	B2	178	▓
93	147	ô	B3	179	│
94	148	ö	B4	180	┤
95	149	ò	B5	181	╡
96	150	û	B6	182	╢
97	151	ù	B7	183	╖
98	152	ÿ	B8	184	╕
99	153	Ö	B9	185	╣
9A	154	Ü	BA	186	║
9B	155	¢	BB	187	╗
9C	156	£	BC	188	╝
9D	157	¥	BD	189	╜
9E	158	Pt	BE	190	╛
9F	159	ƒ	BF	191	┐

Hex	ASCII	Character	Hex	ASCII	Character
C0	192	└	E0	224	α
C1	193	┴	E1	225	β
C2	194	┬	E2	226	Γ
C3	195	├	E3	227	π
C4	196	─	E4	228	Σ
C5	197	┼	E5	229	σ
C6	198	╞	E6	230	μ
C7	199	╟	E7	231	τ
C8	200	╚	E8	232	Φ
C9	201	╔	E9	233	Θ
CA	202	╩	EA	234	Ω
CB	203	╦	EB	235	δ
CC	204	╠	EC	236	∞
CD	205	═	ED	237	Ø
CE	206	╬	EE	238	ϵ
CF	207	╧	EF	239	∩
D0	208	╨	F0	240	≡
D1	209	╤	F1	241	±
D2	210	╥	F2	242	≥
D3	211	╙	F3	243	≤
D4	212	╘	F4	244	⌠
D5	213	╒	F5	245	⌡
D6	214	╓	F6	246	÷
D7	215	╫	F7	247	≈
D8	216	╪	F8	248	°
D9	217	┘	F9	249	•
DA	218	┌	FA	250	·
DB	219	█	FB	251	√
DC	220	▄	FC	252	n
DD	221	▌	FD	253	^{2}
DE	222	▐	FE	254	■
DF	223	▀	FF	255	(blank)

Linking Pascal to Machine Language

If you are a Pascal programmer, you may often wish that you could write part of your program in Pascal and another part in machine language. IBM's implementation of Pascal is very powerful and quite complete; however, it lacks some desirable machine-specific commands, especially where the screen is involved. For example, there is no way to clear the screen or do graphics in Pascal. In this appendix, you will learn how to combine Pascal and machine language programs.

The LINK Program

Up to now, you have used the "LINK.EXE" program to convert .OBJ files into .EXE files. The abilities of the LINK program go far beyond this. It can also join different object modules (your .OBJ files) together into a large program. The .OBJ files can come from any source, from the assembler, the Pascal compiler, even the FORTRAN compiler; the LINK program doesn't care where the object files come from. In this appendix, we will use the LINK program to combine Pascal and machine language programs.

The Rules of Pascal

There are a number of rules that must be followed to combine machine language with Pascal. You must follow these rules to the letter when you write your machine language routines if you hope to make Pascal and machine language work together in harmony. The rules pertain to parameter passing and affected registers (if you haven't already done so, we suggest that you read through Chapter 6 before continuing).

To begin with, Pascal treats all machine language object modules as procedures or functions. When you write your Pascal program, you must use the EXTERN command to tell the Pascal compiler that the procedure or function will be added to the program when it is linked. Let's consider a simple procedure which we will call a machine language routine:

PROCEDURE SAMPLE(VAR PARAM:INTEGER); EXTERN;

Notice how the EXTERN command is used. The name of the example procedure is *sample*. Sample takes one value, an integer.

When your Pascal program uses this procedure, the value of the parameter must be passed to the routine SAMPLE. This is done via the stack in what is referred to as a FRAME. Pascal uses the BP register as a *Frame Pointer* to access data in the *frame*. The frame constructed when SAMPLE is used takes the following format:

Address of the parameter (relative to DS)
RET address (to return to the caller)

The RET at the end of the routine must remove any parameters put onto the stack by the calling program. The routine can modify any of the registers except BP and DS. In other words, it is free to change AX, BX, CX, DX, SI, DI, and ES; but BP and DS must be preserved.

When a function is used, the rules are a little different. For example, consider the following function declaration:

FUNCTION TEST(VAR PARAM:INTEGER):WORD; EXTERN;

The function's name is TEST. As with SAMPLE, our example procedure, TEST takes one value. TEST, however, must also return a word to the calling program. This word must be stored in AX on return from the function.

The rules for returning values from a function can be summarized as follows:

- If the function returns a 16-bit quantity (an INTEGER, WORD, or ADR value), the number must be in AX when on return from the subroutine.
- If the function returns a two-word quantity (a four-byte INTEGER or an ADS value), the number must be stored in the register pair AX:DX, where AX holds the less significant word.

However, returning other values is more complicated:
- If the function returns anything else (a four-byte REAL, an eight-byte REAL, an ARRAY, a RECORD, a SET, or a pointer to a SUPER ARRAY type), then the value/values are expected in a temporary variable set up by the calling routine. The address of the temporary variable is the last value pushed onto the stack before the function is called. On return from the function, AX must point to the temporary variable.

This rule slightly changes the format of the frame. Now there is another word pushed onto the stack before the function is called. The frame now looks like

Address of the parameter (relative to DS)
Address of temporary variable (relative to DS)
RET address (to return to the caller)

Note that the RET at the end of functions must still remove *all* of the parameters pushed onto the stack by the calling routine. Remember that, as with functions, only BP and DS need to be preserved.

In general, unlike routines written to be used by BASIC, there are no restrictions on the amount of stack space you can use.

Writing the Machine Language Routine

Now that you have Pascal's rules at hand, we can examine the general structure of a machine language procedure and function. The segment declarations are slightly different when you are writing machine language programs to be linked with Pascal. If your object module needs a data segment, you must define it like this. The segment MUST be named DATA.

DATA   SEGMENT PUBLIC 'DATA'
**   [put any needed data here]**
DATA   ENDS
DGROUP   GROUP DATA

When the Pascal program calls your routine, the DS register will already be pointing at this data segment, so there is no need to change DS. You define the code segment as you always have:

segment name **SEGMENT**

The PROCedure declaration is also the same:

proc name **PROC FAR**

But you must add the command

PUBLIC *proc name*

after the procedure declaration. The name of the procedure here must be the same as the name of the function or procedure you declare in your Pascal program (see the example programs at the end of this appendix).

Your ASSUME statement must also be a little different. It should look something like

ASSUME DS:DGROUP,SS:DGROUP,CS:*segment name*

Note that DGROUP is used as the name of the DS and SS segments, not DATA.

Now you must write your machine language routine. The first two instructions are generally

PUSH BP
PUSH DS

Remember that BP and DS must be preserved by the routine; all other registers can be changed as required.

Generally, the next step is to access the parameters that are stored on the stack. The simplest method is to use BP as an offset register into the stack. For procedures, the last parameter pushed onto the stack will be at SP + 8 (after you push BP and DS onto the stack). If there is more than one parameter passed, they will be stored on the stack at SP + 10, SP + 12, etc. Remember that the calling program passes the addresses (relative to DS) of the data, not the data itself. For our example procedure SAMPLE, the beginning of the code might look something like

PUSH BP
PUSH DS
MOV BP,SP
MOV BX,[BP+8]
MOV AX,[BX]

AX now holds the parameter passed by the calling program. At the end of this example procedure, we must remember to POP BP and DS from the stack, and we must use the RET 2 command. This will remove the one parameter passed by the calling program.

Functions are slightly different. If the function returns a byte, word, or double-word value, that value must be stored in AL, AX, or the AX:DX pair on return from the subroutine. Remember that for more complex data structures, the last parameter passed by the calling program is the address of a temporary variable set up to hold the value(s) returned by the function. On return, AX must hold the address of the temporary variable. The beginning of the code for our sample function, TEST, might look something like

```
PUSH BP
PUSH DS
MOV BP,SP
MOV DI,[BP+8]    ;get the address of the return variable
MOV BX,[BP+10]   ;get the passed parameter
MOV AX,[BX]
```

As with procedures, remember to POP BP and DS from the stack before returning to the calling program. Also, remember that you must remove any passed parameters before returning; this means that the function TEST must end with the RET 4 command.

In general, machine language subroutines written to be linked to Pascal will take the following format:

```
;Comment Header
;
DATA        SEGMENT PUBLIC 'DATA'
            [put any needed data/variables here]
DATA        ENDS
DGROUP      GROUP DATA
;
cseg        SEGMENT
program     PROC FAR
            PUBLIC program
            ASSUME DS:DGROUP, SS:DGROUP, CS:cseg
            PUSH BP
            PUSH DS
            MOV BP,SP
            [access the passed parameters and perform the
            procedure/function]
            [For functions only: set AL/AX/AX:DX to value to
            return to calling program, or set AX to address of
            temporary variable (for procedures, AX and DX can
            hold any value)]
            POP DS
            POP BP
            RET n
```

You can substitute your own segment and program names for *cseg* and *program*. The value of n for the RET n command depends on two things: whether you are writing a procedure or a function, and how many parameters are passed to the machine language routine. Generally, n will be

(number of parameters passed) * 2

for procedures, and

(number of parameters passed) * 2 + 2

for functions.

An Example Procedure

There are two sample routines included here. The first is a procedure that changes the screen attribute of the entire screen. Notice that this sample procedure requires some variables, so the data segment is used. Also notice that the name of the procedure defined in the machine language program is SCREEN (Program F-1). This is the name we must use when we declare the procedure in Pascal. Notice that we use the code

MOV BP,SP
MOV SI,[BP+8]
MOV AL,[SI]
MOV ATTRIB,AL

to get the value of the passed parameter (a byte in this case) into the machine language variable ATTRIB. The rest of the machine routine is fairly easy to understand, and it is well-commented.

Now turn to the Pascal program called "USESCRN.PAS" (Program F-2). The line

PROCEDURE SAMPLE(VAR PARAM:BYTE); EXTERN;

declares the procedure for the Pascal compiler. The name of the variable (the PARAM) is arbitrary; we could have used anything. The name of the procedure, however, must be the same as the name of the procedure you declare in your machine language program. The rest of the Pascal program is straightforward. It inputs a value from the keyboard, and uses this value as the parameter for the machine language program. If you enter 255 for the attribute, that attribute will fill the screen, and the program will be terminated.

Now that you understand how these programs work, enter and run the Pascal compiler on the Pascal program, and the assembler on the machine language program. Do not link either program. Now that you have the two object files, run the LINK program. We must now tell LINK the names of the object modules we want to link together.

From the Object Modules [.OBJ]: prompt, enter:

USESCRN + SCREEN

LINK will automatically add the .OBJ extensions to the filenames. Enter the desired names for the .EXE, .MAP, and .LIB files as always. LINK will now join the Pascal object module (with its associated routines from the Pascal library file) with the machine language routine SCREEN. If all goes well, you should have a working version of USESCRN.

An Example Function

The second example program for this appendix is a function which gives you easy access to the BIOS video input/output interrupt (10H). The name of the function is VIDEO_IO. It passes a record which holds the values to be used in the AX, BX, CX, and DX registers. The function returns an identical record which holds the values of the registers returned by the BIOS function which was called.

For ease of use, the record was defined as the byte registers (using AH, AL, BH, BL, etc., not AX, BX, etc.). The machine language routine VIDEOIO accepts a record defined this way, and returns a record like that. Thus, video functions which return parameters can also be used. Notice how the routine places the contents in the temporary variable. This variable is addressed with DI (of course, you can use any base or index register). There are some example procedures and functions using VIDEOIO in the sample Pascal program "VIDEO.PAS."

You link the object module for the program VIDEO_IO.ASM and VIDEO.PAS just as you linked the example procedure. Answer the link program's first question with VIDEO + VIDEO_IO. When the linking is complete, execute the "VIDEO.EXE" program.

It is important to keep two things in mind when you link files. First, there is no limit to the number of object files you can link together. Second, when linking a Pascal file to machine language routines, the Pascal file *must* be the first one named.

This appendix has explained only one method of joining Pascal with machine language. This is one of the simplest. The manual from Pascal Version 2.00 has a complete discussion of this process (See Chapter 11, "Interface of Pascal with Assembler and FORTRAN," in the Pascal Compiler, *Fundamentals* book).

Program F-1. SCREEN.ASM

```
; SCREEN.ASM
;
; sample procedure
;
; stack set up as:
; offset    description
; 8   --  address of attribute
; 4   --  far return address
; 2   --  saved BP
; 0   --  saved DS
;
data      segment, public 'DATA'
attrib    db ?              ;new attribute
max_col   dw ?              ;number of columns on screen
column    db ?              ;column we are changing
row       db ?              ;row we are changing
dpage     db ?              ;which display page to use
old_row   db ?              ;where the cursor was when we started
old_col   db ?
data      ends
dgroup    group data
;
cseg      segment
screen    proc far
          assume cs:cseg,ds:dgroup,ss:dgroup
          public screen
```

```
        push bp
        push ds

        mov ah,15              ;how many columns on screen?
        int 10h
        mov al,ah              ;make number of columns a word
        cbw
        mov max_col,ax         ;store number of columns
        mov dpage,bh

        mov ah,3               ;get row/col and page
        mov bh,dpage
        int 10h
        mov old_row,dh         ;save current cursor pos
        mov old_col,dl

        mov bp,sp              ;get the new attribute
        mov si,[bp+8]
        mov al,[si]
        mov attrib,al          ;store in attrib

        mov row,0              ;zero row counter
        mov cx,24              ;number of rows
        push cx
l1:     mov cx,max_col         ;number of columns
        mov column,0           ;zero column counter
```

```
l2:
    push cx
    mov ah,2        ;set cursor position
    mov dh,row      ;row/col
    mov dl,column
    mov bh,dpage    ;page
    int 10h
    mov ah,8        ;read character at cursor
    int 10h
    mov ah,9        ;write new char and attrib
    mov cx,1        ;only one character
    mov bl,attrib   ;new attribute
    int 10h
    pop cx
    inc column      ;do next column
    loop l2

    pop cx
    inc row         ;do next row
    loop l1

    mov ah,2        ;restore cursor pos
    mov dh,old_row
    mov dl,old_col
    mov bh,dpage
    int 10h

    pop ds
```

```
        pop bp
        ret 2
screen  endp
cseg    ends
        end
```

Program F-2. USESCRN.PAS

```pascal
program usescrn(input,output);

procedure screen(var attrib:byte); extern;

var number:byte;

begin
  repeat
    write('Input a new attribute:');
    readln(number);
    screen(number);
  until number=255;
  for number := 1 to 25 do writeln
end.
```

Program F-3. VIDEO_IO.ASM

```
; VIDEO.ASM
;
; accesses VIDEO I/O interrupt
;
        page ,96
;
; the FRAME will be set up as follows:
; offset    --   description
;   10      --   Address of argument record
;    8      --   Address of return record
;    4      --   Address for FAR return to caller
;    2      --   Saved BP
;    0      --   Saved DS
;
; The record must be defined in Pascal as:
;
; TYPE  Registers = RECORD
;                       AL,
;                       AH,
;                       BL,
;                       BH,
;                       CL,
;                       CH,
;                       DL,
;                       DH:BYTE;
;                   END;
```

```
;
cseg    segment
video_io proc far
        public video_io
        assume cs:cseg
        push bp
        push ds
;
        mov bp,sp                ;set up BP to address stack
        mov si,[bp+10]           ;record passed to routine
        mov di,[bp+8]            ;record routine passes back
        mov ax,[si]              ;get the passed registers
        mov bx,[si+2]
        mov cx,[si+4]
        mov dx,[si+6]
        int 10H                  ;call the interrupt function
        mov [di],ax              ;store registers to pass back
        mov [di+2],bx
        mov [di+4],cx
        mov [di+6],dx
        mov ax,di                ;give AX address of temp var

        pop ds
        pop bp
        ret 4                    ;return to caller
;
video_io endp
cseg    ends
        end
```

Program F-4. VIDEO.PAS

```pascal
program video_test(input,output);

type
  register = record
    al,
    ah,
    bl,
    bh,
    cl,
    ch,
    dl,
    dh:byte;
  end;

var
  parameters:register;
  row,column:byte;

function video_io (var input:register):register; extern;

procedure set_mode (mode:byte);
begin
  parameters.ah := 0;
  parameters.al := mode;
  parameters := video_io(parameters)
end;
```

```
procedure pos_cursor (page, column, row:byte);
begin
    parameters.ah := 2;
    parameters.bh := page;
    parameters.dh := row;
    parameters.dl := column;
    parameters := video_io (parameters)
end;

function cursor_row (page:byte):byte;
begin
    parameters.ah := 3;
    parameters.bh := page;
    parameters := video_io (parameters);
    cursor_row := parameters.dh
end;

function cursor_column (page:byte):byte;
begin
    parameters.ah := 3;
    parameters.bh := page;
    parameters := video_io (parameters);
    cursor_column := parameters.dl
end;

procedure write_dot (xpos,ypos:word; color:byte);
begin
    parameters.ah := 12;
```

```
  parameters.al := color;
  parameters.dl := ypos mod 256;
  parameters.dh := ypos div 256;
  parameters.cl := xpos mod 256;
  parameters.ch := xpos div 256;
  parameters := video_io (parameters)
end;

function read_dot (xpos,ypos:word):byte;
begin
  parameters.ah := 13;
  parameters.dl := ypos mod 256;
  parameters.dh := ypos div 256;
  parameters.cl := xpos mod 256;
  parameters.ch := xpos div 256;
  parameters := video_io (parameters);
  read_dot := parameters.al
end;

begin
  set_mode(2);
  pos_cursor(0,10,20);
  writeln('This is at column 10, and line 20');
  row := cursor_row(0);
  column := cursor_column(0);
  writeln('The current cursor position is:',row:1,',',column:1)
end.
```

Glossary

Absolute addressing: In absolute addressing, the desired memory location is loaded directly into the appropriate addressing register. It is not a displacement value, but a true position in memory.

Addressing mode: A method of obtaining an effective address.

Assembler: A program which converts your assembly source code into machine executable object code.

Assembly time: When something happens at assembly time, it happens while the program is being assembled. Certain calculations are performed only during assembly and not while the program is executed.

Auxiliary carry flag: This flag indicates a carry out of the third bit into the fourth. It is provided on the 8088 primarily for compatibility with the 8080 microprocessor.

Backspace key: On the PC keyboard, the Backspace key is the gray key above the Enter key. On it is an arrow pointing to the left. Do not confuse this key with the Delete key.

Based addressing: Addressing in which the offset is the sum of a base register (BX or BP) and a displacement stored with the instruction. This is nearly identical to indexed addressing and is similar to register indirect addressing.

Based indexed addressing: Addressing in which the offset is the sum of a base register (BX or BP) and an index register (SI or DI). This is similar to based indexed addressing with displacement.

Based indexed addressing with displacement: Addressing in which the offset is the sum of a base register (BX or BP), an index register (SI or DI), and a displacement stored with the instruction. This is similar to based indexed addressing.

Base register: Either BX (base register) or BP (Base Pointer register).

BASIC: Beginner's All-purpose Symbolic Instruction Code. This is probably the most used computer language in the personal computer field. BASIC was designed as a simple language which people could use to learn to program. It is generally an interpreted language, although there are many BASIC compilers available for the IBM PC.

Batch files: These files are executed by the DOS command program. DOS reads the file and executes the commands in it as if they were typed from the keyboard. Batch files make using the computer easier since one instruction issued to DOS can mean a long chain of commands.

Binary: The system of base 2 numbering. It is the numbering system used internally by all digital computers.

Binary Coded Decimal (BCD): Refers to a method of storing numbers in which four bits are used to hold one decimal digit. See Chapter 8 for a complete explanation.

BIOS: Basic Input Output System. BIOS handles the simpler tasks of running the computer, such as printing to the screen and reading the keyboard. This is the lowest level at which you can access the computer without actually managing the hardware yourself.

Bit: Binary Digit. This is the smallest representable piece of information available on a digital computer. A bit can exist in one of two possible states (hold a 1 or a 0 value).

Buffer: A *First In, First Out*, or FIFO, storage system. Buffers are frequently used during data transmission, particularly when one of the devices is slower than the other. The buffer holds the data which is about to be sent or was just received. DOS uses buffers to hold data coming from the disk drive.

Byte: A chain of eight bits, representing a binary number to the computer. It is a standard unit of information, large enough to hold the numbers 0 to 255 (unsigned). A single typewritten character can be contained in a byte. The terms *characters* and *bytes* are often used interchangeably when referring to memory or disk storage size.

Carry flag: Used to indicate a carry out of the highest bit after addition or a borrow into the highest bit after subtraction. If the flag is set, there was a carry or borrow; otherwise, the flag is clear.

Central Processing Unit (CPU): Often referred to as the brain of the computer. The CPU is the part of the computer which runs all of the programs. The CPU in the IBM PC is an 8088, designed by Intel. There is another CPU in the keyboard, and probably one in your printer as well.

Clear: When a flag is clear, it has the value of 0.

Clock cycle: The microprocessor paces itself with clock pulses at a rate of 4.77 MHz. One pulse is the same as one clock cycle.

Color Graphics Adapter: This printed circuit board gives IBM PCs and compatibles the ability to drive an RGB or composite monitor. This card supports color and graphics. The PCjr has a built-in display driver which is compatible with the PC's Color Graphics Adapter.

Compatibility: The ability of one kind of computer to execute programs intended for another. There are many IBM PC compatibles which claim the ability to run most, if not all, of the software intended for IBM Personal Computers.

Compiler: A program which translates a high-level computer language source file into a machine language object file. Compiled languages include Pascal, FORTRAN, and COBOL.

Default: The assumed value, or state which exists if you do not make any changes.

Delete key: On the PC's keyboard, the Delete key is on the bottom row of the keyboard. It has a decimal point on it. Do not confuse this with the Backspace key.

Device driver: A program which DOS loads to handle (drive) some special peripheral (or device) installed in your computer. DOS calls this program whenever a program requests the device. The DOS 2.00 manual gives an example of a device driver which creates a RAM disk (a floppy disk emulated in RAM). The RAM disk is only one example of a device driver.

Direct addressing: Addressing in which only a displacement, stored with the instruction, is used as the offset to locate the data.

Direction flag: This flag indicates whether string operations should be performed up in memory or down in memory (whether the pointer registers should be incremented or decremented).

Displacement: A byte or word which is stored with an instruction. It can act as an address or is added to the contents of other registers to find the address of data. A displacement can represent a positive or negative number.

Documentation: The material which accompanies a program. It tells you what the program does and how it should be run. The term *documentation* also refers to notes within the program source code. There has been a push in recent years for program self-documentation. Essentially, this means that the labels and symbols used in the program should have clear and significant names. A well-documented program should be clear enough so that any person familiar with the language can read and understand the source code. This applies to *all* languages, not just machine language.

DOS: The Disk Operating System, a set of programs which allow the computer to communicate with the disk drives. DOS has many features and subroutines available to the machine language programmer through the DOS function call.

DOS-compatible files: Files which have no special control codes (such as those added by many word processors for formatting purposes) and are terminated by a Ctrl-Z. Only DOS-compatible files (often called *pure ASCII* files) can be assembled using the *IBM Macro Assembler*.

Editors: Programs which allow you to manipulate program source files. They are often thought of as simple word processors.

Effective address: The effective address is the calculated memory location of a piece of data. It has two components, a segment, and an offset.

Extension: Refers to the three letters which appear after the filename. For example, in the filename SAMPLE.EXP, EXP is the extension.

Far: Refers to certain kinds of JMPs and CALLs. Far JMPs or CALLs are *inter segment.*

Flags: These are bits within the status register of the microprocessor which indicate the result of an operation.

Floating-point numbers: These are numbers which have decimal points and a fractional portion.

General register: Any register in the 8088 except a segment register (CS, DS, ES, or SS) or the flags. It generally refers to a word register, but not always.

Hexadecimal: The preferred number system for machine language. It refers to a base 16 system. It is convenient because each hexadecimal digit corresponds to four binary digits.

High-level computer languages: COBOL, FORTRAN and Pascal, BASIC, Logo, and APL are all examples of high-level languages. They are separate from the machine in which they operate. The user of a high-level computer language writes programs with wordlike instructions such as PRINT or GOTO. These high-level instructions must then be interpreted or compiled into machine language instructions which the microprocessor can execute directly. High-level languages are often defined by national or international organizations.

Immediate value: A value which is stored with the machine language instruction.

Indexed addressing: Addressing in which the offset is the sum of an index register (SI or DI) and a displacement stored with the instruction. It is nearly identical to based addressing and is similar to register indirect addressing.

Indexing: Refers to the use of a subscript variable in an array.

Index register: Refers to either SI (Source Index register) or DI (Destination Index register).

Indirect addressing: In indirect addressing, the location of the data is stored in memory, not with the instruction itself.

Interpreter: An interpreter is a program which translates high-level source code into machine code for the microprocessor. For example, BASIC interprets as it executes a BASIC program.

Interrupt: A way of stopping the microprocessor so that it can check for some event (such as a keypress) in the system.

Interrupt enable flag: When this flag is set, the microprocessor accepts all software- and hardware-generated interrupts. If this flag is clear, all hardware-generated interrupts, except the NMI (Non-Maskable Interrupt), are ignored. Software-generated interrupts (those called with the INT command) are always processed.

Inter segment: Between two segments; this refers to a jump or call to a label in a different code segment. Jumps or calls of this kind load new values into the IP and CS registers.

Intra segment: Within a segment; this refers to a jump or call to a label within the same code segment. Jumps or calls of this kind change only the IP register. The CS is not changed.

Labels: Used to identify locations within a program for jumps or calls.

LIFO: The storage method used by a stack. It stands for *Last In, First Out*. See *Stack* for more details.

Long: Another term for FAR or Inter segment.

Loop: A structure for repeating a set of commands. In BASIC, a loop is often performed with the FOR-NEXT commands.

Machine language: The native (binary) language of the computer; the instructions which the microprocessor can execute directly.

Macro: A shorthand way of referring to a larger piece of code.

Main loop: See *Main routine.*

Main routine: The uppermost level in a program. It is the part of the program which calls other subroutines.

Microprocessor: See *Central Processing Unit.*

ML: An abbreviation for machine language.

Mnemonic: A symbol used to help the programmer remember something. For example, DIV is the three-letter mnemonic for the machine language *divide* instruction.

Modems: Devices which allow two computers to communicate with one another over a phone line. There are many modems on the market. Some plug directly into the IBM PC (using up one of the expansion slots), while others plug into an RS-232 serial port. IBM offers an internal modem for the PCjr.

Monochrome Screen Adapter: This printed circuit board can be installed in an IBM PC or hardware-compatible computer. It drives the IBM monochrome display. It does not support graphics, but has the ability to display normal, flashing, underlined, and high-intensity text. The adapter board includes a parallel printer interface. This product cannot be used in the PCjr.

Near: Refers to intra segment jumping or calling.

Nybble: Half a byte. In other words, a nybble is one hexadecimal digit, or a chain of four bits. It can represent the numbers from 0 to 15.

Object code: The program which the LINK program will convert into an executable file. It's basically the machine language version of your source file.

Octal: Similar to hexadecimal, except that octal is base 8 numbering. There are three bits per digit rather than four.

Operand: The part of the instruction which is operated upon. In the example ADD AX,3, the operands are AX and 3.

Operation: The instruction itself. In the instruction DIV BL, DIV is the operation.

Overflow flag: This flag is set when an addition or subtraction unintentionally changes the sign of the result. This is often the case when two large positive numbers are added together. This flag is also used to indicate the size of a product after multiplication. If the flag is set, then both the lower and upper halves of the product are relevant. The flag is clear if the upper half is only a sign extension of the number.

Parameter passing: Refers to transferring values from a calling program to a routine (or vice versa).

Parameters: The values that are passed between a calling program and a routine.

Parity flag: The parity flag (PF) is set to one if the result of an operation has an even number of 1 bits in the lower byte; otherwise, this flag is cleared. The parity flag's primary use is in communications software.

Pascal: A highly structured and standardized language, created by N. Wirth and named in honor of Pascal, a French mathematician.

Pass 1 and 2: The assembler assembles your source file in two passes, once to locate all of the variables, and again to produce the actual code.

Path names: Refers to the names of the subdirectories where a file can be found. Since you can have subdirectories within subdirectories, DOS needs some way of finding files. A path name describes to DOS how to find the file by naming the different directories it must trace through to find the directory with the file in it.

Program Segment Prefix: This is set up by DOS each time a file is loaded and executed. It contains information DOS needs to run the program.

Pseudo-operations: Commands in the source code which are interpreted by the assembler, but don't actually produce any machine language instructions.

Real numbers: See *Floating-point numbers.*

Recursive routines: Routines which call themselves.

Register indirect addressing: Addressing in which the offset is the quantity stored in a base register (BX or BP) or an index register (SI or DI).

Registers: Special locations within the microprocessor which can hold word-sized data. There are a number of special registers which are used to address the program, data, and the stack. See also *General register.*

Relative addressing: In relative addressing the location of the address is not stored directly, but a displacement value (added to some register) is used.

Runtime: Refers to the execution of the program. If something happens during runtime, it happens while the program is executing.

Segment registers: Used to define memory segments, these are CS (code segment), DS (data segment), ES (extra segment), and SS (stack segment).

Segments: 64K blocks of RAM pointed to by one of the segment registers.

Set: When a flag is set, it has the value of 1.

Short: A SHORT JMP uses one byte as an offset for IP. Short JMPs are limited to 127 bytes forward and 128 bytes backward. All conditional jumps and LOOP commands use short jumps.

Sign bit: The highest bit of a number. For an eight-bit number, it is the bit with the value of 128. It is also used to indicate the sign of a binary number; if the highest bit is 1, the number is negative; otherwise, the number is positive.

Sign extended: A number which has been expanded or extended into a higher byte or word. If the number is negative the extension is all binary 1's. If the number is positive, the extension is 0.

Sign flag: This flag indicates the resulting sign of the last operation. It reflects the status of the sign bit of the result. If this flag is set, the last result was negative. If this flag is clear, the last result was positive.

Source code: The file that you type into the computer. It is the human-readable form of your program. The process of assembly converts this into actual machine language instructions.

Stack: The stack is a *Last In, First Out* (LIFO) storage system. Values are PUSHed onto the stack, and POPped off when needed again. The stack is used to store return addresses during subroutine calls, and can be used by the programmer to temporarily store registers or pass parameters to subroutines.

Stack-oriented computer: Computers of this type use a stack much like the 8088 uses its registers. The stack is used to hold and manipulate data. The Forth computer language and all HP calculators are stack-oriented.

Subroutine levels: Refers to how many times subroutines call other subroutines. In other words, if a program calls a subroutine, which in turn calls another routine, which in turn calls another, you are three levels down in subroutines.

Subroutines: Called with the GOSUB command in BASIC. They are similar to PROCedures and FUNCtions in Pascal. In machine language, subroutines are activated with the CALL command.

Symbols: A generic term for labels and variables.

Trap flag: When this flag is set, the microprocessor enters its trap or single-stepping mode. An INT 1 is automatically performed after every instruction (with the exception of instructions which affect the segment registers). DEBUG uses this mode of the microprocessor to perform the TRACE operation.

Word processors: Programs which let you enter, edit, and print text.

Words: A word is a 16-bit number (there are two bytes per word). In some circumstances, however, word can refer to any number larger than a byte.

Zero flag: This flag is set when the result of an operation is 0. It is used to indicate equality after a CMP command. This flag is sometimes confusing because it is set (has a value of 1) when the result is 0, and is clear (has a value of 0) when the result is nonzero.

Index